Welcome to the EVERYTHING® Profiles line of books—an extension of the bestselling EVERYTHING® series!

These authoritative books help you learn everything you ever wanted to know about the lives, social context, and surrounding historical events of fascinating people who made or influenced history and religious thought. While reading this EVERYTHING® book you will discover four useful boxes:

Factum: Definitions and additional information
Discussion Question: Questions and answers for deeper insights
Symbolism: Explains a concept or symbol
Fallacy: Refutes a commonly held misconception

Whether you are learning about a figure for the first time or are just brushing up on your knowledge, EVERYTHING® Profiles help you on your journey toward a greater understanding of the individuals who have shaped and enriched our lives, culture, and history.

Visit the entire Everything® series at *www.everything.com*

The
EVERYTHING®
Mary Magdalene Book

Dear Reader,

For almost as many years as I can remember, I have gone to bed at night with a book. Usually it is a biography of a holy person or a saint. They were ordinary people who lived extraordinary lives. Many were intriguing, but, for me, none more so than Mary Magdalene.

She walked with Jesus along the dusty paths and byways of ancient Palestine. She was his faithful, loving supporter and follower, yet mentions of her in the New Testament Gospels are few. That would be the sum of her story if it were not for a spectacular discovery in Nag Hammadi, Egypt, in 1945 of some ancient gospels, including one called the Gospel of Mary [Magdalene]. The discovery of these lost texts has become the impetus for new interest and scholarly research into the life of this amazing woman.

Using the New Testament Gospels and those texts excluded from the Bible, I have pieced together as many details as I can find about the life of Mary Magdalene. My desire is to share with you all the information and resources about Mary Magdalene so that you, too, may have a better understanding of not only her life and role in the life of Jesus and the earliest days of Christianity, but her enduring legacy for our world.

Meera Lester

THE
EVERYTHING®
MARY MAGDALENE BOOK

The life and legacy of Jesus' most
misunderstood disciple

Meera Lester

Adams Media
Avon, Massachusetts

*This book is dedicated to Mary Magdalene,
in celebration of her life and legacy, and to my readers*

• • •

Publishing Director: Gary M. Krebs
Associate Managing Editor: Laura M. Daly
Associate Copy Chief: Brett Palana-Shanahan
Acquisitions Editor: Gina Chaimanis
Development Editor: Jessica LaPointe
Associate Production Editor: Casey Ebert
Technical Reader: Dr. James B. Wiggins

Director of Manufacturing: Susan Beale
Associate Director of Production:
Michelle Roy Kelly
Cover Design: Paul Beatrice, Matt LeBlanc,
Erick DaCosta
Design and Layout: Colleen Cunningham,
Holly Curtis, Sorae Lee

• • •

An Everything® Series Book.
Everything® and everything.com® are registered trademarks of F+W Publications, Inc.

Published by Adams Media, an F+W Publications Company
57 Littlefield Street, Avon, MA 02322 U.S.A.
www.adamsmedia.com

ISBN: 1-59337-617-0

Printed in the United States of America.

J I H G F E D C B A

Library of Congress Cataloging-in-Publication Data
Lester, Meera.
The everything Mary Magdalene book : the life and legacy of
Jesus' most misunderstood disciple / Meera Lester.
    p.   cm.
Includes bibliographical references and index.
ISBN: 1-59337-617-0
1. Mary Magdalene, Saint. I. Title: Mary Magdalene book. II. Title. III. Series: Everything series.

BS2485.L465 2006
226'.092—dc22
          2005034596

This publication is designed to provide accurate and authoritative information with regard to the subject matter covered. It is sold with the understanding that the publisher is not engaged in rendering legal, accounting, or other professional advice. If legal advice or other expert assistance is required, the services of a competent professional person should be sought.

      —From a *Declaration of Principles* jointly adopted by a Committee of the
American Bar Association and a Committee of Publishers and Associations

Many of the designations used by manufacturers and sellers to distinguish their products are claimed as trademarks. Where those designations appear in this book and Adams Media was aware of a trademark claim, the designations have been printed with initial capital letters.

*This book is available at quantity discounts for bulk purchases.
For information, please call 1-800-872-5627.*

Contents

Foreword xii

Introduction xiii

part I

Mary Magdalene in the New Testament Gospels 1

1 The Woman from Magdala 3

Who Was Mary Magdalene? 4

A Flourishing, Corrupt Magdala 6

Mary Magdalene Receives a Divine Healing 7

Jesus the Christ 10

Following Jesus 12

Mary Magdalene's Female Companions 14

A Woman of Independent Means 15

Could She Claim Royal Lineage? 18

2 For the Love of Jesus 21

Leader, Follower, Friend, and Confidante 22

Witness to the Resurrection 24

Vigil with Mother Mary and John 27

First Witness and Commission from Jesus 30

Apostle to the Apostles 33

3 Jesus' Other Loyal Followers 37

Mary, Mother of Jesus 38

James, the Lord's Brother 40

John the Baptist 42

The Apostle Peter 44

The Apostle Paul 46

The Last Apostle 49

4 Influential People in Early Christianity 51

Flavius Josephus 52

Marcion 54

Clement of Alexandria 56

Origen 58

Arius 60

Eusebius of Caesarea 62

Diocletian 64

The Apologists 66

Domitian 70

Constantine 72

5 Mary Magdalene's First-Century World 75

Turbulent Times 76

Diversity Within Judaism 77

Roman Law Versus Mosaic Law 79

A Woman's Place in Society 80

Roman Treatment of Women and Children 83

Jesus' Radical Shifting of the Status Quo 84

Challenging the Patriarchy 87

6 Mary Magdalene's Life Begins Anew 89

After the Resurrection 90

Patriarchal Entrenchment 92

Paul's Letters Reveal Early Struggles 94

Women in Leadership Roles 96

The Importance of Apostolic Succession 98

Misogyny and Patriarchal Restriction 100

7 Mary Magdalene in Legend 103

Danger of Persecution 104
Fleeing the Holy Land 106
Mary Magdalene and John on Ephesus 107
Arriving on the Shore of Gaul 109
Proselytizing to the Populace 110
Retreat from the World 112
Relics and Reliquaries 113
Icon Veneration 115

8 Ancestral and Apostolic Seeds Are Sown 117

A Myth Is Conceived 118
A Homily Hurts Mary Magdalene's Reputation 119
The Church Perpetuates the Myth 121
Celibate Male Apostolic Succession 123
The Apostolic Church 125
Long-Term Consequences for Other Women 128
Modern Stained-Glass Ceilings 130

9 Magdalene and the Early Church Crisis 133

The Struggling Jesus Movement 134
A Gospel for Pagans and Non-Jews 136
The Definition of an Apostle Narrows 137
The Hysterical Female Charge 138
Differing Views about Women's Church Roles 139
Oral Tradition Before Written Texts 142
Was Mary Magdalene's Scriptural Presence Diminished? 143
Presbyters, Bishops, and Women in the Early Church 145
The Orthodox Viewpoint on Women Priests 146

10 Pivotal Events in Early Christianity 149

Tumultuous Timeline of Early Christianity 150
Creating the Vulgate Bible 153
The Council at Nicaea 155

Apostle John Writes Revelation 157

The Death of Stephen 159

The Great Jewish Revolt 161

The Siege at Masada 164

part II

Mary Magdalene in the Gnostic Gospels 167

11 Gnostic Veneration of Mary Magdalene 169

An Untidy Beginning to Christianity 170

Flourishing of Gnosticism 173

At Variance with Literalist Christianity 175

Mary Magdalene in the Gnostic Texts 176

The Pagan Goddess Cults 178

Early Christian Fathers Root Out Heresy 179

12 Rituals and Beliefs of Early Christians 185

Almsgiving 186

Burial 187

Baptism 188

Healing 189

Conversion 190

Pilgrimage 191

The Three Pillars 192

Christian Holy Seasons and Prayers 195

13 A Woman's Gospel 197

The Manuscript Found in Cairo 198

Other Pieces of the Gospel of Mary 199

Six Missing Pages 200

Peter Invites Mary Magdalene to Teach 201

Mary Magdalene Shares Her Vision 202

Where the Truth Is to Be Found 203

Seven Female Christian Mystics 205

14 Reaction to Mary Magdalene's Vision 209

Peter Does Not Believe Mary 210
Levi to the Rescue 211
Why Peter Denounced Mary Magdalene 212
Spiritual Adeptness Is More Important than Gender 213
Make No New Law 214
Conflicting Attitudes Toward Prophecy 216
Founding the Church on Peter 219

15 Mary Magdalene Shines in Other Gnostic Texts 221

Mary Magdalene in the Inner Circle 222
Conflict with Peter 223
The Ancient Story of Sophia 225
Mary Magdalene and the Sacred Feminine 227
Examples Predate Christian Scripture 229
Jesus' Promise to Mary Magdalene 231

16 Mary Magdalene in the Gospel of John 233

What's Different about the Fourth Gospel? 234
Questions about the Anonymous Beloved Disciple 235
Founder and Leader of the Johannine Community 237
Who Wrote the Gospel of John? 238
Did Mary Magdalene Write the Fourth Gospel? 240
Suggestions of Redaction 242

17 Her Place in Esoteric Christianity 243

A Goddess Archetype 244
Heavenly Mother 245
Vesica Piscis—Sacred Feminine 247
Magdalene in Other Doctrines 248
The Mystery Traditions and Magdalene's Role 249
Esoteric References in the Apocrypha 251

part III
Mary Magdalene in Modern Times 253

18 Mary Magdalene Through Artists' Eyes 255

Early Portrayals and Icons of the Magdalene 256
Artist Renderings During the Middle Ages 257
Renaissance Depictions of Mary Magdalene 259
Nineteenth-Century Symbol of Eros 261
A Model for Twentieth-Century Artists 263

19 Under the Scholars' Microscope 265

Historical Reinterpretations of Magdalene 266
The Magdalene and Unwed Mothers 267
Feminist Theologians Have Their Say 268
Male Gender, Status, and Power 270
Strife and Conflict in the Early Church 271
The Roman Catholic Position 274
Mary Magdalene Is the Glue 275

20 Relevance and Resonance for Modern Women 277

Speaking with Authority and Conviction 278
Hollywood Offers Its Distorted View 278
The Da Vinci Code Sparks Heated Debate 280
Modern Seekers Exchange Ideas 283
A New Generation Looks Beyond the Myth 284
Restitution Worldwide 285
Mary Magdalene Pilgrimage Sites 286
Diverse Ways She Is Venerated 287
Recounting Her Many Roles 289

Appendix A: Glossary 290

Appendix B: Web Site Resources 293

Appendix C: Bibliography 296

Index 299

Top Ten Interesting Facts
You'll Learn about Mary Magdalene

1. Mary Magdalene was Jesus' pre-eminent female disciple and the leader of a branch of the early movement of Christianity that promoted women's leadership.

2. Infamous as a repentant fallen woman, Mary Magdalene was, in fact, never a prostitute. You'll learn exactly how this myth was created and perpetrated for centuries.

3. She was the primary witness to the Resurrection. Jesus commissioned her to proclaim the Good News of his victory over death and this act earned her the appellation of Apostle to the Apostles.

4. Catholics consider her a saint. Her feast day is July 22 on the Roman calendar.

5. She is mentioned only fourteen times in the Gospels, sometimes as just a name in a list of women's names. However, her name often appears first, an indication of her stature and importance after Jesus' mother, Mary.

6. That the message of the Resurrection was entrusted to Mary Magdalene and other women is proof, scholars say, of the historicity of the Resurrection accounts. The testimony of women in Mary Magdalene's time was not accepted.

7. Writings related to early Christianity reveal that entire communities of faithful believers grew up around Mary Magdalene's ministry.

8. Mary Magdalene and other Christian women led prayerful fellowship and worship sessions in house-churches. Their leadership roles were diminished or eliminated when they moved into larger public places.

9. A Gospel named after her was excluded from the Bible. No complete version of the Gospel of Mary exists, but fragments tell a story different from the New Testament Gospels.

10. Some sources speculate that Mary Magdalene was the Beloved Disciple. Also, she may have either written or provided the eyewitness testimony for the Gospel of John.

Foreword

Mary Magdalene—saint or sinner, or both? She is sometimes identified as Apostle to the Apostles. The history of this woman, and her role and reputation within Christianity, is quite a remarkable story. She is held up by some as a figure who has been demeaned and discounted by the patriarchy that has so dominated the leadership of Christianity for more than 2,000 years. The claim for the authority of the apostolic successors has been the theory for the governance of Catholic Christianity since the early decades of the first century B.C. Mary Magdalene, according to her defenders, attempted to divert the patriarchal (male-dominated) interpretation of Jesus' message toward a far more radically inclusive interpretation known as "Gnosticism." If this understanding of the meaning of Jesus' teachings had prevailed, the history of Christianity would be radically different.

Biographical data about Mary Magdalene produces a complex picture. She may have been a wealthy woman who was sufficiently attracted by Jesus and his teachings to follow him and to provide material support for him and his other disciples. Her close connection to Jesus may have evoked jealousy and ridicule from his male disciples after his death. She was falsely identified as a prostitute by Pope Gregory I in the sixth century with the intention of testifying to the forgiving grace of God through Jesus the Christ. This story was meant to illustrate that even a fallen woman receives the mercy of God. Alongside that tradition, Mary Magdalene has been venerated as a saint for many centuries (her saint day is July 22). Some argue that Mary was the author of, or the source for the author of, the Gospel of John in the New Testament. Others insist she provided the material for the document that was lost for many centuries called the Gospel of Mary.

Read this book and you will learn much about this fascinating, alluring woman. I hope you will also find that the story of Mary Magdalene deepens your understanding of Christianity as a whole. I'm sure you'll agree that there is much to ponder.

Dr. James B. Wiggins

Introduction

Mary Magdalene's life, perhaps more than any other biblical figure, remains shrouded in myth, misconception, mystery, and controversy. The Bible reveals that Jesus cast out of her seven devils. Right away, that conjures up questions of what "devil" meant to the first-century Palestinian Jews. All four Gospel accounts credit her with being the eyewitness to the Resurrection and being commissioned by Jesus to tell the others the Good News of his victory over death. Few would dispute her close proximity to Jesus or her status as preeminent female among the disciples. Mary Magdalene served Jesus as a faithful companion, confidante, follower, supporter, benefactor, and friend.

Considering her importance to him, one would think that her life's story would have been told and retold; no detail would ever be left out. Yet, just the opposite may be true. The New Testament Gospels were written by men during the first or early second centuries—during a particularly patriarchal time when women could not serve as legal witnesses, hold office, or participate in the temple as men did. Scholars have been studying Mary Magdalene's life for a long time and what they've been able to ascertain is that she may have gotten a raw deal.

She was depicted as a fallen woman and marginalized in the texts that were deemed acceptable for inclusion in the Bible. Artists and writers have portrayed her as a repentant prostitute, sensual seductress, and pious contemplative. Most recently, she has been imagined as everything from Jesus' romantic companion and wife, a wealthy heiress, author of the Fourth Gospel, the real Holy Grail, the leader of an early Christian sect whose ideas varied from orthodox Christianity, an Isis temple worker, Jesus' heir designate, and the mother of a child who became the ancestress to a line of medieval French kings. Legends about her still circulate in Provence, Ephesus, and England; cookies have been named after her in France; and churches are dedicated to her in many places in the world.

But as scholars have noted, Mary Magdalene was the perfect disciple. Spiritually adept, she was an eloquent spokesperson for Jesus' words, giving all credit, honor, and glory to him. The Vatican cleared Mary Magdalene's name in the 1960s and revised its Missal. Pope John Paul II called her "Apostle to the Apostles." Women today who desire to serve in their churches and synagogues find Mary Magdalene to be an inspiring role model, for they, like her, also face issues of a male-dominated clergy and often a seemingly impenetrable stained-glass ceiling.

This book will help you learn about Mary Magdalene and her life in first-century Palestine under Roman occupation. You will also gain a basic understanding of her time with Jesus and his fledgling movement as it metamorphosed into one of the most far-reaching religious movements of all time. In a frank examination of her portrayal in the Bible, scholarly texts, legends, books, art, and popular culture, you will discover a beautiful mosaic of this holy woman's intriguing life.

Great effort was made to verify the facts in this work; however, scholars sometimes disagree, so whenever such discrepencies arose, the interpretation of a majority of the sources was the one used in this book.

I

Mary Magdalene
in the New Testament Gospels

chapter 1

The Woman from Magdala

Mary Magdalene, perhaps more than any other woman in the Bible, has fired the imaginations of historians, theologians, writers, and artists for more than two millennia. Venerated as a saint and maligned as a prostitute, she had an important role in the birth of Christianity. You might assume the details of her life—before meeting Jesus as well as during and after his lifetime—would be well documented, but you would be wrong. However, recent investigations are raising her profile and generating even more questions.

Who Was Mary Magdalene?

Today she bears the name of Mary Magdalene, but in the Aramaic language of Jesus, she was known as Miryam (an alternate spelling is Miriam) of Magdala. Mary Magdalene was ethnically Jewish—a Palestinian Hebrew woman who suffered from a serious affliction (the nature of which is still being debated), was healed by Jesus, and became his devoted follower. The canonical Gospels (the texts approved for inclusion in the Bible) do not tell us her age, status in society, or family connections or whether she ever had a husband and children.

Did She Have a Family?

Married women in the patriarchal cultures during Jesus' time were addressed first by their given names and then by their relationship to the most prominent male in their families, whether father, husband, or brother. For example, Salome might be called Salome, wife of Zebedee; and Mary might be called Mary, sister of Lazarus. However, this is not true for Mary Magdalene, either in the New Testament Gospels or the Gnostic texts. So, it is easy to assume that she must have been either single or possibly widowed with no family attachment.

What Drew Her to Jesus?

Did she choose to follow Jesus because he healed her? Or did his teachings about tolerance, forgiveness, and love resonate with her? Like so many questions swirling around this woman at the center of the New Testament Gospels, we don't have the answers. She lived under Roman occupation at a time when there was great upheaval in the sociopolitical and religious climate. Jesus' egalitarian treatment of women may have appealed to her. His group quite possibly afforded her a measure of protection and safety as well as spiritual support.

Women and Men under Mosaic Law

Being Jewish, Mary Magdalene would have been raised by her parents to obey and respect Mosaic Law. She would have understood a woman's place in the male-dominated culture of her time. Women were often betrothed while still quite young. Unlike men, they generally were not educated. Men participated fully in society, courts, and synagogues. A woman's place was subordinated to her father first and later, after marriage, to her husband. A woman bore the responsibility of caring for the home and the family. Women were forbidden to read the Torah in public. They sat separate from men and were excluded from religious office. They were considered unclean during their menses. Finally, they could not be legal witnesses.

discussion question

Who were the other Marys who followed Jesus?
Mary Magdalene was one of six Marys who enjoyed the companionship and teachings of Jesus and formed part of his inner circle that included his mother; the wife of Cleophas; the mother of James the Less and Joses; Mary of Bethany; and Mary, mother of John Mark.

So it is ironic that the four male writers of the New Testament Gospels all included references to Mary Magdalene in their accounts. Though details of their stories may differ somewhat, they basically agree on Mary Magdalene. She must have been a powerful force for those writers to mention her. Perhaps her role in the Passion and the Resurrection of Jesus and leadership in his movement was simply too important and too well known to be ignored.

Modern Thinkers Debate and Wonder
Feminist theologians assert that the label of repentant prostitute was a way for the patriarchal church to minimize her. The archetype of a fallen and redeemed woman rendered Mary Magdalene more useful to those who needed a strong example of the forgiving nature of Christianity.

Scholars and biblical historians and members of the clergy alike wonder what it was about Mary Magdalene that made societies of different centuries denigrate her. Was she beautiful, sensual, brainy, competent, spiritual, and independent? Did she eschew traditional women's roles? Was she a free thinker who considered spiritual development more important than marrying, bearing children, and doing traditional women's work of managing a household? These questions continue to provoke debate and discussion among scholars and historians. Who was this woman from Magdala?

A Flourishing, Corrupt Magdala

Many sources suggest that Mary Magdalene came from Magdala, a Galilean town mentioned in the Gospel of Matthew immediately following the fishes and loaves story: "And he sent away the multitude, and took ship, and came into the coasts of Magdala" (15:39).

Magdala was located along the banks of Lake Gennesaret between the cities of Capernaum and Tiberias in Galilee, an area where Jesus ministered. The Magdala place name appears in the writings of Flavius Josephus, a first-century Jewish historian for whom early church fathers had high regard because of the historical accuracy of his writing.

factum

Magdalene and Magdala derive from the Hebrew word *migdal*, meaning tower. Migdal in Greek and Aramaic (the language of Jesus) is Magdala. The Greek translation of Magdala Nunayya is "tower of fishes." Mary Magdalene's name has been associated with the strength and fortification imagery that a tower represents and the place name of the prosperous fishing community that was her hometown.

The Magdala place name also appears in the Talmud, a collection of Hebrew writings dating to the second century. The Talmud cites two Magdalas, one known as Magdala Gadar and the other called Magdala Nunayya. The latter, according to the Talmud, was a flourishing town situated on a lake located about three and a half miles north-northwest from Tiberias.

This Magdala is likely the same town that Josephus calls Taricheae (Greek for "place of pickling houses"). Pickling houses for preserving fish certainly fit in with a fishing community such as Magdala Nunayya, which is believed to have been an important center for the fishing industry as well as for ship building and trading. The town was once a fort. According to the Talmud, the Romans destroyed the town because of the moral depravity of its inhabitants and their involvement in the Jewish revolt against the Romans. The town of Mejdel occupies the site today.

Mary Magdalene Receives a Divine Healing

Mary Magdalene, whom others may have referred to as the "tower of strength," is mentioned more often in the New Testament Gospels than any other female follower of Jesus. Scholars say that is a sure indication of her importance to Christianity. Some theologians and scholars of the early beginnings of Christianity say that without Mary Magdalene, the Jesus movement would have ended. The Romans had put to death other leaders of sects, knowing that when the leader of the movement dies, the movement itself eventually dies, too.

Today, Mary Magdalene is being credited as being the "glue" that kept the Jesus movement together after Jesus' death and resurrection. She comforted the grieving apostles who wanted only to return to their homes and resume their lives, and turned their minds back upon Jesus' good works and teachings. But she could never have accomplished this without being healed by Jesus.

Different Accounts of Healing

The Gospel of Mark reveals that Mary Magdalene was possessed by seven devils (devils represented a metaphor for illness) that Jesus cast out, suggesting that he treated and healed her: "Now when

Jesus was risen early the first day of the week, he appeared to Mary Magdalene, out of whom he had cast seven devils"(16:9). The orthodox view this "casting out" as an exorcism, while the non-orthodox suggest that Jesus enabled some kind of healing to take place.

In the Gospel of Luke, which most scholars agree was written after the Gospel of Mark, Mary Magdalene is also introduced as someone who has been healed: "And it came to pass afterward that he [Jesus] went throughout every city and village, preaching and showing the glad tidings of the kingdom of God: and the twelve *were* with him, and certain women, which had been healed of evil spirits and infirmities, Mary called Magdalene, out of whom went seven devils" (8:1–2).

The Gospel of Luke actually does not say directly that Jesus healed Mary Magdalene, but it infers as much. Whether she suffered from melancholy, severe depression, or epilepsy, the restoration of her health could certainly have been a powerful motivator for Mary Magdalene to remain in the Jesus movement, near him, ministering to his needs, as the canonical Gospels state she did.

What Was Her Ailment?

It is clear that Mary Magdalene suffered from some kind of serious illness. Modern scholars suggest that Mary Magdalene's illness may have been depression or epilepsy, and the nature of it may have been protracted, as suggested by the number seven. The writers of the Hebrew and the New Testament texts used the number seven symbolically to suggest something exaggerated or "in the extreme." Jesus, for example, used the number seven to advocate an exaggerated and total sense of forgiveness. "Then came Peter to him, and said, Lord, how oft shall my brother sin against me, and I forgive him? till seven times? Jesus saith unto him, I say not unto thee, Until seven times: but, Until seventy times seven" (Matthew 18:21–22).

What "possessed" Mary Magdalene? Did she hear sounds or voices or see visions or sense things that she didn't fully comprehend? Could her ailment have been epilepsy? Or, did Mary Magdalene suffer from a form of depression? Modern scholarship suggests she most likely suffered from one of these ailments.

Epilepsy is one of the most common of all neurological conditions. Stroke itself can cause epilepsy. But epilepsy can also be triggered by infections such as meningitis. Some people are born with lesions on their brains that cause epilepsy. If Mary Magdalene had epilepsy, she would not have been the only biblical character to suffer from the illness. The Old Testament prophet Ezekiel possessed all the symptoms of temporal lobe epilepsy, according to American neuroscientist Dr. Eric Altschuler at the University of San Diego. Ezekiel displayed common signs of the illness, such as fainting spells and the inability to speak at times.

discussion question

Can people have different types of hallucinations with epileptic seizures?
Yes. The Epilepsy Foundation, which provides information to suffers and those interested in the disease, states many different kinds of epileptic seizure cause a variety of symptoms that can include olfactory, auditory, and visual hallucinations.

Modern scholars theorize that Mary Magdalene may have suffered from epilepsy because the canonical Gospels refer to the devils that Jesus cast out of her. The people of the first century attributed any physical, spiritual, or emotional dysfunction to the presence of evil spirits (or devils, as the Gospels of Mark and Luke called them). Some sufferers of epilepsy experience panic attacks, depression, and bouts of melancholy as well as seizures. Could Mary Magdalene have been plagued by such severe symptoms that people around her believed she was possessed? We may never know exactly what ailed Mary Magdalene, but the scriptures *never* say that her illness was a result of sexual sins.

Jesus the Christ

Mary Magdalene's story might never have been told if it were not intertwined with Jesus' Resurrection narrative. She was the first eyewitness to the risen Savior, commissioned by Jesus to go forth and spread the Good News, and mentioned by all four Gospel writers. Although her story shines in its own right, Jesus' story dwarfs all others for he was the founder of Christianity and the beloved teacher of Mary Magdalene and all the other believers through the ages.

Background

The date of his birth is fixed in Matthew 2:1 as occurring "in the days of Herod the King." Most timelines place the birth at the beginning of the first century or at around 4 B.C. Christian history states that his mother was Mary, a virgin who conceived Jesus by the power of the Holy Spirit. At the time, Mary was betrothed to Joseph, a carpenter who served as Jesus' stepfather. Jesus was born in Bethlehem, located in the Judean province, which was part of the Roman Empire. The infant Jesus and his family did not remain for more than two years in Bethlehem because of Herod's decree to kill all infants under the age of two (this was in response to a prediction of a threat to Herod's power by another would-be king).

factum

Luke's narrative about the birth of Jesus relates how the shepherds were watching their flocks; an angel of the Lord appeared, proclaimed the news of the birth of the Messiah, and told them how to find him.

Eight days after his birth, Jesus received circumcision and his name, which the angel had told Mary during the Annunciation. Both acts incorporated him into the people of Israel. When the time for purification had passed, Mary and Joseph took Jesus to the Temple, in keeping with Mosaic Law. There they presented Jesus to the Lord. The Gospel of Luke states that two people recognized the infant as the Messiah—Simeon, a righteous man who blessed them, and Anna, a prophetess of the tribe of Asher, who gave thanks to God.

Early Years

Not a lot is known about the early years of Jesus. He may have lived a normal Jewish boy's life as the son of a carpenter and a loving mother. The New Testament, however, tells the story of one Passover trip to Jerusalem, when Mary and Joseph could not locate Jesus after leaving the city and they had to return. They eventually found him in the Temple discoursing with learned rabbis. When Mary asked him why he had not stayed with them, Jesus answered that he needed to be in his father's house. "How is it that ye sought me? wist ye not that I must be about my Father's business?" (Luke 2:49).

Baptism and the Beginning of Public Ministry

Jesus' cousin John the Baptist, who had a large following of his own, baptized Jesus in the River Jordan. When Jesus asked John to baptize him, John at first refused because he felt unworthy. But at Jesus' insistence, John performed the rite of baptism whereupon Jesus retired to the desert to fast for forty days and nights. Although he faced many temptations by Satan, Jesus prevailed in order to carry out the plan he believed God had for him.

The Gospel of Luke and the works of Josephus the Jewish historian set the beginning of Jesus' ministry when he turned thirty. A group of followers soon gathered, including, of course, his mother, Mary, and Mary Magdalene. Jesus' ministry consisted of teaching through the literary devices of stories, fables, anecdotes, prayers, sayings, and parables as well as healings, miraculous works, signs, and the like. His followers were so devoted that they often sacrificed their lives rather than renounce their beliefs.

Passion and Death

The arrest and trial of Jesus is called his Passion. The Gospel of Mark 15:42 states that Jesus died on a Friday (Jews celebrate sundown Friday to sundown Saturday as their Sabbath) on a Passover weekend. He perished on the cross, was removed to the garden of Joseph of Arimathea, wrapped in linen and spices, and subsequently entombed. On the third day, scripture says he arose and appeared to Mary Magdalene. It is because of her role as a loving and loyal disciple during his Passion and His Resurrection that her place in the history of Christianity is ensured for all time.

Following Jesus

Biblical historians familiar with the sociopolitical and religious conditions of Jesus' time say that he didn't just one day appear and declare he was establishing a new religion and calling it Christianity. He was a Jew and Mary Magdalene and his earliest followers were as well. The Jesus movement began as a Jewish sect at a time when influences from other cultures, especially the Roman Empire, were informing the lives of those living in Palestine.

How Did They Meet?

Jesus may have been one of a number of charismatic healers who traveled the countryside doing good works and teaching religious ideas. But for women to move around the countryside with a man or men would have been unusual in the first century. It was considered scandalous for a woman to even speak to a man in public or to let him see her hair unbound. So how did Mary Magdalene and Jesus cross paths? Perhaps she had heard about the itinerant preacher and the crowds he attracted. Perhaps she wanted to see him and hear his message. Maybe she sought healing from Jesus. However that fateful meeting came about, Mary Magdalene heeded an inner urging to follow Jesus, and no other.

The prevailing opinion is that she wasn't "called" by him, as were his twelve male disciples. The Bible sheds no light on this subject, so it's difficult to know the sequence of events that connected their lives. But she did follow Jesus. And she wasn't the only woman to embrace his ideology and values. His mother, Mary, and other women were part of his traveling coterie of disciples and followers.

fallacy

It's a fallacy that Mary Magdalene was ever a prostitute. Biblical scholars have found no evidence to support that myth, which was created by Pope Gregory the Great to illustrate the forgiving nature of Christianity. After unfairly portraying Mary Magdalene for centuries as a redeemed harlot, the Roman Catholic Church in 1969 reversed its position and revised its Missal. It now calls Mary Magdalene "Apostle to the Apostles."

How Jesus Treated Women

The egalitarian Jesus offered a new view of how to treat women that elevated their status from a rank below beasts of burden to one of equality with men. The Jewish men around him must have seen this as a radical departure from the traditional way women were viewed in their culture. Some might have even been threatened or thought he was crazy. Jesus liberated women from their established traditional roles as wives and mothers.

For Mary Magdalene and her female companions in the Jesus movement—especially those women considered social outcasts because of physical defects, illnesses, and sins—Jesus' compassion and respect must have seemed as refreshing as a sip of cool water on a hot Galilean day. Jesus gave them hope, purpose, and a reason to live. He forgave the sins of Jewish and Gentile women alike, healed their ailing and broken bodies, saved them from death by stoning, and restored their dignity.

Mary Magdalene is accorded a prominent position, even a pre-eminent one, as a follower of Jesus in the Gospels when her name often appears first in lists of women who followed Jesus. Unless a woman had social prominence, she would not be named in any texts. Since Mary Magdalene's name is included along with other women's names, perhaps wealthy women helped fund Jesus' Galilean mission.

Mary Magdalene's Female Companions

Often in the New Testament Gospels, Mary Magdalene's name is mentioned along with other women who, like her, traveled with Jesus. She must have forged relationships with these women as they moved from town to town, helping Jesus, learning from him as he spoke to the crowds, and talking with his disciples.

Mary, Mother of Jesus

Jesus' mother would have kept company with Mary Magdalene while traveling with Jesus in his ministry. All Christians hold Mary in high esteem; Catholics, in particular, venerate her as the Queen of Heaven, the Immaculate Conception, and the sinless mother of Christ.

Mary Jacobi

The mother of James the Less and Joses, Mary Jacobi was one of the women contributors (perhaps a financial supporter) who followed Jesus throughout Galilee. She also accompanied Mary Magdalene and the other women to Jesus' death, burial, and resurrection.

Mary, Mother of John Mark

The mother of John Mark (a friend of Peter's and namesake of the Gospel of Mark), this Mary held a group prayer session that Peter attended on his release from prison. Her son, John Mark, may have been the youthful disciple who fled when Jesus was arrested.

Mary, Wife of Cleophas

The wife of Cleophas (modern spelling is Clopas) and thought to be the sister-in-law of Jesus' mother, this Mary stood vigil at the cross with Mary Magdalene and Jesus' mother during Jesus' crucifixion and death.

Salome

Wife of Zebedee and the mother of James and John, Salome was among the women who went to anoint Jesus' body with sweet spices.

Martha

The sister of Mary of Bethany and Lazarus (whom Jesus raised from the dead), Martha oversaw the running of the home where she and her siblings lived. She labored to prepare a meal while Mary remained seated at Jesus' feet. Mary anointed Him with scented oil. Martha told Jesus that her brother would not have died if Jesus had not waited four days to come. Even after all that time, Jesus raised Lazarus from the dead. Although the Eastern Church has always kept Mary Magdalene and Martha's sister, Mary, separate, some Western traditions have fused the two identities while others have distinguished between them.

A Woman of Independent Means

Mary Magdalene may have had the financial means to contribute to the needs of Jesus and his coterie. The Gospel of Luke states that Mary and some of the women healed by Jesus not only accompanied him and his apostles as they traveled through cities and villages but that the women ministered "unto him of their substance" (Luke 8:1–3). Along with Mary Magdalene who provided support to the Jesus movement, the Gospel of Luke also mentions Joanna, the wife of Chuza, Herod's steward. The passage in Luke certainly seems to suggest that these women had financial resources at their disposal.

Feminist theologians say that it is important to remember that although the Gospel of Luke often mentions women, Mary Magdalene and other women are cast in traditional roles as patrons and benefactors rather than as leaders, preachers, healers, prophetesses, and visionaries within the movement. The Gospel of Luke also states that Peter first saw the risen Christ, not Mary Magdalene as proclaimed by the Gospels of Matthew, Mark, and John. The Gospel of Luke, according to some feminist theologians, subtly erodes the primacy of Mary Magdalene as an important member of the Jesus movement and relegates her to roles appropriate for women of those times. In the role of benefactor, she might have arranged or contributed to the purchase of food, clothing, and shelter for Jesus and his group. This would certainly fit in with a lesser role accorded her by Luke. It begs the question, however: What was the source of Mary Magdalene's income?

factum

Mary Magdalene's titles of respect or monikers are "Thirteenth Apostle," "the All," "the Apostle to the Apostles," "Equal to the Apostles," and the "Woman Who Knows the All." Some have even called her "Christianity's Founder" in veneration of her role as the first apostle.

Theories of Mary Magdalene's Wealth

Some believe that Mary Magdalene may have descended from a well-to-do family. Theologians reason that since she came from Magdala Nunayya, and it was known to be a prosperous place, perhaps she had some beneficial connection to a successful enterprise there. Perhaps she had some prominence in that town and that is why she was called Mary of Magdala. However, seaports, especially a prosperous one like Magdala Nunayya, have traditionally been associated with unsavory reputations—places where bacchanalian sailors could drive the age-old trade of prostitution.

Others say she was most likely a widow of some inheritance although scholars say that Palestinian Hebrew women were quite poor during Jesus' time. They lived tenuous lives, unable to inherit and at the mercy of husbands who could divorce them for the slightest provocation (like burning a meal). They had no right to divorce and even if they did, the consequences were disastrous in terms of their survival.

Was She Mary of Bethany?

Still others believe a connection exists to support the fusing of Mary Magdalene's and Mary of Bethany's identities. A careful reading of the Gospel of John seems to confirm that Mary of Bethany is indeed Mary Magdalene (11:2). Mary of Bethany may have been of noble lineage and had considerable resources. The Eastern Church has always kept these two Marys separate, but certain Western traditions have combined them. The Roman Catholic Church long ago merged Mary Magdalene and Mary of Bethany with the Gospel of Luke's unnamed sinner, a fallen woman, or prostitute. In Luke's account, this anonymous woman's story precedes the reference to Mary Magdalene, perhaps causing the confusion in the first place.

> *And behold, a woman in the city, which was a sinner, when she knew that Jesus sat at meat in the Pharisee's house, brought an alabaster box of ointment, and stood at his feet behind him weeping, and began to wash his feet with her tears, and did wipe them with the hairs on her head, and kissed his feet, and anointed them with the ointment. Now when the Pharisee which had bidden him saw it, he spake within himself, saying, This man, if he were a prophet, would have known who and what manner of woman this is that toucheth him: for she is a sinner* **(Luke 7:37–39)**.

The Pharisee certainly knew this woman was a sinner. What was the nature of her sin? It's a good bet it had something to do with her sexuality. If she didn't conform to first-century society's traditional view of womanhood, then she stood outside of what was culturally acceptable. Such women were judged fallen, forbidden, or outcast—and were usually judged in terms of their sexuality or sexual sins. It was outside the realm of traditional Old Testament Hebrew thinking that a woman could be both a sexual and a holy being.

In Chapter 8, you'll read about how a well-meaning pope combined these women's stories. The Catholic Church has now officially separated this repentant sinner from the two Marys. But some still believe that Mary Magdalene and Mary of Bethany were the same woman. The Gospels suggest they both anointed Jesus.

symbolism

In art, she is most frequently pictured with the icon of an ointment box or unguent jar (often made of alabaster). In Byzantine iconographic images, Mary Magdalene also holds an egg as a symbol of the Resurrection, hope, and promise.

Lest there be any confusion about what anointing is, here's a brief overview of that act. Anoint means to apply holy oil on objects, people, and places to sanctify and consecrate them to God. The Hebrews often used perfumed oil (olive oil mixed with spices) for both secular and sacred purposes, including medicinal uses such as applying it on wounds. Even in modern times, some churches use holy oil to anoint the sick. In Jesus' time, Jews customarily used perfumed oils to refresh themselves and also anointed their guests as an act of hospitality. In addition, they anointed their dead before burial. Following the Jewish Sabbath, Mary Magdalene, according to the Gospel of Mark, went to anoint the body of Jesus: "And when the sabbath was past, Mary Magdalene, and Mary the mother of James, and Salome, had brought sweet spices, that they might come and anoint him" (16:1).

Could She Claim Royal Lineage?

There's a great deal of confusion about the Marys in the Gospels because there were so many women who had that name. In fact, Mary was a popular name for Hebrew women in Jesus' time. Also, many of them were followers of Jesus. Some anointed him. Mary of Bethany, sister to Martha and Lazarus, was one of them, according to the Gospel of John. She is the Mary most often associated with Mary Magdalene. Could they have been the same woman?

A Case for Being Martha's Sister

"Now a certain man was sick, named Lazarus, of Bethany, the town of Mary and her sister Martha. (It was that Mary which anointed the Lord with ointment, and wiped his feet with her hair, whose brother Lazarus was sick)" (John 11:1–2). Mary lived with Martha and Lazarus in a house in Bethany. The canonical Gospels reveal that Jesus loved them and visited them. On one occasion mentioned in the Gospel of Luke, Jesus stays for a meal. While Martha completes the preparations, her sister sits with Jesus. The Gospel of Luke describes this particular incident.

> Now it came to pass, as they went, that he entered into a certain village: and a certain woman named Martha received him into her house. And she had a sister called Mary, which also sat at Jesus' feet, and heard his word. But Martha was cumbered about much serving, and came to him, and said, Lord, dost thou not care that my sister hath left me serve alone? bid her therefore that she help me. And Jesus answered and said unto her, Martha, Martha, thou art careful and troubled about many things: but one thing is needful; and Mary hath chosen that good part, which shall not be taken away from her *(10:38–42)*.

If Mary Magdalene was the same person as Mary of Bethany (as suggested by some authors who have conjectured that the latter woman was possibly a Benjamite heiress), it would explain her having resources to use to minister to Jesus. Biblical scholar and writer Margaret Starbird theorizes that Mary of Bethany may have belonged to the tribe of Benjamin and that her tribe remained so close and loyal to the tribe of Judah (the House of David from which Jesus descended) that the tribes' histories were entwined. For a nation chafing under Roman occupation, an alliance between this royal daughter and Jesus would have given hope to the Jewish people. However, many do not believe that Mary Magdalene and Mary of Bethany were the same person. And scriptures do not say that Mary of Magdala descended from royalty.

factum

There are several references in the Bible to Christ as the Anointed One. The Greek word christos means "anointed one." The Hebrew equivalent is meshiach or messiah. The ancient Hebrews believed a Redeemer (descendant from the House of David) would reunite Israel and Judah to usher in a messianic age. The promised Deliverer in the Old Testament is called the "Anointed." The New Testament Gospels and letters declare that Jesus is that Anointed Messiah or Christos (John 1:41; Acts 9:22, 17:2–3, 18:5, 18:28).

Mary Magdalene the Apostle

While many curious Christians have turned to the scriptures to discover anew Mary Magdalene's story, others have not and may still believe in the penitent prostitute myth, despite lack of evidence. In that way, she is still being maligned. Most scholars now agree that Mary Magdalene was Jesus' closest friend (some say, his confidante). She is venerated in the Eastern Orthodox Church and the Roman Catholic Church as a saint. She has been called Apostle to the Apostles by church fathers, from Saint Augustine, who viewed women as inferior, to the late Pope John Paul II. Her other titles are "the Thirteenth Apostle" and "the Woman Who Knew the All."

chapter 2

For the Love of Jesus

For more than 2,000 years, Mary Magdalene has been falsely portrayed as a woman with an unsavory past in the flesh trade who was forgiven her sins by Jesus. Modern scholarship has corrected the untruth about her past and is revealing a Mary Magdalene who loved her teacher and selflessly served him and his earthly ministry in many roles, some traditional and others that elevated her stature from that of a traditional Hebrew woman of her time.

Leader, Follower, Friend, and Confidante

Most Christians believe that Mary Magdalene was a faithful follower of Jesus and that their relationship may have evolved until she became a close friend and confidante. Experts say that a good predictor of future leadership lies in past leadership behavior and skills. Mary Magdalene might have been a leader or a woman of significant standing in her community before meeting Jesus and may have put her leadership skills to use in the movement after the Resurrection.

Generous Benefactor

As previously mentioned, she provided for Jesus out of her own resources—perhaps she sold woolen items that she had woven or had a business concerned with fish or baked goods. No one knows for sure what revenue streams were available to her, how much money she had, or whether she even engaged in financial enterprise. What the Gospel accounts say is that she provided for Jesus out of her resources. When lodging was required or food items needed to be purchased, Mary Magdalene and the other women took care of what was needed. But more than her monetary resources, Mary Magdalene bore a great love for Jesus and freely gave of that as well. She showed her devotion, loyalty, courage, leadership, and commitment to Jesus in many ways in the Gospel accounts—ministering unto him, standing vigil at the cross, returning to the tomb to anoint him after the Jewish Sabbath had ended, weeping when she found the tomb empty, begging the man she thought was the gardener to tell her where the body of Jesus had been taken, and, upon discovering that the man wasn't the gardener but the risen Savior, faithfully following his directive to tell the others of his victory over death.

In the Gospel of Matthew, Mary Magdalene is represented as Jesus' benefactor along with some other women who ministered to him (27:55–56). Accompanied by "the other Mary," Mary Magdalene took spices to the tomb to anoint Jesus' body. The women experienced a great earthquake because the angel of the Lord had descended from heaven, rolled the stone away from the tomb, and sat on it. The angel wasted no time in telling them that Jesus had risen and that they must go and tell his disciples (Matthew 28:1–7).

factum

A myrrhbearer was a woman who acquired and prepared gums or resins, perfumed oil, and spices for anointing. In ancient times, myrrh served as an excellent preservative and drying agent and was therefore used to anoint the dead.

The Last Supper

The Last Supper refers to the meal that Jesus shared with his twelve disciples during that momentous Passover before he was arrested and crucified. This meal was the covenant meal in which Jesus introduced the bread (his body) and wine (his blood) as new symbols of his sacrificial death. The Reformation churches generally use the term *Lord's Supper* to signify the ingesting of bread and wine in symbolic remembrance of Jesus' great sacrifice for humankind. Many Christian churches refer to this sacrament as communion. In the Catholic Church, it is the sacrament of the Eucharist. Just as during Passover the Jews shared a celebratory meal that marked their redemption and deliverance out of Egypt, the Last Supper signified the deliverance and salvation of God's people through the Messiah and his ultimate sacrifice. From then until now, the taking of communion in Christian churches re-enacts Jesus' sacrifice, something he enjoined his faithful followers to do.

Was Mary Magdalene present during the Last Supper when Jesus dined with the Twelve in the upper room? Nowhere in the Gospels does it say that she attended that last meal, either as a participant or as a cook or server. Since Jewish families marked the holy occasion of Passover with the symbolic Seder (or meal), Mary Magdalene would certainly have been familiar with the event and the foods prepared and consumed.

symbolism

Jewish people celebrate Passover with a Seder, or religious meal that includes blessings, prayers, the reading of the Haggadah (the book that contains the liturgy for this holy occasion), the singing of traditional songs, and the eating of foods that symbolize the bondage of the Jews in Egypt and their subsequent exodus.

A More Important Role?

For many, Mary Magdalene stood then as now as an important exemplar for a model disciple. But did she have an elevated role in the Jesus movement following the Resurrection? Could she have served the fledgling community as a visionary prophetess, a healer, a preacher, and a church leader with her own following? Some scholars believe that is exactly what happened while others discount it as pure speculation. Some of the apostles had their own circle of disciples, and those disciples, in turn, had their own followers. Learn more about this in Part II; Mary Magdalene is discussed in the context of the Gnostic texts and those writings excluded from the Bible. In her book, *Mary Magdalene*, Lynne Picknett differentiates the focus of the New Testament Gospels from the Gnostic writings by pointing out that the canonical Gospels are concerned with Jesus' mission and the chronological sequencing of events of his life interspersed with miracles and parables. The Gnostic Gospels deal with inner spiritual work to gain knowledge and attain perfection of the soul.

Witness to the Resurrection

Jesus' Resurrection account depends upon the testimony of women. The Gospels reveal that Mary Magdalene, Salome, Joanna, Mary (the mother of James and Joses), and other women disciples escorted Jesus to his death. Mary Magdalene witnessed his transcendent form, and Jesus gave her a message to carry to the others. Biblical scholars think this represents strong proof of the historical event of the Resurrection because men would not have included women in a society that rejected women as legal witnesses.

The Synoptic Gospels

In the Gospel of Mark, Mary Magdalene is one of the women who ministered to Jesus and witnessed his death (15:40–41). Mary Magdalene, accompanied by Mary, mother of James the Less, and Salome, purchased sweet spices to anoint Jesus (15:47, 16:1). So here again, Mary Magdalene performs a traditional woman's role of one who ministers and anoints.

factum

The synoptic Gospels are the first three books of the New Testament: Matthew, Mark, and Luke. They contain certain accounts in common about Jesus' life and work as well as parables. The Gospel of John, also known as the Fourth Gospel, differs from the synoptic Gospels with a literary voice and a theological understanding that casts doubt it was written by John, the fisherman.

In the Resurrection narrative of the Gospel of Luke, Mary Magdalene is a myrrhbearer and a messenger. She and the other women with her went to Jesus' tomb and found the stone rolled away. They "beheld the sepulchre and how his body was laid" and "prepared spices and ointments" (23:55–56). Two men in dazzling garments tell the women that Jesus is not there. The women return to the other disciples and share the news about the empty tomb and that Jesus has risen but the disciples do not believe them. So here, too, Luke portrays Mary Magdalene in roles traditionally belonging to women.

The three synoptic Gospels generally cover the ministry of Jesus in Galilee. Mentions of Mary Magdalene are few and show her in the traditional roles of benefactor, myrrhbearer, and messenger. As messenger, however, she isn't believed, perhaps precisely because she's a woman.

The Fourth Gospel

The Gospel of John, also referred to as the Fourth Gospel, stands apart from the synoptic Gospels in its depiction of Mary Magdalene and also because of its content, narrative style, and selection of events (it deals with Jesus' work in Judea and includes some events not included in the other Gospels, suggesting a reliance on some other material). This Gospel focuses on the theological interpretations of Jesus' life and work and provides a fuller accounting of the Passion and Resurrection of Jesus. The Gospel of John also differs from the synoptic Gospels because it puts a spotlight squarely on Mary Magdalene.

discussion question

Who were Jesus' seven companions who were holy myrrhbearers? Mary Magdalene; Mary, the wife of Cleophas; Joanna, wife of Chuza (steward of Herod Antipas); Salome, mother of the sons of Zebedee; Susanna; and Mary and Martha, sisters of Lazarus.

John places Mary Magdalene at the Crucifixion, however, she isn't merely one of the women who had ministered to Jesus or who brings spices. The Fourth Gospel shows Mary Magdalene in a primary role in the Easter story. She is present at the Crucifixion and observes the placing of Jesus' body in the tomb. She laments at the empty tomb and desperately seeks information on the whereabouts of Jesus' body when she finds the tomb empty. Mary Magdalene is the sole eyewitness to the transcendent form of the risen Christ. And he commissions her to carry the news to the other disciples (some say this is the first commission by Jesus to preach).

How the Gospels Agree

With John's Gospel echoing Matthew's, Mark's, and Luke's accounts of the Resurrection, the centerpiece of Christian theology, there is no credibility of a single eyewitness. In the synoptic Gospels, no one person witnessed each of the events surrounding the Passion and the Resurrection. In the Gospel of John, Mary Magdalene becomes that person. She witnessed not just one part but the entire unfolding of these events so central to the Christian faith. She provides continuity and credibility; scholars say that her role suggests the historicity of these events because women could not be legal witnesses.

fallacy

It's a fallacy that women were never crucified. While women made up a tiny fraction of the crucified (who were mostly male slaves and criminals), it was not completely unheard of for a woman to be executed in this way. One ancient text, Sanhedrin 6.5, states that in the community of Ashkelon, seventy or eighty women—considered sorceresses—were hung on crosses.

All four Gospel writers included Mary Magdalene in their accounts of the last days of Jesus, which suggests that she performed roles far too important to be excluded. Some feminist theologians say that references to her were almost certainly minimized by the Gospel writers (and possibly editors/revisionists) and a church that was evolving out of an Old Testament Jewish male-dominated culture.

Vigil with Mother Mary and John

Mary Magdalene did not desert Jesus when he was tortured and nailed to the cross. Even as the soldiers cast lots for his coat,

Mary Magdalene took stood vigil. The Gospel of John's narrative explains:

> Now there stood by the cross of Jesus his mother, and his mother's sister, Mary the wife of Cleophas, and Mary Magdalene. When Jesus therefore saw his mother, and the disciple standing by, whom he loved, he saith unto his mother, Woman, behold thy son! Then saith he to the disciple, Behold thy mother! And from that hour the disciple took her unto his own home *(19:25–27)*.

For those gathered at Golgotha, the place of the cross, the hours must have been agonizingly long. And how horrific it must have been for them to stand by helplessly with only prayers to offer as they witnessed and awaited the death of the one they loved most.

The Gospel of Mark says that present during Jesus' death was Mary Magdalene and other women looking on from a distance: "There were also women looking on afar off: among whom was Mary Magdalene, and Mary the mother of James the Less and of Joses, and Salome; who also, when he was in Galilee, followed and ministered unto him; and many other women which came up with him into Jerusalem" (15:40–41).

No one can deny it took an enormous act of character and faith for Mary Magdalene to keep vigil with Jesus' mother and his disciple through the grueling hours that followed the Crucifixion. After watching him, they heard his heart-wrenching cry: "*Eloi, lama sabachtani?*" which means, "My God, my God, why hast thou forsaken me?" The Gospel of Mark says that a centurion who stood nearby heard Jesus cry out in a loud voice and "give up the ghost" then that man said, "Truly this man was the Son of God" (15:39).

And so it was finished. While Jesus' mother, Mary Magdalene, and the "disciple whom Jesus loved" stood vigil at Golgotha, the other disciples hid themselves out of fear that they might be arrested and put to death as well. Perhaps those who feared for their lives did not think the Romans would hurt Jesus' mother or Mary Magdalene because of their gender.

Significance of the Cross

It might have been difficult for Mary Magdalene to put the punishing image of Jesus on the cross out of her mind. Even grasping the meaning of his death would not have lessened the agonizing experience of watching the one she loved most in the world die in such an excruciating way. She could not know then that Christian churches throughout the centuries would be recognized by their crosses and how different they would look, even though the symbolism remained the same: He paid the ultimate sacrifice for the sins of humankind.

factum

While the crucifixion of women was rare, stoning was a more common method of executing women who sinned, such as those believed to have committed adultery or those others presumed to have had sexual intercourse while menstruating, which was strictly forbidden. Menstruation lasted about seven days; during this time, known as niddah, women were unclean until they purified themselves with the ritual purification bath known as a mikvah.

In some ancient texts, the method of death by crucifixion could be on a tree or a wooden pole cut from a tree. The most rudimentary cross or *crux simplex* was simply a stake. Later, a horizontal beam was anchored to a vertical post or stake. The person being put to death was either tied or nailed to the cross. Making the sign of the cross may have early origins because the Montanist follower Tertullian (155–230) mentioned tracing the sign upon the forehead before undertaking mundane actions such as eating, bathing, or lighting lamps. It is believed that he was speaking about making the sign of the cross. One of the earliest examples of the cross in art appears on a fifth-century Vatican sarcophagus. Cross shapes evolved from the *crux simplex* or simple cross to other forms such as the St. Andrew's cross, which forms an X, St. Anthony's cross, and St. Philip's, in which the structure forms a T, *tau* shape. There is some speculation that the *tau* shape was borrowed from the Druids who worshiped the pagan god Thau. The Greek version of the Gospels say Jesus was crucified on a *stauros*, which means a vertical post without a horizontal pole crossing it. Today, the cross is used both as a religious symbol and as an artistic design in ornamentation. There are more than 400 different variants of the cross.

First Witness and Commission from Jesus

As you have already learned in this chapter, Mary Magdalene went to anoint the body of Jesus after the Jewish Sabbath ended. She had walked to the tomb with her spice jar in the predawn darkness. Such work was not to be done on the Sabbath so Mary Magdalene had to wait until the first day of the week. When she saw the stone had been removed, she ran to Simon Peter and to the disciple whom Jesus loved and told them. Of course, the disciples then went to the tomb to see for themselves, but then they went home.

Grief and Joy

Mary Magdalene remained, standing outside the tomb, and wept. In her grief, she leaned down and looked into the sepulcher and saw two angels clad in white. One of them was sitting where Jesus' head had previously lain. The other was seated where his feet had been. "Woman, why weepest thou?" the angels asked. Mary replied, "Because they have taken away my Lord, and I know not where they have laid him" (John 20:11–13).

Mary Magdalene, like anyone in the deep throes of grief, must have felt utter despair; she didn't react at seeing the angels. She simply turned back and saw the figure of a man standing nearby. Seeing him through eyes that surely shimmered with tears, she must have wondered who he was.

And when she had thus said, she turned herself back, and saw Jesus standing, and knew not that it was Jesus. Jesus saith unto her,

Woman, why weepest thou? whom seekest thou? She, supposing him to be the gardener, saith unto him, Sir if thou hast borne him hence, tell me where thou hast laid him, and I will take him away. Jesus saith unto her, Mary. She turned herself, and saith unto him, Rabboni, which is to say, Master (John 20:14–16).

One can only imagine the incredible exhilaration and joy Mary Magdalene experienced in that moment when Jesus called her name and she recognized him in his transcendent form. She must have reached out to touch him or dropped to her knees to embrace him for the Gospel of John goes on to say: "Jesus saith unto her, Touch me not; for I am not yet ascended to my Father: but go to my brethren, and say unto them, I ascend unto my Father, and your Father, and to my God, and your God" (20:17).

discussion question

Why did Jesus tell Mary Magdalene not to touch him but told Thomas the opposite?
He may have wanted Mary Magdalene to understand that she must release the desire to hold on to his physical form; her relationship would now be with his spirit. Because Thomas could not believe what he couldn't feel or see, Jesus provided proof.

Mary Spreads the News
Jesus bestowed a great blessing on his faithful companion Mary Magdalene that day. She became the first to see the risen Christ. And with the blessing came a directive. He chose her to carry the news of his victory over death to his brethren. "Mary Magdalene came and told the disciples that she had seen the Lord, and that he had spoken these things unto her" (John 20:18).

The Gospel of John states that after Mary Magdalene told the disciples about the Resurrection appearance, Jesus came and stood in the midst of the disciples that evening where they had assembled behind closed doors. Thomas was not present and when the disciples told him the news, he doubted them. He told them he would believe Jesus had risen from the dead only if he could put his finger into the print of the nails on Jesus' body and thrust his hand into Jesus' side. Eight days later, Jesus appeared to the disciples again and this time instructed Thomas to touch his wounds.

factum

Noli me tangere is Latin for "touch me not." The phrase has inspired many works of art depicting the resurrected transcendent Jesus and Mary Magdalene in the garden near the empty tomb that first Easter morning.

When Mary Magdalene recognized Jesus in the garden at the empty tomb, she reached out to touch him, prompting Jesus to tell her not to touch him. Those who study the Bible have vigorously debated the issue of *noli me tangere*. Some have suggested that Jesus encourages Thomas to touch him to strengthen the man's faith. As for Mary Magdalene, Jesus may have wanted her to learn to keep company with his spiritual essence rather than his earthly physical presence. And this was a woman he knew so well. Mary Magdalene quite possibly was Jesus' brightest pupil. The Pistis Sophia, a Gnostic text, states that Jesus tells Mary Magdalene that he would reveal the Divine mysteries to her because her heart was pure and reaching toward heaven. Mary Magdalene most certainly would have known how to turn inward in prayer, contemplation, and meditation to be in his presence.

The Risen Jesus Magnifies Her

The apostles carried forth the news of the Resurrection to others, but Jesus asked Mary Magdalene to carry it to his apostles. Jesus could have just as easily shown himself first to his mother or the Beloved Disciple or Salome—anyone but Mary Magdalene, but he chose her for this supreme blessing and her most important role.

According to some of the Gnostic texts (discussed in Part II), Mary Magdalene so excelled at insightful questioning of Jesus and skillfully grasped the subtle nuances of his teachings that he complimented her. It seems clear from those Gnostic texts that she held a place of esteem in Jesus' heart. She must have been a spiritual adept, a hard worker, and generous with her resources. Even the Apostle Paul writing in his letter to the Romans honored Mary Magdalene as he singled out women and men who shared in the work of preaching: "Greet Mary, who bestowed much labor on us" (Romans 16:6), meaning she both served and supported the movement through its difficulties and dangers.

Mary Magdalene must have felt magnified by the risen Jesus as she glorified him through the work that she and the other disciples carried forward. One can only marvel that the grief-stricken woman found the strength to seek and draw out the disciples from where they hid, then comfort them, and turn their minds away from the despair and darkness to the light that Jesus' teachings and words of comfort represented.

Apostle to the Apostles

Who saw the risen Jesus first and why does it matter? The Gospels differ on this question. In Matthew, an angel tells Mary Magdalene and the other Mary that Jesus has risen. And as they run to tell his disciples, Jesus meets them (Matthew 28:1–7). Mark states it simply and boldly: "Now when Jesus was risen early the first day of the week, he appeared first to Mary Magdalene, out of whom he had cast seven devils" (16:9). John agrees with Mark and explains what transpired in this way: Mary Magdalene stood outside the empty sepulcher weeping. She asked a man she believed to be the gardener to tell her where they had taken Jesus' body. When Jesus calls out her name, she instantly recognizes him (20:16). So, Matthew, Mark, and John are in accord that Mary Magdalene first witnessed the risen Jesus. That her name is singled out in the Gospel accounts suggests her prominence among the women surrounding Jesus.

discussion question

What's the textual evidence for the Resurrection?
Jesus' message depends on the testimony of Mary Magdalene, Salome, Joanna, Mary, the mother of James and Joses, and other women. Biblical scholars agree that this testimony suggests the historicity of the event. If men had made it up, they would not have included women as witnesses in a society that rejected women as legal witnesses.

However, the Gospel of Luke says that Peter first saw the risen Savior on the road leading to the village of Emmaus. Further, Luke says that Peter and Cleopas spoke with Jesus. Then the two went to Jerusalem, met with the eleven apostles who were gathered, and told them that the Lord had risen. Jesus appeared in their midst and opened their minds and hearts so that they could understand the scriptures (Luke 24:10–31). The Roman Catholic Church traces its apostolic lineage, power, and authority back to Peter, not Mary Magdalene.

Women and the Great Commission

A point of contention among scholars is whether at that point the disciples were considered apostles. Also, did Jesus' words amount to an assignment that was or was not associated with the apostolic leadership position? Were Mary Magdalene and the women witnesses at the same gathering as the eleven disciples (Matthew does not say)? They certainly believed that Jesus had risen. They fell down, held on to his feet, and worshiped him. Their hearts were not hardened (which was the reason Jesus upbraided the men). The women witnesses loved Jesus, served him, ministered to him, witnessed his transcendent form, and shared the Good News as they had been told to do. It is difficult for some to believe that Jesus would deny them apostleship when they could serve him as leaders, spreading the teachings, and administering sacraments like baptism—in short, using their gifts of Spirit in their communities and in the greater world beyond.

In the Gospel of Mark, Jesus appears first to Mary Magdalene. She tells the others, but they do not believe her. Then Jesus appears in another form to two others as they are walking in the countryside. When they share the news, they are not believed either. Later, Jesus appeared to the eleven as they sat eating and chastised them for not believing those who had told them he had risen. Then he says: "Go ye into all the world, and preach the gospel to every creature. He that believeth and is baptized shall be saved; but he that believeth not shall be damned" (Mark 16:15–16).

The Great Commission seems to have two major points: to evangelize, making disciples of all nations, and to preach the gospel. Scholars believe that Mary Magdalene accomplished these things in her life following Jesus' death. She is believed to have served as a leader of prayer services and spiritual fellowship in homes of followers of the movement. Her legends suggest that at some point she may have evangelized southern Gaul and possibly Ephesus, where traditions venerating her continue to the present and many churches have been erected in her honor. Did she perform baptisms? No source says she did, but none say she didn't.

chapter 3

Jesus' Other Loyal Followers

No one knows exactly when it was that Mary Magdalene met Jesus, but she would have known at least some of the other followers. She certainly knew his mother, Mary, and possibly his brother, James. Unquestionably, she had contact with Peter. Any meeting between Mary Magdalene and the apostle Paul is a point of speculation since Paul never physically met Jesus. Many people walked with Jesus from time to time, but Mary Magdalene was constantly by his side.

Mary, Mother of Jesus

In the New Testament Gospels, mentions of Mary Magdalene often appear with the name of Mary, Jesus' mother. The two women were members of a coterie that traveled with Jesus during his ministry. They stood together at Golgotha during his crucifixion. John 19:26–27 states that Jesus entrusted the care of his mother to his Beloved Disciple from the cross. Both women witnessed the death of his earthly body.

Foreshadowing in the Old Testament

Genesis 3:15 foreshadowed the role of Mary in that it states the destroyer of Satan [Christ] would be the seed of a woman [his mother]. The house of David, according to the Gospel of Matthew, was promised the incarnation of God would come through a virgin. "Now all this was done, that it might be fulfilled which was spoken of the Lord by the prophet, saying, Behold, a virgin shall be with child, and shall bring forth a son, and they shall call his name Emmanuel, which being interpreted is, God with us" (Matthew 1:22–23). Mary fulfilled the prophecy and the promise.

Background

Ann and Joachim, an infertile couple who prayed to God for a child, had their desire fulfilled with the birth of Mary. Sinless from birth, Mary became known through the centuries by one of her many monikers, the Immaculate Conception. When she was a young woman, she was betrothed to the carpenter Joseph. Luke 1:26 states that God sent the angel Gabriel to the city of Galilee in Nazareth to find Mary and tell her that God favored her and that she would conceive and give birth to a boy whom she was to call Jesus. The angel explained that the Holy Ghost would come over her and make the conception possible. Mary replied, "Behold the handmaid of the Lord; be it unto me according to thy word" (Luke 1:38).

Contradictory Accounts of Mary

The details of Mary's life are found in a wide assortment of biblical and apocryphal narratives and some contradict others. Her childhood was spent, according to some sources, in the Temple, a sacred Jewish environment, but also an exclusively male conclave. A good Jewish girl, she lived from her preteen years in Galilee, thought by some to be one of the most pagan-minded areas of Greater Judea. She was born a virgin and in her sinless state ascended into heaven instead of dying and being interred. Mary, the Blessed Virgin, who never knew a man in the carnal sense, came to be called Queen of Heaven, which was also the moniker given to the Mesopotamian fertility goddess.

Devotion and Inspiration

Mary is revered as the mother of the Savior. Early church fathers referred to her as *Christotokos* (Christ Bearer) and *Theotokos* (God Bearer). Traditionally, Mary is Queen of Heaven, and the faithful often ask her to carry their prayers on her heart to her son, Jesus. She serves as an advocate and a mediatrix. Today, she is venerated and honored all over the world. Some of the most beautiful cathedrals in Europe are dedicated to her. Miraculous sightings of Mary have occurred from ancient to modern times.

factum

One of the most important Latin prayers in veneration of Mary is the Ave Maria or Hail Mary. It combines the angel Gabriel's salutation to her in the Gospel of Luke with later worshipful words used in prayer to Mary in her role as mother of God. Other important prayers to Mary are the Angelus and the Memorare.

For centuries, Christians, especially Catholics, have recited the Hail Mary as part of the rosary. The repetition of the prayers while handling the beads is believed to create a sacred space for the minds and hearts of the faithful to receive the blessings of God. The rosary begins with recitation of the Apostles' Creed followed by the

Our Father and three Hail Marys, followed by the prayer Glory Be to the Father and continuing from that point on.

Through the centuries, the many faces of Mary, as well as her story, have inspired artists, writers, and musicians from all countries and cultures. In art, depictions of her run the gamut from famous works such as Michelangelo's *Pieta* and Diego Velasquez's *The Immaculate Conception* to lesser-known portraits of Mary on holy cards created by sisters in holy orders. Whether the image is of an unwed girl with an angel whispering in her ear or the sorrowful mother holding the body of her slain son, the mother of Jesus never ceases to inspire.

James, the Lord's Brother

Did Mary Magdalene know James, the Lord's brother, since she traveled with Jesus and the other disciples? No documents prove that she knew James, but it seems likely she may have met him. James is called "the Lord's brother" in Paul's letter to the Galatians 1:19: "But other of the apostles saw I none, save James the Lord's brother." This raises the question of whether Mary had other children or if James was Joseph's son and to indicate a brotherly spiritual relationship.

James's Life and Family

Tradition of the Russian Orthodox Church asserts that James was the son of Joseph and further relates that when Joseph was dying, he doled out his property to his sons and wanted also to give something to Jesus. That idea was thwarted by one of his sons who did not see Jesus as a brother. James, however, declared that he would share his portion with Jesus. James lived by Jesus' teaching. He consumed no oil or fat but rather bread and water, and remained chaste throughout his life.

James, also called James the Just, became one of Jesus' apostles and saw the risen Jesus after he had appeared to others: "And that he was seen of Cephas, then of the twelve: after that, he was seen of above five hundred brethren at once; of whom the greater part remained unto this present, but some are fallen asleep. After that he was seen of James; then of all the apostles" (1 Corinthians 15:5–7). James served as the bishop of Jerusalem for thirty years.

discussion question

Did James write the first liturgy?
The Russian Orthodox Church claims that James followed the Lord's instructions and wrote the first liturgy. Later church fathers Saint Basil and Saint John Chrysostom edited the liturgy to shorten it because they believed it was too long for Christians of that time.

James had brothers and possibly a wife. His brothers are mentioned in Matthew 13:55: "Is not this the carpenter's son? is not his mother called Mary? and his brethren, James, and Joses, and Simon, and Judas?" When Paul asks in 1 Corinthians 9:5, "Have we not power to lead about a sister, a wife, as well as other apostles, and as the brethren of the Lord, and Cephas," the inference is that James, the Lord's brother, is married.

One of Many

Just as there are many women called Mary in the New Testament, so, too, there are many men called James. James is one of four named in the New Testament texts. He was not one of the Twelve, which included James, son of Zebedee and brother of John the Divine, and James, son of Alphaeus, also known as James the Younger or James the Less. James, the Lord's brother, was undoubtedly the author of the Epistle of James since the other James (son of Zebedee and brother to John) was already martyred by the time the letter was written.

James Writes a Letter to the Twelve Tribes

The General Epistle of James, included as part of the canonical New Testament, opens with James declaring himself a servant of

God and of the Lord Jesus Christ. He writes to the attention of the twelve tribes (not in Jerusalem) that were scattered.

The letter offers practical advice for living a Christian life. Among other things, James admonishes against temptation and encourages believers to be pure in heart and not just a listener to the word of God as taught by Jesus but also a doer. "Wherefore, my beloved brethren, let every man be swift to hear, slow to speak, slow to wrath: for the wrath of man worketh not righteousness of God. Wherefore lay apart all filthiness and superfluity of naughtiness, and receive with meekness the engrafted word, which is able to save your souls. But be ye doers of the word, and not hearers only, deceiving your own selves" (James 1:19–22).

James's Martyrdom

James presided over the council of elders and apostles in Jerusalem. He fell afoul of the high priest Ananias, who, with the other Jewish elders, decided to get rid of him. They encouraged him to climb up onto a roof and speak out against Jesus as the Son of God. However, when James spoke, it was in favor of Jesus. According to the Russian Orthodox legend, the high priest and Jewish elders then pushed James off the roof. He hit the ground but was still alive until someone bashed in his head with a blow so vicious that his brains spilled out. James, the Lord's brother, was sixty-three.

John the Baptist

Of all the people mentioned in the New Testament along with Jesus, his mother, and Mary Magdalene, John the Baptist ranks as one of the most familiar. John and Jesus were related since John's elderly mother Elizabeth and Jesus' mother were cousins. Zechariah, John's father, was a Temple priest whose job included burning incense. They were Levites.

John the Wild Man

John lived in a mountainous area of Judah between the Dead Sea and Jerusalem. He wore clothes made of camel hair supported by a leather belt. His basic diet consisted of locusts and honey. He began his ministry at age twenty-seven preaching repentance of sin and baptizing crowds from Samaria and throughout the Judean wilderness. Jesus asked John to baptize him. After he baptized Jesus, John instructed his disciples to follow Jesus, whom he believed to be the Messiah.

factum

John's great destiny was to baptize his cousin Jesus. Interestingly, John was born six months before Jesus and died six months before Jesus was crucified. The conception of both boys was announced by the angel Gabriel appearing separately to their mothers. Zechariah did not believe and so was struck dumb until the birth of John.

John radically condemned the Jewish establishment of his lifetime, and his ministry grew so popular that people thought he was the messiah. To this John replied: "He that hath the bride is the bridegroom: but the friend of the bridegroom, which standeth and heareth him, rejoiceth greatly because of the bridegroom's voice: this my joy therefore is fulfilled. He must increase, but I must decrease" (John 3:29–30).

Other Names

Today John the Baptist is known by many other names, including Joannes Baptista, John the Baptizer, John the Forerunner, and Juan Bautista. He is sometimes called simply the Baptizer. Jewish historian Josephus suggested that John called people together in religious community through the act of baptism. His followers made up a distinct group who believed that baptism did not remove sin but purified the body and consecrated a heart already purified by righteousness to God.

John's Downfall and Death

John incurred the wrath of Herod Antipas and also of Herodias, Herod's wife. Herod thought John was behind a popular movement that might pose a political threat to him, and Herodias was upset that John had denounced her marriage as illegal. Herod imprisoned John, and scholars say that marked the beginning of Jesus' Galilean ministry. Herod beheaded John at the behest of Salome, daughter of Herodias. Salome danced for Herod, and he asked her what gift she wanted in return. She was instructed by Herodias to demand John the Baptist's head on a platter, which she did. One tradition states that Herod would stab the tongue with a dagger from time to time.

The Apostle Peter

Simon Peter was one of Jesus' most prominent disciples. Some modern theologians suggest that tension existed between Peter and Mary Magdalene because of her gender (Peter was patriarchal) and because Jesus favored her over the other disciples (according to some non-canonical sources). However, to Peter, Jesus said, "Upon this rock I will build my church; and the gates of hell shall not prevail against it" (Matthew 16:18). While many Christians interpret this verse literally, others say Jesus was speaking of the unshakeable rocklike belief that he intended to instill in his disciples and not specifically that Peter had to be the sole pillar.

Background and Character

Peter came from the fishing village of Bathsaida, which was located not far from Capernaum. A rural fisherman by trade with his brother Andrew and father, Jonah, Peter could likely read and write Aramaic and perhaps speak a little Greek. He was married, partners with James and John, and a follower of John the Baptist before his brother introduced him to Jesus.

Peter was characterized by boldness, strength, and straightforwardness. He was curious, sometimes violent (with enemies), but he was also loving and loyal. Peter possessed several qualities that made him an excellent spokesperson for the Lord: He was friendly, self-confident, and enthusiastic. But Peter was also hot-tempered and occasionally got into situations that required an apology in order to extricate himself. The New Testament Gospels reveal that Peter denied Jesus three times before the cock crowed, just as Jesus had predicted. Also, when the soldiers came to take Jesus away, Peter tried to protect him using weapons for which Jesus rebuked him.

discussion question

Why did Peter say that Jesus loved Mary Magdalene more than the rest of the disciples?
Perhaps Mary Magdalene's spiritual maturity and her ability to understand Jesus' teachings better than all the others set her apart and endowed her with a legitimacy as a leading disciple and eloquent spokesperson for the teachings of the Savior.

Peter's Personal Motive

According to some sources, Peter initially had a personal motive for following Jesus: He saw Jesus as the potential messiah for the Hebrew people. By aligning himself with Jesus, Peter thought he could enhance his status. Jesus demonstrated a loving patience with Peter's ebullient ways. In the Nag Hammadi texts, Peter is critical of Mary Magdalene, who enjoys an elevated status; in the orthodox texts, Peter's status is elevated. Jesus favors Peter, giving him the responsibility of leading the movement.

A Ministry Far and Wide

After the death of their beloved teacher Jesus, the disciples went to Galilee where Peter suggested they return to fishing. During an unsuccessful fishing trip, Jesus appeared and caused the second miraculous catch of fish. He asked if they'd caught anything and the disciples told him no.

And he said unto them, Cast the net on the right side of the ship, and ye shall find. They cast therefore, and now they were not able to draw it up for the multitude of fishes. Therefore that disciple whom Jesus loved saith unto Peter, It is the Lord. Now when Simon Peter heard that it was the Lord, he girded his fisher's coat unto him, (for he was naked) and did cast himself into the sea (John 21:6–7).

After Jesus' death and ascension, Peter became the leader of the early church and remained in Jerusalem until Stephen was martyred and widespread persecution began. Peter traveled to other areas such as Samaria, Lydda, Joppa, Antioch, and possibly Corinth. There is disagreement about whether he ever went to Rome, but tradition says that he became that city's first bishop and Catholics consider Peter the first pope even though there is no documentation in any biblical text.

A Revered Saint

The New Testament Gospels state that Peter was a miracle worker and that Jesus told Peter that he would give him the keys to the kingdom of heaven. According to tradition, circa A.D. 64, Peter was crucified head downward because he felt unworthy to be crucified upright as Jesus was. Peter is the patron saint of bakers, bridge builders, clock and watchmakers, fishermen, longevity, ship builders, and numerous cities including St. Petersburg, and Philadelphia.

The Apostle Paul

If Mary Magdalene was still in Jerusalem circa A.D. 33, the year of Jesus' death, she may have witnessed or heard about the stoning of Stephen for his Christian beliefs. Acts 8:58 states that as Stephen was being stoned to death, a Pharisee named Saul stood watching over the executioners' coats. This man, who was so opposed to the followers of Jesus, later experienced a life-altering conversion and changed his name to Paul.

Saul of Tarsus

Saul was born in the city of Tarsus in the province of Cilicia, an area that now lies in modern Turkey. He was an Israelite of the Diaspora (those Jews dispersed or scattered from Palestine to other lands after the Babylonian captivity). His exact birth date is not known. His family belonged to the tribe of Benjamin and young Saul spoke Aramaic. As the boy grew to manhood, he became a devout Pharisee with strict adherence to the Torah.

By virtue of his birth in the province of Cilicia, Saul was a free Roman citizen. Since the area of Cilicia in the first century had a Greek culture, a Roman political climate, and was a crossroads of commerce, Saul would have been exposed to those influences. He was most likely taken to Jerusalem for a period of formal education in rabbinical studies. The grandson of Hillel (founder of the most influential school of rabbinical Judaism during that time), a rabbi named Gamaliel became Saul's teacher. At some point in his education, Saul became fervently opposed to Jesus and his followers and participated fully in their arrest and trials.

factum

Gamaliel, interestingly, succeeded his father to become president of the Sanhedrin, the very body that condemned Stephen after he delivered a passionate and eloquent defense of the faith. The Sanhedrin, Judaism's highest ecclesiastical tribunal, had seventy-one members.

Saul Undergoes a Violent Conversion

With the blessing of the high priest, Saul left Jerusalem for Damascus, Syria (which is about 130 miles from Jerusalem), to find the followers of this movement and bring them back for trial. He was stricken by a blinding light and a voice asked, "Saul, Saul, Why persecutest thou me?" (Acts 9:4). According to the biblical narrative, the men with Saul took him into the city where the disciple Ananias laid hands on him (baptizing him), whereupon Saul's sight was restored and he was filled with the Holy Spirit.

Apostle to the Gentiles

Paul stayed for a time in Tarsus. He then went to Syria, Cyprus, and Asia Minor. He traveled with Barnabas and Barnabas' cousin, young John Mark, who would later write the Gospel of Mark. Paul had to defend his claim to apostleship because he had never met and traveled with Jesus and he had not witnessed the resurrected Jesus. Still, just as Mary Magdalene is remembered as the Apostle to the Apostles, so Paul is remembered as the Apostle to the Gentiles.

Paul's Epistles and Other Writings

Paul traveled widely during his lifetime as a missionary for Jesus and the Christian faith. On some occasions, his life was threatened, and he barely escaped. He made at least one trip to Jerusalem to meet with Peter and James, the Lord's brother. Paul also wrote letters to house-churches and new Christian communities. His letters often encouraged those new to the faith to stay strong in their convictions. He penned more New Testament letters and texts than anyone else, and from his letters, in particular, scholars and historians have learned details about Christianity at its beginnings and what the followers of Jesus believed.

discussion question

Was Paul anti-Jewish?
Paul was accused of teaching men all over the Roman world to go against the Jews, against the Mosaic Law, and against the Temple. Perhaps even worse, he brought non-Jews (Greeks) into the Temple, thereby polluting it (Acts 21:28).

The first Church historian Eusebius, who was bishop of Caesarea in the fourth century, wrote that at the time the Roman Emperor Nero was murdered, Paul was executed in Rome. As a Roman citizen, Paul was entitled to a quick death and so he was beheaded. His death occurred sometime after A.D. 68, the end of the period when Nero was persecuting Christians.

The Last Apostle

After Judas betrayed Jesus and hung himself, the disciples gathered to elect someone to replace him as the last apostle. The Bible states that the meeting took place in an upper room in Jerusalem and included about 120 disciples—both men and women, including Mary, mother of Jesus. Scholars assert that Mary Magdalene probably would have been present as well for the coterie that made up the Jesus movement had become her "family." The book of Acts states that the group commenced praying: "These all continued with one accord in prayer and supplication, with the women, and Mary the mother of Jesus, and with his brethren" (1:14).

fallacy

The first disciples in the Jesus movement were not regarded as anything other than Jewish. They were not called Christians after Jesus' death because they were Jewish and were viewed as such within their world.

Any potential candidate, they decided, had to meet certain criteria. The new apostle must have accompanied Jesus during his whole ministry (from Jesus' baptism to his death) and have witnessed the Resurrection. The group settled on Joseph (called Barsabas) Justus and a man named Matthias. The group prayed and asked the Lord to guide them before they cast lots. They chose Matthias.

49

chapter 4

Influential People in Early Christianity

During early Christianity's first few centuries, historians, heretics, apologists, persecutors, and Roman emperors all had roles to play in shaping the theology, practice, persecution, and leadership of the infant Christian church. As these individuals played out their roles, Mary Magdalene's reputation was besmirched and her leadership status diminished. Her views, considered Gnostic by some, would have been problematic for conservative Christian fathers fighting heresies. Some feminist theologians assert that she fell victim to increasingly rigid patriarchal elements within the young church.

Flavius Josephus

Mary Magdalene may have never met Flavius Josephus, but he certainly knew about Jewish events prior to and during the first century. Modern scholars researching Mary Magdalene and the beginnings of Christianity often reference his work. His writings about historical incidents that occurred during his lifetime, beginning a few years after Jesus, have provided information for church fathers and scholars alike.

Background

Flavius Josephus was born Joseph ben Mattathias in Jerusalem in A.D. 37, four years or so after the death of Jesus. His father was a descendant of Hasmonean kings and priests, and young Josephus was born into a family of privilege. As a teenager, he dazzled others with his understanding of Jewish law. During his mid-teens, he embarked on a spiritual search, observing the teachings and practices of the Pharisees, Essenes, and Sadducees.

In his twenties, Josephus went to Rome to secure the release of some priests that the Roman emperor Nero had imprisoned. Josephus then returned home to discover a Jewish revolt brewing against Roman occupation. Despite concerns that the Romans had more soldiers, weaponry, and resources than the Jews, Josephus became commander of a rebellious force in Galilee. He boasted of being a Pharisee and a patriot to the Jewish cause, yet he eventually ended up serving the Roman emperor. Both Romans and Jews may have seen Josephus as an opportunistic, self-serving fellow.

Saved by His Cunning

In the summer of 66, the Jewish war began, sacrifices for the emperor were halted in the Temple, and the Zealots seized Masada. Josephus was taken prisoner by the Roman general Vespasian when the latter's forces overpowered Jotapata, a city Josephus was defending. Pretending to be a seer, Josephus told Vespasian about an ancient messianic prophecy predicting the rise of a world ruler from the land of Judea and convinced the general that he was that man. Vespasian kept Josephus as an interpreter.

discussion question

How did Josephus ben Mattathias get the name of Flavius?
Eventually Vespasian became emperor of Rome, and he freed Josephus, adopted him, and bestowed upon him the family name Flavians. From then on, Josephus was known as Flavius Josephus.

Destruction of the Second Temple

Vespasian's son Titus commanded the Roman forces in Judea against the Jewish uprising. After Josephus tried unsuccessfully to negotiate with the Jewish rebels, Titus seized the city and torched it, burning the Temple. The Hebrew people refer to this point in their history as the destruction of the Second Temple (the first marked the beginning of the Jews in Babylonian exile in 423 B.C.). Josephus could have retired then and stayed near Jerusalem, but he decided to return with Titus to Rome.

His Literary Works Endure

Circa 71, Josephus became a Roman citizen, and Vespasian commissioned him to write about the Jewish revolt. Initially, he wrote the account in Aramaic and later translated it into Greek since that was the language most often used throughout the Roman Empire. The *History of the Jewish War* was published circa 78; it was considered factually accurate but clearly favored his benefactor.

By the time Josephus wrote *Antiquities of the Jews*, *Against Apion*, and *The Life of Josephus*, he had been married three times and had three sons. The exact date of his death is not known but is thought to be around 107. Most scholars used the writings of the apostolic fathers as the source for Christianity in the late first and early second centuries. Without the writings of Josephus, there would be little known about the first-century struggles between the Jews and the Romans and the Jewish views on the earliest beginnings of Christianity.

Marcion

Marcion was a North African shipping magnate, born near the end of the first century, who initially supported the church and donated a substantial amount of money only to have the money returned when church leaders denounced and banished him. The heresy of Marcion and his followers seriously threatened orthodox Christianity during the early second century. His writings have not survived, so scholars have had to piece together his life from the writings of those who opposed him and his beliefs.

Life and History

Marcion was born circa 85 at Sinope on Pontus, a fishing port on the south shore of the Black Sea some 600 miles northeast of Ephesus. His family may have been wealthy, but Marcion certainly acquired wealth in his lifetime as a ship owner and merchant. His father was a Christian bishop who ran a house-church.

factum

Recently, scholars have asserted that the Roman church formulated the Apostles' Creed as a way of opposing Marcionism.

Young Marcion, who claimed to be austere and chaste (and was portrayed as such in the writings of certain church fathers), was expelled from his father's house-church for seducing a consecrated virgin. Modern scholars assert that the virgin tale is libel by another church father against Marcion and suggest instead that the virgin may have been a metaphor for the young Christian church.

Sometime between 135 and 140, Marcion made the long trip to Rome to give 200,000 *sesterces* to the church. He stayed and developed his theology, falling under the influence of a Syrian named Cerdo, a Gnostic who became his teacher.

Was He a Gnostic?

Cerdo taught Marcion, among other things, that matter was the creation, not of the Highest God, but of the Demiurge. Jesus appeared on Earth without being born of Mary. In fact, he believed that Jesus didn't need to be born as man. So, Marcion was saying Jesus did not have a human body. His foremost disciple took this thinking one step further and asserted that Christ's body was an astral body of superior substance.

discussion question

What happened to Marcionism after Marcion's death?
Marcion died circa 160. The movement bearing his name remained strong throughout the third century. By the fourth century, however, it had been absorbed into Manichaeism, which was informed and influenced by the writings of the apostle Paul.

Three church fathers—Irenaeus, Tertullian, and Hippolytus—branded Marcion a Gnostic. Even modern scholars have disagreed over whether his ideas were truly Gnostic. The Egyptian Gnostic Valentinus, perhaps the most influential of all the Gnostic heretics, did not agree with Marcion that Christ did not have a body of human flesh. Valentinus believed that the Savior's body merely passed through Mary from above as it would pass through a channel, but it did not acquire anything from her or the channel.

Marcion's Bible

Marcion, who was anti-Jewish, rejected the Old Testament in favor of the New Testament, in part because, as he understood things, Jesus rejected certain points of the Torah. But Marcion thought the New Testament also needed some editing. He was aggressive in cutting and manipulating the rest of the New Testament to create his own version of the Bible. His version had one less gospel and only ten letters from Paul.

Marcion Seeks to Rejoin the Church

While in Rome, Marcion asked to be readmitted to the Roman church but the church turned him down, saying that it could not admit someone who had been expelled by his bishop without some communication from that bishop (the bishop had died).

Following his break with the church, Marcion's monetary gift was returned to him. Scholars say that it is likely that Marcion was already a consecrated bishop. His gift of money may have gone along with the condition that he submit a confession of faith. If not a bishop, how else would he have had the power and authority to threaten church leaders with splitting the church with such force that it would remain divided for centuries?

Clement of Alexandria

After Jesus' ascension, Mary Magdalene, for a while at least, may have been the leader of an important group of early Christians (Gnostics) who believed in the equality of men and women to receive and share spiritual truth. A century later in Alexandria—a place where the peculiar mixing of pagan and Christian beliefs found leavening—such radical thinking was more commonplace. Alexandria was a trading crossroads, a cultural melting pot. Many Christians were affluent. It was there in Alexandria that a man named Clement developed into a Greek theologian and a Christian writer.

Background and Ideology

Titus Flavius Clement was born circa 150 to Greek pagans, perhaps in Athens. He was educated as a young man in a catechetical school located in Alexandria. His teacher there was a Christian philosopher named Pantaenus. As an adult, Clement found work as an assistant to Pantaenus and eventually succeeded him as a teacher. Although a pagan, Clement converted to Christianity and was later ordained as a presbyter (or priest). He tried always to be faithful to the Scriptures.

Clement studied all branches of Greek literature and systems of philosophy but found his greatest satisfaction in Christianity. He wrote about the transfigured life. He had a philosopher's mind and believed it was important to be a Christian first but also to bring reason to bear even while adhering to established ecclesiastical rules. He wrote about such religious topics as fasting, charitable giving, and evil thinking. Clement enjoyed describing the perfect Christian as a true Gnostic.

factum

The church eventually came to suspect some of Clement's ideas. He was known in the Alexandria religious community and in Antioch but never attained status within the church as a popular and important leader or as a theologian. In that regard, his brilliant student Origen eclipsed him.

Clement's Important Writings

Some scholars assert that three of Clement's works stand out: *Exhortation, Tutor,* and *Miscellanies.* He dealt with the issue of Christian display of wealth and excess through dress and behavior in public in *Paedagogus.* In another text aimed at affluent Christians, *Can the Rich Be Saved,* Clement warned that material wealth does not bring people closer to God. Scholars point out that the most notable thing about Clement was that he was well read and rather fanatical about collecting facts and notations to use in his homilies or writings.

The Perfect Christian

Clement thought that the science of faith was refined in the perfect Christian who used reasoning to gain insights into the mysteries of humans, their natures, their virtues, and their world. This type of Christian was compelled to lead a life of devotion through union with God in prayer. Clement wrote about the Godhead as a Trinity and called the second person of the Trinity the Word. He was more sympathetic to the Gnostics and desired to learn about their approach to the Divine even though he also defended the church against Gnosticism.

Fleeing Persecution

Under the threat of religious persecution during the reign of Roman Emperor Septimius Severus, Clement left Alexandria for Caesarea. His student Origen succeeded him at the school and went on to become one of the Christian church's greatest theologians. Circa 215, Clement died in Jerusalem, where he had taken refuge with Alexander, a former student who had become bishop of that city.

Origen

Origen came from a devoutly Christian family and lived during a period of the Roman Empire when persecutions were widespread and invaders threatened the Roman hold on Europe. He received an excellent education in Christianity and Hellenistic studies, including Greek philosophy. When he took over as headmaster of the Christian Catechetical School at Alexandria, he was still in his teens. He has been called the church's first systematic theologian. His contribution to Christianity consisted of a brilliant elucidation of Scripture and a system of theological beliefs.

Background

Origen was born circa 185. When he was seventeen, the persecution of the Church of Alexandria began and his father, Leonides, was imprisoned and martyred. The Romans confiscated Leonides' fortune, leaving Origen to support his mother and six brothers. Origen taught as well as wrote and sold his manuscripts and was supported, in part, by a rich female benefactor who appreciated his talents.

During a trip to Greece, Origen was elevated to the priesthood by the bishop of Caesarea and the bishop of Jerusalem. However, upon his return home, he discovered that his own bishop, Demetrius, was offended that Origen had been ordained without his (Demetrius') knowledge. Later church fathers say that Demetrius was simply envious of Origen's sphere of influence.

Origen decided to leave Alexandria. Subsequently two different councils were held, one banished Origen and the other deposed him. He left for Caesarea, a city located in Palestine. While in Caesarea, Origen established a new school with a friend Theoctistus. The school soon attracted a new group of pupils. Origen made few trips (to Greece and Arabia) and began to devote himself to writing.

fallacy

Origen was not only a Christian writer. Pagans and Christians alike were attracted to his school. Plutarch, the Greek biographer, frequented it. Origen attended philosophic schools, including the one associated with Ammonius Saccas. Origen enjoyed studying the works of Plato and the Stoics. His work at Alexandria was interrupted by five different trips during his tenure.

Prolific Writer Persecuted

Origen's advancing age did not slow his work. When he wrote *Contra Celsum* (*Against Celsus*) and *Commentary on Saint Matthew*, he was over sixty. Work on those two projects, however, was interrupted by persecution. In 253 or 254, at the age of sixty-nine, Origen died, most likely from the trauma of persecution and imprisonment.

Origen's sepulcher was placed behind the high altar in the Cathedral of Tyre. Today, the cathedral is in ruins and the precise location of Origen's tomb is unknown.

The number of Origen's works ranged from fewer than 2,000 to up to 6,000, including homilies, letters, treatises, books, tracts, and other written texts. The exact figure is not known, and scholars have only estimates made by other early church fathers.

His Influence Spreads after Death

Origen projected a great influence during his lifetime. In his work on the Scriptures, he focused on three approaches: homilies, scholia (interpretation), and commentaries. He spent his final days in Tyre and was buried as a confessor of the faith. Following Origen's death, his reputation spread. He was well regarded, and when disputes arose over a schism, suspected heresy, or simply a theological point, Origen's name was often invoked.

Arius

Arius was a Christian presbyter who expounded views at variance with orthodox Christian theology and was excommunicated for his heretical beliefs. Arius was thought to have been of Libyan descent. Many Syrian religious clergy followed him in 321, when more than one hundred Libyan and Egyptian bishops officially condemned him. The conflict that Arius and his ideas introduced to the fledgling church was the first major struggle it faced after Emperor Constantine made Christianity legal in the Roman Empire.

History and Public Image

Arius was born circa 250 in Libya. Some scholars say he was born in Alexandria. By most accounts, Arius received his education from a presbyter in Antioch named Lucian. Arius occupied a position of authority as presbyter in the Church of Alexandria and most likely could have been highly esteemed when trouble began to brew over his views concerning the equality of the Son and the Father and Christ's eternal deity.

discussion question

What were Arius' theological beliefs?
Arius asserted that the Father created the Son, who was therefore of essentially a different essence; thus, he was inferior to the Father. His views set him at odds with prevailing orthodox Christian thinking. It was particularly offensive to Bishop Alexander.

Arius has been described as a learned man of austere habits with an impeccable moral character and positive nature. However, he had a quarrelsome side as well. The disagreement between Arius and Bishop Alexander may also have been rooted in the fact that Arius was not elected bishop, for which he blamed Bishop Alexander.

The Conflict Grows Wider

The entire synod of Alexandria in 320 or 321 (according to one source) pronounced its decision: Arius was condemned. He left Alexandria and went to Caesarea where Eusebius, another church father, took him in. Eusebius and the Asiatic churches were much more sympathetic to Arius' doctrinal ideas. In time, relations were patched between Arius and Bishop Alexander, but the conflict broke out once again. It spread around the eastern Mediterranean where Arius had many followers and influence.

The First Council of Nicaea in 325

The assembly of bishops took up the issue of Arian doctrine. After much discussion, they condemned it and formulated a creed that would state what orthodox Christians believed. It became known as the Nicene Creed and is recited even today by Catholics and some Protestants. Arius' ideas were deemed heretical and his books were burned. Arius was exiled to Illyria. In Alexandria, his friends and followers began to make trouble.

The Winds Shift Again

Eusebius and friends took the cause of Arius to Constantia, the emperor's sister, who apparently listened sympathetically and elicited the help of her brother. Emperor Constantine recalled Arius from exile and permitted him to go to Alexandria. The emperor also ordered the church to reconcile with Arias. As an assembly was set to convene in Constantinople and to accept Arius back into the church, Arius passed away. Some say he was poisoned; others believe it was divine intervention. Arius was eighty years old.

factum

On the death of Arius, a particularly gruesome account states that his bowels suddenly failed him in an attack of conscience and regret. As he sought a place of privacy, he suffered a massive hemorrhage and expulsion of his intestines, causing his death.

Eusebius of Caesarea

Eusebius was a presbyter, a scholar, and an early church father in Caesarea. He wrote the history of Christianity (a religion that was illegal prior to his lifetime) in ten volumes. Eusebius was the first church historian and became known as the Father of Church History. Because of him, modern Christians can read about the origins of their religion and of apostolic succession as Christianity spread and grew in areas of the ancient world. Eusebius' interest in antiquities ensured that he maintained and preserved the library established by his predecessor Pamphilius.

From Birth to a Bishop

Eusebius was born circa 260 in Caesarea. Pamphilius, a student of Origen, taught Eusebius the texts of the Bible. Scholars say that although he was widely read, Eusebius was deeply influenced by the ideas of Origen. He visited Palestine in 296 where he saw Constantine. Some time after, Pamphilius was put into prison. Eusebius succeeded Agapius to become bishop of Caesarea.

Eusebius was already a well-known author and bishop when Constantine convened the Council at Nicaea to deal with the Arian heresy. Eusebius played an important role as a leader among the 300 bishops and presbyters at that historical event. He proposed the confession of faith that formed the framework for the Nicene Creed, which is still recited today.

Scope of His Work

Initially, Eusebius focused on writing biblical criticism; later, he wrote about Christian martyrs. Following that, he turned his attention to church history (which included the history of the Jewish people and the heathens), and finally he addressed the history of the world. His writing ranged from apologetics (explaining Christian beliefs to those who did not understand) and a biography of his teacher Pamphilius, to a polemic treatise *Against Marcellus*, and eulogies that praised Constantine in *The Life of Constantine* (*Vita Constantini*).

His greatest and best-known works are *Chronicle* (written first) and *Church History*. In *Church History*, Eusebius covered many subjects, among them: the bishops in important regions and their successors, teachers of Christianity and their history, the heresies of the church, and martyrdoms of Christian faithful. He also wrote *Preparation for the Gospel* (*Praeparatio Evangelica*), which was an introduction to Christianity for pagans.

The Preservation of Sources

During his lifetime, Eusebius garnered respect and a reputation for being a learned man, a widely read historian, and a meticulous compiler who had to sift through mountains of material to extract and chronicle historical information. He is remembered as an early church father who distinguished himself through a carefully compiled literary legacy that preserved the history of Christianity (up to and through his lifetime).

discussion question

What happened to his writings after Eusebius died?
Eusebius died in 339 (some sources say 340) at the age of seventy-four. His legacy included, among other texts, a geography of the Bible, books that cleared up discrepancies found in the Gospels, and commentaries on Psalms and the book of Isaiah from the Old Testament.

Eusebius faced a daunting task in writing about Christianity. Since before his lifetime, the Roman Empire considered the religion illegal. Not only did Eusebius write about the origins of the religion and details of apostolic succession as Christianity spread and grew throughout the ancient world, his works contained ancient sources and other minutiae. Such attention to detail preserves the sources he used as well as certain historical facts. That Eusebius wrote about these things is important because, through the centuries, many of the original source materials have been lost or destroyed.

Diocletian

Diocletian was a man of lowly birth who rose to become a powerful Roman emperor and ushered in a new phase of the Roman Empire. Eager to regain control of the army, to establish secure borders against invading barbarians and put down rebellions, to mend the economy, and to shore up the governance of the vast empire, he instituted many reforms, including the tetrarchy, or rule of four (two Augusti and two Caesars). Subsequently, the new phase of the empire was to be referred to as the "Tetrarchy."

The Life of a Soldier

Diocletian was born circa 236 or 237 on the Dalmatian coast, although some historians assert that Diocletian was born at Salona. He was married to a woman named Prisca, a Christian or Christian sympathizer. They had a daughter, Valeria, who was raised Christian.

Diocletian joined the Roman army and was assigned to defend an area of the lower Danube known as Moesia. He was what we today would call a results-oriented kind of person. He sought success rather than fame and glory. An officer by the name of Carus was serving as the praetorian prefect in the upper Danube when, in 282, the legions serving under him proclaimed him emperor. Diocletian ingratiated himself with Carus and was elevated to count of the Domestics and, subsequently, in 283, given a consulate.

While fighting the Persians, Carus was hit by lightning and died. The empire then became the concern of his two sons. Young

Numerian died mysteriously, leaving Diocletian in charge as the new emperor of the eastern part of the Roman Empire. Then in 285, the other son was killed in battle. Diocletian took control of the western empire.

Diocletian Makes Bold Changes

Diocletian felt it was imperative to take whatever steps were necessary, regardless of how brutal or bizarre, to take back control of the increasingly lawless Roman army. He broke the army into two entities: palace troops (which he led) and border troops (militias of Roman citizens that had little power). With the armies under his control, Diocletian turned his attention to ruling the entire empire.

Once Diocletian decided to establish the Tetrarchy, he became a monarch. His subjects had to address him as Lord and Master and to prostrate themselves before him. He assumed the attributes of the god Jupiter.

To remedy the ailing economy, Diocletian swiftly instituted reforms that would restore confidence in the currency. He shifted the empire from a money-based economy to one based on payment "in kind," which is how he paid his soldiers. He also instituted compulsory service by tenant farmers, soldiers, bakers, and others.

factum

In an effort to unify the empire through a state religion, Diocletian enacted punishment for those who refused to recite a pledge of allegiance to the imperial cult. His action became known as the "Great Persecution."

Diocletian's Time Ends

In 305, Diocletian retired and ordered his co-regent Maximianus to do the same. The two Caesars who had been serving under them became the new *augusti*, or regents, and new Caesars were chosen to replace them. Diocletian enjoyed the next eleven years at his palace on the coast of Croatia. He died in 316.

The Apologists

Apologists are generally authors who write books, tracts, and treatises defending the religion to opponents and outsiders. Tertullian and Justin the Martyr are two significant Christian apologists whose works continued to influence Christianity long after their deaths.

Tertullian came to be known as the Father of the Latin Church. His ideas were brilliant and bold. He practiced his faith as an orthodox Christian and later in life became a member of the cult of Montanists. No Christian church ever pronounced him a saint despite his contributions as a church leader and a prolific writer of material about Christianity. He was a controversial figure in the church—ordained a presbyter (priest) and married. He wrote two books for his wife.

Justin the Martyr wrote a number of Christian apologies. Although he referred to himself as a Samaritan, historians say he was more likely of Greek or Roman descent through his father's line, and he was reared as a pagan. He studied enough philosophy to decide to convert to Christianity, believing it to be the true philosophy. He is remembered as a philosopher, a teacher, an apologist (with a sizable legacy of works), and a Christian martyr.

Tertullian's Life and Theology

Born Quintus Septimius Florens Tertullianus in Carthage circa 155, Tertullian's father, an aide-de-camp in the Roman army, was stationed in Africa. Tertullian received an excellent education, specializing in the study of law. Roman advocates considered him a terrific orator with excellent reasoning skills. He was roughly forty-two when he converted to Christianity circa 97 or 98. He became an ordained presbyter in the Church of Carthage.

A Break with Orthodox Christianity

Tertullian coined the term *Trinity* and is credited with coming up with the concept of the Godhead being three persons, one substance. But in 207, Tertullian left the orthodox Christian church to embrace Montanism, a movement started by Montanus and two women who prophesied the impending apocalypse and practiced a strict asceticism.

discussion question

Why did mainstream Christians object to Montanism?
The Christians were offended by the Montanists, who claimed superiority because their theology arose from inspired prophecy. Tertullian became a Montanist leader and an eloquent and passionate proponent of the cult.

Despite his own schism (his departure from the Christian church to Montanism), Tertullian continued to fight the heresies that threatened the church, particularly Gnosticism. That work continued until his death. Cyprian and later Augustine were students of Tertullian's writings and doctrinal studies, including works that railed against paganism or that addressed Christian morals and the establishing of a Christian religious life. The writings of Tertullian's later life included Christian apologetic (defending, explaining, and exploring Christian beliefs) and polemic material. He wrote no fewer than five books against the heresies of Marcion, a Gnostic.

Scorn for Aristotle and Plato

Tertullian was realistic, practical, and pragmatic; he was not interested in the ideas of Greek philosophers such as Aristotle and Plato. In Tertullian's opinion, they simply set the stage for Jesus the Christ and the Christian Gospels. In his polemic writing on heretics, he dubbed them the patriarchs of the heretics. Tertullian did not accept the idea of the pre-existence of the soul, as Plato did, nor the belief that the soul reincarnates, as the Pythagoreans did, rather he believed that the soul was its own entity in bondage to Satan until baptism.

67

Beliefs and Legacy

Among other things, Tertullian believed in chiliasm and the continuation of prophecy as a gift of the Holy Spirit. Certain Christian denominations today hold to this belief and others believe that this will be the period of battle with the antichrist. Another word for chiliasm is millennialism. Tertullian believed that baptism did not bestow the Holy Spirit but prepared the way for its expression.

symbolism

Chiliasm refers to the thousand-year reign of Christ between the Second Coming and the world's end. Even in modern times, various religious cults have embraced the apocalyptic ideas of millennialism, with their leaders prophesying the end of the world as imminent.

Tertullian died circa 230. He is remembered as a formidable defender of Christianity. He was one of the most insightful and articulate interpreters of the rules of the faith during his time. Although a Montanist who later established the sect of Tertullianists, he is remembered as one of the great fathers of the church who advocated strict observance to the rules and practice of Christian faith.

Justin the Martyr

Justin's was born around 100, at the end of the lifetime of the original apostles. His birthplace was Flavia Neapolis (modern Nablus in Palestine). He attended schools in Ephesus and Alexandria and studied philosophy and history. Some sources note that he was anti-Semitic.

Enamoured for a while with Stoicism, Pythagoreanism, and Platonism, Justin turned away from pagan philosophy toward Christianity. He was particularly interested in the Christian martyrs. Although a teacher of philosophy, he converted to Christianity, writing that his soul was lit by fire over the love of Christ and his followers and prophets.

Writings

Justin wrote one *Apology* for Antoninus, his sons, and the Roman senators and a second *Apology* for Marcus Aurelius and Lucius Verus (co-emperors). He also wrote *Dialogue with Trypho, the Jew*. While modern historians agree that Justin wrote these three works, some question the authorship of other works attributed to him such as the *Hortatory Address to the Greeks, On the Resurrection*, and *On the Sole Government*. Scholars say that *Discourse to the Greeks*, sometimes attributed to him, is believed to have been a Jewish treatise.

In *Apology,* which he wrote to the emperors, Justin asserted that the persecution of Christians was not justified and that Christianity was the true philosophy. He told them that he is among those persecuted; he defended the Christians and presented an argument for how Christian belief (especially in the Resurrection) leads to a perfect morality. Christians, Justin explained in his writings, are the true people of God. Further, he wrote that Christianity is the new law for all humankind.

factum

Justin the Martyr wrote to the pagan emperor Antoninus in the second century about how Christians celebrate the Eucharist. His explanation reveals that the fundamental structure of the eucharistic celebration during the church service remains the same today.

The Consequences of Teaching Christianity

A new chapter in Justin's life began when he opened a school where he taught Christian philosophy. He taught, wrote, and debated. But a debate with a man named Crescens, a philosopher of the Cynic school, was Justin's undoing.

discussion question

What did the early church fathers think of Justin's writings?
Early church fathers such as Irenaeaus, Tertullian, Hippolytus, and others praised Justin in various ways, some for his philosophy and others for his apologetics. He participated in debates with pagans, Jews, heretics, and non-Christians in an effort to explain the superiority of the Christian philosophy.

The Acts of Justin the Martyr is the record of Justin's trial. Crescens, it has been noted, may have lost the debate with Justin. Whether or not it was Crescens who turned him in, Justin went afoul of the Roman political leadership by practicing a religion that was not officially recognized or authorized by the state. It is likely he antagonized Jews as well through his anti-Semitic writing.

Justin was brought before Rusticus, the Roman prefect. He demanded that Justin renounce his Christian faith, which Justin refused to do. Rusticus then sentenced Justin to a quick death, the right of Roman citizens, by beheading. Six of Justin's students, including one woman, were put to death as well.

Domitian

In the years after Mary Magdalene had witnessed the resurrection of Jesus but before the Jewish revolt, a son was born to Roman Emperor Vespasian named Titus Flavius Domitianus (A.D. 51–96). Vespasian already had another son, Titus, who would fight in that rebellion and eventually succeed his father to the throne. Domitian would be remembered as one of the Roman rulers famous for his womanizing, dismal performance as an administrator, lackluster military leadership, and merciless persecution of Christians.

Ambition and Family

Domitian was a loner. By the time he was a teenager, he had already suffered periods of isolation; his mother had died, his father was absent for long periods, and his brother Titus was ten years older. Domitian received an excellent education, as did the elite senatorial class of his day. He married the daughter of a well-respected general whom Nero had forced to commit suicide. When Domitian's infant died, he had his wife exiled. He later asked her to return to the palace with him where she remained until he died. When their father died, Titus, not Domitian, succeeded Vespasian as emperor. Domitian, too, was ambitious, but he was also patient. He was named to several positions, but none of them carried much responsibility or power. When Titus died, Domitian finally ascended to the throne as emperor. He was a despotic ruler, whose seat of power was through his court.

Persecution of Christians

Their religion forbade the worship of false idols, yet Christians were expected to pay homage to the Cult of Domitian. Under the threat of persecution and pressure to conform, many Christians may have questioned their beliefs or abandoned their faith. Some sources say this is exactly the kind of prevailing atmosphere in which the apostle John the Divine undertook the writing of the Revelation on the island of Patmos, where Domitian had exiled him.

Domitian's Reign Inspires Apocalyptic Writing

The Revelation of Saint John the Divine is an apocalyptic text in the New Testament in which Christians are encouraged to remain strong; when the Savior returns, he will reward the believers and punish the nonbelievers and all who persecute the faithful. This text, more than any other in the New Testament, is filled with symbolic language and is considered to be the most difficult to understand. It was composed, according to one source, as resistance literature against a crisis of faith and must be read in the context of the historical milieu in which it was written.

Domitian's Demise

Paranoia about conspiracies may have been Domitian's undoing. He replaced his own Praetorian Guards with new men. Concerned that their services would be short-lived, the Praetorians engaged the freedman Flavia Domitilla the Younger to assassinate Domitian. The emperor's wife was an accessory to the plot. One account states that the Roman ruler did not die with the first blow; the conspirators together hacked Domitian to death.

Constantine

Who are Christians and what do they believe? Constantine, known as the first Christian emperor, tried to answer these questions. He was one of the four tetrarchs (emperors) ruling the Roman Empire. Although Constantine was not baptized a Christian until his death, his mother may have been sympathetic to practitioners of the faith.

discussion question

What did Constantine do to help Christians?
Besides ending the persecution of Christians, Constantine advanced a policy of widespread religious tolerance, permitted Christians to own property (thus they could build and own their churches), and made Christianity the official state religion in the Roman Empire.

Background and Military Career

Constantine was born in 285 (although it may have been as early as 272) in Naissus, located in Upper Moesia, to Constantius Chlorus and a woman named Helen, a local innkeeper's daughter. The two may not have been married. When his father was promoted to Caesar, young Constantine entered Diocletian's court. In 306, after Diocletian abdicated, Constantine, now a military officer serving Galerius, went with his father, who actually ranked higher than Galerius, on a campaign to Britain. When his father died, the soldiers proclaimed Constantine their new Augustus, but Galerius refused to acknowledge him as such and, instead, proclaimed him a Caesar.

Constantine married a woman named Fausta. Her father, Maximian, one of the rulers in Rome, proclaimed Constantine Augustus. Even when the other Roman rulers met at a conference in 308 and demanded Constantine give up his title, he refused. Later on, Maximian turned against Constantine in a power struggle that Constantine won.

Constantine Ends Persecution of Christians

Galerius died in 311. The other rulers fought for dominance. Legend states that Constantine won control of the entire Western Roman Empire with a battle at Milvian Bridge in Rome in 312. Before the battle, he prayed (perhaps as his mother had taught him) and saw the Chi-Ro (a symbol for the Christ) in a beam of light above the sun. Considering it a sign from God, Constantine urged his soldiers to embellish their shields with the symbol, and he put it on his standard. He won the battle and from that moment on considered himself emperor of all Christians in the Roman Empire.

Constantine's efforts stopped the widespread persecutions and religious intolerance of Roman rulers against the religious minority. While ruler of the Western Roman Empire, he ended the persecution of Christians in Gaul, Spain, and Britain where a campaign had taken him. The ruler of the eastern part of the Roman Empire followed Constantine's example.

The Edict of Milan and the Council of Nicaea

Maximinus, the ruler of Egypt, continued to persecute Christians. He journeyed from Asia Minor to Europe to confront Licinius (who prayed as Constantine once had in the Christian manner). Licinius prevailed, and an era of religious freedom began. Constantine's decree that all should live in religious freedom was called the Edict of Milan. It served as the example for future laws ensuring religious tolerance.

factum

Legend says that Constantine, convinced that his wife, Fausta, had committed adultery with his son Crispus (her stepson), had him executed. His wife then killed herself. Although this gruesome detail is part of Constantine's legend, he is best remembered as the emperor who stopped the persecution of Christians and convened the council that would be commemorated by the Nicene Creed, the statement of faith that it formulated.

Constantine convened the religious council at Nicaea in 325. The purpose for calling together all the Christian bishops was to condemn Arianism as a heresy. The Nicene Creed, which defined who is a Christian and what a Christian believes, was drafted at that council and is still recited by Catholics today.

chapter 5

Mary Magdalene's First-Century World

uring the time Mary Magdalene accompanied Jesus in his ministry, Jews who had not joined a particular sect of Judaism lived their lives in the regular religious cycles without paying much attention to the theological debates and positioning going on around them. Yet, diversity of religious belief and interpretation was certainly part of the scene in ancient Palestine. It might be helpful to examine the turbulent political and religious environment simmering in the region when Jesus of Nazareth began his work.

Turbulent Times

Not only were the Jews of first-century Palestine contending with outside cultural influences but also with various sects that emerged. When Jesus first began to preach publicly, his message might have initially been received as religious ideology from another preacher with a different viewpoint. In fact, Judea was filled with rabbis, teachers, tribes, magicians, clans, sects, healers, and prophets (also false prophets). Add to the mix Greek and Roman pagan worship, polytheistic religious practices, and mystery cults, and it's nothing short of amazing that the Jesus movement survived to the end of the apostolic age (when the first generation of apostles began to die) and then not only remained viable but grew stronger and spread throughout the Roman Empire, to the West, and eventually around the world.

Under Roman Law

Some Jews in first-century Judea adapted well enough to Roman rule while others (the Zealots) advocated resistance. In Galilee, Roman colonization and rule may have changed the character of the place, but the Galilean Jews lived by their own religious traditions, spoke Aramaic, and were known to favor resistance to Rome.

discussion question

What are the Torah and the Talmud?
The Torah contains the laws of the Old Testament and the Talmud includes commandments and commentaries. Together, these books contain the laws of the Lord and the commandments, teachings, beliefs, interpretations, and practices for living a Jewish life.

Together, these groups constituted the fragmented portrait of Judaism at the time of Jesus. They all followed the commandments and rules of living laid out in the Torah and Talmud since these sacred texts governed Jewish life. As a Hebrew woman, Mary

Magdalene would certainly have known about the rules contained in the Torah and the Talmud, but whether she could read them is debatable since women weren't educated. That's the big picture, so how did women, in general, and Mary Magdalene, in particular fit into that world?

Mary Magdalene in Her Community

Mary Magdalene undoubtedly knew many of the other Jewish families dwelling in her coastal fishing community. Perhaps the community leaders or at least the women also knew her. Maybe she had heard sedition whispered among the women who might have learned it from their men who might have had contact with the Zealots.

Possibly, she was too ill to be concerned about the political climate or the religious and cultural influences coming into Judea from surrounding countries. Cured of her terrible illness, the Gospels tell us, she followed Jesus and ministered to him out of her means (probably pooled with the resources of the others in a communal pot). Was the Jesus movement—the primitive foundation of Christianity—financed by wealthy women patrons and followers such as Mary Magdalene? If the fishermen had no time to ply their trade and the tax collector wasn't collecting taxes after becoming full-time followers of Jesus, how could they pay for food and lodging except for the generosity of the women who were willing to put money into the community purse?

Diversity Within Judaism

The New Testament Gospels mention Jesus and his followers' interactions or interrelationships with four main Jewish groups: the Essenes, the Sadducees, the Pharisees, and the Zealots. What follows is a brief description of each group along with its main ideology.

The Essenes

This Jewish separatist group is likely to have been the same sect as the one at Qumran (northwest of the Dead Sea). The Essenes' original writings make up the *Dead Sea Scrolls*, called by some the Essene library. The *Dead Sea Scrolls* were discovered in 1947. Some people believe that John the Baptist and perhaps Jesus either came from the Essenes or borrowed from their teachings. Many other scholars dispute that assumption. The Essenes were monastic in that they preferred to keep to themselves and away from the outside world. They called themselves "children of light." Their theology included apocalyptic ideas such as cataclysmic events and God's intervention at important times in history. They cultivated the virtues of temperance, obedience, truthfulness, and justice. They believed slavery, which existed in first-century Judea, was wrong.

Sadducees

The Sadducees were the dominant Jewish group and were comprised of the aristocratic priesthood that controlled ritual observances in the Temple. The Sadducees traced their lineage to the tribe of Levi and the Zadok family. The only law they recognized and rigidly interpreted was the written Torah. The Sadducees were conservative and closely associated with the Sanhedrin or Jerusalem's city council.

fallacy

It's a fallacy that Jesus rejected the Pharisees outright. Obvious parallels exist between the Jesus movement members and the Pharisees, but there were also differences. Jesus told his followers to obey the teachings of the Pharisees, and yet he admonished them to not engage in their (the Pharisees') hypocrisy (Matthew 23:3–7).

Pharisees

This group adhered to the teachings of the Torah and believed that practice and adherence to the written law of the Torah (given by Moses) would make them righteous and lead them to God. Study of the Torah and implementing its teachings into daily regimens (for example, discussing, reading, debating) was important to the

Pharisees who gathered for group fellowship, ate together, and studied the Torah under the tutelage of a teacher.

Zealots

The Zealots espoused both religious and political discontent and were considered seditionists. Much like a passionate religious group that seeks to establish a theocratic state, the Zealots were behind the First Jewish Revolt (A.D. 66–70). The Gospels do not tell us whether Mary Magdalene knew Simon the Zealot (also known as Simon the Cananaean, which derives from the Aramaic word for "zealous one"), but he was certainly one of the Twelve so it's conceivable that she did.

Roman Law Versus Mosaic Law

In addition to knowing something about Mosaic Law, Mary Magdalene might have also been aware of some of the Roman civil laws. Mosaic Law differed from Roman law in that it came from God by way of Moses and included the Ten Commandments as well as the rules and observances of the Pentateuch. This was the law that Jesus' earthly family and his Jewish followers were raised to honor and obey. Jesus admonished his disciples neither to make new laws (beyond what he had already given them) nor to promulgate any new law. For Mary Magdalene and the women around Jesus, both the Old Testament Mosaic Law and the Roman law were patriarchal. There were few, if any, provisos for women.

During Mary Magdalene's time, Jews who ran up against Roman law discovered that the polytheistic Romans dealt with the legal actions between people swiftly and succinctly. The Romans focused on individual rights more than on the law of the nation. Three main areas of Roman law dealt with goods, obligations, and families. It has been said that Roman law was of such quality that its far-reaching influence has affected lawyers of all subsequent times and places.

factum

Early Jewish followers of Jesus did not immediately call their religion Christianity or Christianismos (the formal name of the religion). The term was not used, scholars say, until roughly a half century after Jesus' death (circa 112 to 115) and not in the Galilean or Judean vernacular but rather by Greeks in Antioch, the capital of Syria.

Though there is no mention of Mary Magdalene having personal experience of Roman law, it is certain that she witnessed the swiftness by which the death decree was decided against Jesus and the implementation of Roman capital punishment by crucifixion. Whenever Christians engaged in what the Romans perceived as acts of insurrection or violations of Roman law, the Romans did not differentiate between the genders when persecuting, imprisoning, or putting those Christians to death. Some scholars and biblical historians speculate that Mary Magdalene may have at some point fled Judea to escape Roman persecution and the threat of death.

A Woman's Place in Society

The historical Mary Magdalene must have had a mother and father. Did they raise her to adulthood or marry her off early? Did her husband's family rear her? That was often the case with girls betrothed early. The Talmud rabbis established the marriage age for girls at twelve. Boys could marry at thirteen. How did Mary Magdalene come to be an independent woman who was free to follow Jesus?

Without some as-yet undiscovered document revealing the whole story of Mary Magdalene's life, biblical historians and scholars must speculate. They try to place Mary Magdalene in the context of her times, in her country's society and culture, and within her socioeconomic status. They fit together the pieces of what is known about the company she kept, the circles she traveled in, and the religion she practiced. Then they make educated guesses. What follows is a brief glimpse into Mary Magdalene's world as a first-century Galilean woman.

symbolism

For Rosh Hashanah (the Jewish high holy day that starts the Jewish New Year), the challah dough (often with sweet raisins added) is shaped round, instead of braided, to represent the life cycle and wholeness of the universe. The seeds (often poppy or sesame) symbolize fertility and abundance.

Life as a Jewish Woman

Life wasn't particularly easy for anyone in ancient Palestine, especially for women. In the male-dominated culture, women and children ranked below beasts of burden on the ladder of value and hierarchy. Couples preferred to bear sons rather than daughters. Daughters were often betrothed to their future husbands while still quite young; once married, they immediately began to have babies. Many girls and young women died in childbirth. Since a woman's life revolved around caring for her husband and children, girls learned early how to manage a household.

For Jewish children, religious education was home-centered. Some say this necessitated women knowing about their religious traditions, beliefs, laws, rules, and practices. The consensus is that women did not study the Torah in public. But they could attend synagogue (which didn't always necessarily mean a physical temple, but a congregational gathering or assembly). However, they sat separate from the men in a designated area.

factum

Orthodox Jewish women had three basic commandments: keep the family pure, light the candles on Shabbat, and keep the law of challah (tithe in bread dough weighing at least 1,600 grams and paid to the rabbi in a symbolic gesture for the prosperity of their families).

As soon as she began to menstruate, a Jewish woman had to deal with regular cycles of being considered unclean (*niddah*); this was true for her bleeding after childbirth as well. These regular weeklong periods of exclusion ended with immersion in a ritual bath called a *mikvah*. Women were also required to light and bless the candles on the Sabbath (and other holy days) and to make the *challah* or bread that would be served with the Sabbath meal. Mary Magdalene would have been well versed in these particular ritual observances, customs, and practices.

symbolism

Blood symbolically represents many different things, including life force, sacrifice, unity, and fertility, as well as a covenant between humankind and God. In the celebration of the Eucharist, the wine symbolizes the blood of Christ. Ancient Jews had many laws about contact with blood including through dietary, sacrificial, disease, menstruation, and childbirth.

Women Outside the Home

Although a woman's primary role was in the home caring for her husband and family, she had to venture out in public to procure foodstuffs and other household items. When women went outside the home, they were expected to conform to certain rules of behavior. They avoided unnecessary contact with men, never unbound their hair in public, and never shared a meal with a man. Any infraction could result in being labeled a "loose" or "fallen woman," which would negatively affect the family. This consequence may have been worse than the damage to the woman's reputation.

Finally, although the primary roles remained wife and mother, some women did work outside the home. They could participate in occupations such as hairdresser, textile worker (spinning, weaving, needlework, and dyeing of cloth), baker (grinding, sifting, kneading, baking, and selling of bread), tent-maker, professional mourner (crying and beating their chests in lamentation), real-estate dealer, and midwife.

Roman Treatment of Women and Children

As previously mentioned, Mary Magdalene lived in Galilee under Roman occupation. Inevitably, she would have had contact with Roman society. Having discussed the life of a Jewish woman's place in society, now we'll explore the life of a Roman woman.

The main purpose in life for a Roman woman, just as for her Jewish counterpart, was the happiness and well-being of her husband and family. She was under the dominion of her husband or the oldest male who was the household ruler and his authority was absolute. His title was *paterfamilias*. He literally wielded power over life and death. For example, if his wife had too many babies, he could decide to keep the newborn or place it on the ground somewhere and allow it to die from exposure. Or, someone might pass by and take the baby to rear as a slave. Deformed infants frequently faced this cruel form of family planning.

Women played an important role in the family whenever they helped their men gain favorable prominence in their communities and bore their husband sons. If a family didn't have any sons, the father could adopt one because the family name had to be continued through the male line. A Roman woman was usually married to an older man. Women married in their teens; men married in their twenties. A woman couldn't vote or hold office.

Jesus' Radical Shifting of the Status Quo

What a friend Mary Magdalene and other women had in Jesus. Cursed by their own biology, their monthly menses made them unclean. Physical contact with a man during niddah meant that the man became polluted and had to undergo a ritual purification. Any man but Jesus might have been annoyed or angered at being touched by an "unclean" woman and might even have pressed charges. Yet, according to the Gospel of Luke, Jesus healed the unclean woman who suffered a bleeding problem. This woman had already spent a dozen years of her life and her money on doctors who could not heal her. She knew touching the hem of Jesus' garment would make him ritually unclean. All women knew this. Jesus, after seeking out the person who had made the "virtue go out of Him" (Luke 8:46), cured the woman, telling her that her faith had made her whole.

factum

The Gospels do not say Jesus ever did any ritual cleansing following these two acts. Why is that? Perhaps, as authors Madeleine L'Engle and Carole F. Chase write in *Glimpses of Grace, Daily Thoughts and Reflections*, Jesus obeyed the higher law of love. He showed not only how to act out of love but that he was Love.

When the woman with the issue of blood touched him, he was on his way to raise the daughter of Jairus (the child had fallen mortally ill). So Jesus was about to engage in yet another taboo act—touching a dead body—and others, who knew of his contact with the woman, knew that he was now already considered ritually unclean. Nevertheless, he touched the child and brought her back to life with the Aramaic words, *Talitha cum* ("Little girl, I say to you arise"). She, however, was now considered polluted and he doubly so.

The Samaritan at the Well

In an incident with a Samaritan woman, Jesus does something else that goes against the status quo. He not only spoke with the Samaritan woman at the well, he also asked her for a drink of water. She was perplexed because she knew he was a Jewish man and that Jews had no dealings with Samaritans. When Jesus began talking about the living water he could give her, the woman pointed out that he had no utensil with which to draw the water. "Jesus answered and said unto her, If thou knewest the gift of God, and who it is that saith to thee, Give me to drink; thou wouldest have asked of him, and he would have given thee living water" (John 4:10).

When the Samaritan woman said she wanted some of that living water, Jesus told her to get her husband. The woman replied that she didn't have one. Of course, Jesus knew at once that the woman had had five husbands and that the current man in her life wasn't her husband. Jesus told her she had spoken correctly and then he proceeded to explain his knowledge of her. Shocked, she called him a prophet. Then Jesus did a remarkable thing. He confessed that he was the Messiah, and he taught the woman that God is a Spirit and, therefore, must be worshiped in spirit and in truth. Any other Jewish man would have avoided that woman as if contact with her equaled a dozen menstruating women. But Jesus asked her for a drink of water, confessed he was the Son of God, and proceeded to teach her. Everything about this incident suggests that Jesus' relationships with women fell in direct opposition to the status quo.

The Samaritan ran back to her community and told the men in her city about Jesus and their conversation. Some of the men didn't believe her. After all, she was a woman. They went to discover the truth and became believers. "And many more believed because of his own word; and said unto the woman, Now we believe, not because of thy saying: for we have heard him ourselves and know that this is indeed the Christ, the Saviour of the world" (John 4:41–42).

After Jesus, the Paradigm Returned

The woman who touched Jesus' hem, the Samaritan woman at the well, and Mary Magdalene represented an invisible, powerless, and outcast sisterhood. Jesus first restored them to wholeness by healing their broken bodies and troubled minds; then, he treated them with love and respect and welcomed them into his circle of fellowship, even his closest discipleship. Mary Magdalene's relationship with Jesus, in particular, exemplifies his egalitarian disposition and treatment of women. Once healed, she served as a strong disciple and primary witness to the Resurrection. This, of course, presented a problem for the New Testament Gospel writers (and editors or redactors) that will be explored in later chapters. The point is that Jesus, through word and deed, began to shift the status quo in a radical way.

discussion question

What are the three methods of baptism and their meanings?
Complete dunking under water symbolizes the death, entombment, and resurrection of Christ, according to the Baptists. Sprinkling, such as done by the Anglicans and Methodists, symbolizes the Blood of Christ that is cleansing the person of their sins. Christians pour water to symbolize the pouring out of the Holy Spirit and the person's receiving of the Spirit.

Modern feminist theologians have theorized that after Jesus' death, women as well as men served equally in leadership roles of the church. For women to evangelize and bring in converts was one thing. Did they also perform baptism and administer other sacraments, such as the Eucharist (bread and wine communion)? The Bible doesn't say. To a patriarchal Orthodoxy, women as priests or priestesses would have been problematic in the early centuries of the church and remains so today for many churches—in particular, the Catholic Church. Jesus made enormous strides to shift the patriarchal paradigm while he was alive, but as modern psychologists might say, homeostasis (a system's tendency to try and maintain internal stability, often reverting back to old behavior) set in after his death.

Challenging the Patriarchy

The mere presence of women in coleadership positions within the early Christian church would have been threatening to those safeguarding existing traditions that kept women legally and culturally in an inferior position. Women were accorded dignity and respect when they became wives and mothers, but what was to be done with an independent woman like Mary Magdalene?

Women Support the Church

She not only became a loyal follower of Jesus, but after his death and resurrection, she likely continued to support the faithful (not only the other women in the movement but the men as well) and may have become an evangelist in her own right. Some sources of biblical history suggest that Mary Magdalene was such a powerful figure in the movement after the Resurrection and Pentecost that faith communities sprouted and grew around her ministry. The efforts of other women are mentioned in Paul's letter to the Romans, including Priscilla, "servant of the church"; Phebe, "helper in Christ"; and Mary, "who bestowed much labor" (Romans 16:1–3).

Patriarchy Persists

Patriarchal traditions were deeply entrenched. Women had their place in the patriarchal world where Jewish men made decisions for them. But later, some Jewish leaders advocated that Gentile men who desired to follow Jesus would have to convert to Judaism *and* be circumcised in order to become Christians. Even Paul, who is known as the "Apostle to the Gentiles," and who spent his life converting other Jews and Gentiles to a belief in Christ, found it necessary to proclaim himself a member of the Tribe of Benjamin (as was Mary of Bethany, whose identity is sometimes intertwined with Mary of Magdalene). His biography states that he was a circumcised Israelite of the Pharisaic tradition who spoke Aramaic and strictly observed the Torah. In Acts, he cries out in the council: "Men and brethren, I am a Pharisee, the son of a Pharisee: of the hope and resurrection of the dead I am called in question" (23:6).

factum

Modern classical Torah scholars say that Jewish women are not obliged to marry. In Orthodox Judaism, women who eschew the traditional roles of wife and mother can find a place within the faith to perform divine service to others because such service is considered virtuous.

Women Devote Themselves to Jesus

Women were the first to convert in numbers and to receive Jesus' teachings. They believed Jesus when he said women are capable of growing in grace and understanding the same as men. Jesus taught them well. They received the gifts of the Holy Spirit. Jesus expected them to fulfill their responsibilities just as he expected the men to do. He would be with them and women did not let him down. They did not ever abandon, deny, or betray him.

Women committed themselves to doing everything they could to spread Jesus' message of love, forgiveness, redemption, and salvation. But after he died, they needed the support of their spiritual brothers to challenge the patriarchal status quo. For those women, change came so excruciatingly slowly that they didn't see it in their lifetimes. Still, Mary Magdalene and her sacred sisters in Christ stand as powerful exemplars for the modern spiritual-seeker.

chapter 6

Mary Magdalene's Life Begins Anew

Life changed for Mary Magdalene and the other disciples following the death and resurrection of Jesus. The disciples, who cowered at Jesus' death, became spiritual warriors after Pentecost. Though the Bible doesn't mention Mary Magdalene after the Easter story, it's a good bet that the stress of being an independent Jewish woman in Judea under Roman occupation did not go away. The patriarchy was strongly rooted even within the Jesus movement.

After the Resurrection

Jesus' followers steadily attracted converts even though they were a minority movement in a Hebrew world of many sects. Initially, these newly converted "believers" were mostly Jewish like Jesus' original followers. Mary Magdalene, who, during Jesus' ministry, was one of the three who walked with Jesus at all times, according to the Gospel of Philip, may have stayed in Galilee and evangelized among her own people. Or, perhaps she went to Jerusalem to be closer to Mary, mother of Jesus, and John, the disciple whom Jesus loved and to whom Jesus entrusted the care of his mother upon his death (there are legends that say she eventually went to Ephesus with John and Mother Mary).

factum

Initially after Jesus died, Mary Magdalene may have enjoyed high apostolic status, but scholars assert that by the time the Gospel accounts were written, her relevance may have been greatly diminished by the Gospel writers and later by well-meaning patristic scribes who struggled with clarifying problematic points and theological problems.

What happened to her after the death of Jesus has been the focus of much scholarly conjecture, supposition, and debate. Because of the love and loyalty that Mary Magdalene bore for Jesus in life, she most certainly would have shared his story and teachings as long as she had breath to do so although there are no biblical accounts stating as much. There is no historical record that she evangelized Galilee or Jerusalem, although she may have. Some writers have suggested that she went to Egypt, perhaps to do missionary work or to escape persecution.

The Coterie Grows

The group continued to evolve and increase despite having to confront some complex issues, rising tensions, and outright conflict. For example, after Stephen, leader of the Greek-speaking Jews, died, his followers began preaching to the Diaspora Jews of Antioch and to the pagans. Soon, a conflict erupted over whether Gentiles had to convert to Judaism, be circumcised, and adhere to the dietary restrictions of the Jews before they could be followers of Jesus.

The apostle Paul (who called himself Apostle to the Gentiles) averted what might have become a small crisis by diplomatically suggesting to the Jerusalem-based followers that the pagans were like new shoots grafted onto the wild olive tree of the Jews, which is sustained by a holy root (Romans 12:16–25). At some point it must have made sense to preach to the Gentiles, because once Paul and others began to penetrate those communities, the Jesus movement took hold and spread rapidly.

Spreading the Gospel in the End-Times

On their own after the death of Jesus, his followers may have felt a sense of disunity and perhaps isolation because they (as members of Jesus' inner circle) were the only ones who truly understood that Christ Jesus (the promised Messiah from King David's bloodline) was going to establish his earthly kingdom upon his return. They may have believed that the Second Coming prophesied by sages of the Old Testament and fought for by the Zealots and Daggermen (resistance fighters against the Romans who carried daggers and killed Jewish opponents of their cause) would happen in their lifetime. Of Jesus' twelve disciples, three were presumed Zealots: Judas Iscariot (the betrayer who hanged himself), Simon the Cananaean (also known as Simon the Zealot), and Thaddaeus (also known as Jude).

Mary Magdalene and her companions might have not thought that their little community, even as it grew, needed formal organization, structure, canon, creed, and texts to remind them of Jesus' remarkable life and teachings. Because they believed the end-time was near, they saw no need. Using oral traditions that preserved Jesus' teachings and miracles, his followers lived and worked within an ethical framework that guided their lives and decisions. They remained focused on spreading the miraculous story of the risen Jesus—his wisdom and ultimate sacrifice for humankind.

Patriarchal Entrenchment

Scholars say that Paul's letters—written to provide counsel and support to new communities of converts—give some idea of the treatment Jesus' female followers faced when Christianity was still in its infancy. Paul's letters, which are included in the canonical New Testament, affirm that women should remember their place and never upstage men. In a letter to Timothy, Paul writes, "I will therefore that men pray every where, lifting up holy hands, without wrath and doubting. In like manner also, that women adorn themselves in modest apparel, with shamefacedness and sobriety; not with braided hair, or gold, or pearls, or costly array; but (which becometh women professing godliness) with good works. Let the woman learn in silence with all subjection. But I suffer not a woman to teach, nor to usurp authority over the man, but to be in silence" (1 Timothy 2:8–12).

discussion question

What is patriarchy?
It is an old form of social organization within a family or tribe. The father is the supreme authority. Children descend through the male line and belong to the father's family. Women have to submit to male authority. Patriarchal thinking was deeply embedded in Jewish and Roman psyches. Thus, Jesus' egalitarian treatment of women was viewed as radical.

Jesus' Radical Treatment of Women

Jesus modeled an inclusive and egalitarian treatment of women and defied oppressive commandments that Jews observed because they were found in Old Testament Jewish law and custom. Through his love, empathy, compassion, wisdom, and respect, he exhibited a new and different way to treat women. The Bible cites these specific instances:

- He taught women the same as men without discrimination (Luke 10:41–42).
- He welcomed women into his inner circle (Luke 8:1–3).
- He ignored the ritual impurity rules embedded in Old Testament and cultural teachings and healed a woman who had a blood issue for twelve years (Mark 5:25–34).
- He appeared first to Mary Magdalene in his risen form (John 20:15–16).
- He commissioned Mary Magdalene with the first apostolic mission (John 20:17).
- He articulated a concern about widows (Luke 20:46–47).
- He spoke to foreign women—the Samaritan woman at the well (John 4:7–10).

Mary Magdalene Encounters Male Resistance

Mary Magdalene no longer had Jesus to protect her against the hot-tempered contentiousness of some of the male disciples. Some must have had a more difficult time than others developing the kind of respect toward women that Jesus had shown. It was a new experience for these men for a woman to challenge them the way that Mary Magdalene did. According to the Gnostic texts, while Jesus was still among them, Mary Magdalene exhibited an inquisitive and facile mind during group discussions that was uncharacteristic for a woman and yet Jesus encouraged her to speak in boldness. The male disciples might have had a problem with her being female and independent.

Paul's Letters Reveal Early Struggles

The earliest biblical accounts of the life of Jesus and Christianity's origins are found in the letters of the apostle Paul. Paul wrote a number of letters (that became part of the New Testament) between the years 50 and 60. Others believe that the letters were written a decade earlier, placing them less than ten years after Jesus' death. Either way, they predate the New Testament Gospels and other historical accounts. Paul's letters to fledgling Christian communities in provinces around the Roman Empire, however, do not contain many details and insights into the events of Jesus' life, but they do shed light on the fledgling movement as it was metamorphosing into the Christian religion.

factum

Jesus spoke Aramaic during his Galilean ministry, and Aramaic was the language they used to converse with him and each other. A Semitic language, Aramaic dates back to the ninth century B.C. The Jewish people, during Babylonian captivity, brought Aramaic to Palestine. However, the Gospels were likely written in Greek to be easily distributed throughout the Roman world.

Many of the letters detail internal struggles and crises within the communities of converts. In the Corinthian church, for example, problems arose out of disagreements of interpretation of the liturgy, neglect of the meaning of the Lord's Supper, head coverings for women, and the shamefulness of women whose hair was cut off. A man had a direct relationship to Christ, but a woman's was through her husband. A man did not have to cover his head in church, but a woman did to symbolize her subordinate relationship. Women who cut their hair very short were equated with prostitutes.

But I would have you know, that the head of every man is Christ; and the head of every woman is the man; and the head of Christ is God. Every man praying or prophesying, having his head covered, dishonoreth his head. But every woman that prayeth or prophesieth with her head uncovered dishonoreth her head: for that is even all one as if she were shaven. For if the woman be not covered, let her also be shorn: but if it be a shame for a woman to be shorn or shaven, let her be covered **(1 Corinthians 11:3–6).**

Despite the internal squabbles and struggles of the movement, its members did what Jesus had commissioned them to do. They had no particular name for themselves, no physical church, no formal organizational structure. They shared their money, dispersed goods to those in need, and took care of each other as comrades. Somehow, the movement's membership held together and grew.

discussion question

Why did Paul not write about the details of Jesus' life?
What Paul (who was a Roman citizen formerly named Saul and intent on persecuting the Jews) knew about Jesus would have been hearsay, since the two never physically met. During Paul's conversion, however, he witnessed the risen Christ and was compelled to proclaim Jesus as the Son of God.

Devout Christians say that the Holy Spirit worked through them drawing others to their message. Others say that the message itself was powerful and compelling. Also, people were naturally curious, and word of mouth worked its magic. This was especially true, scholars say, in Jerusalem, where some of the original followers remained and thus encountered increasing numbers of Diaspora Jews. However, Jerusalem also became the site where the seeds of disharmony may have sprouted once the population of Diaspora Jews swelled disproportionately to Jesus' original group.

Women in Leadership Roles

Scholars believe that Mary Magdalene and her sisters in the movement forged ahead faith-sharing, hosting prayer meetings, bringing others into a belief in the risen Jesus while also supporting their spiritual brethren as they undertook similar endeavors. Some sources say that women joined as converts in greater numbers than men. However, the prevailing thought was that men should always make the decisions for the family because men had the benefit of an education, were better informed, and could therefore reason through the best decisions for their families. But women successfully evangelized other women.

factum

Shrines and churches dedicated to Mary Magdalene throughout the world often are adorned with art, icons, paintings, sculptures, and beautiful friezes. Among the many sites frequented by pilgrims are churches in southern France at Sainte Maximin-La Sainte-Baume and in Burgundy at Vézelay. In Salt Lake City, Utah, stands a particularly beautiful Romanesque cathedral built in honor of Mary Magdalene.

Inspired by the Holy Spirit

After Jesus' death, Mary Magdalene had to seek his companionship and counsel in prayer, meditation, and contemplation. In the quiet of her soul, she received the guidance she sought for the trials and tribulations she faced in daily life. But did her spoken words (based on inner guidance from Jesus) fall on deaf ears? As Mary

Magdalene pushed forward in her work to share Jesus' message and address others as a woman who had learned at the feet of her master, would others remember that he had singled out one sister and commended her for her learning as she sat at his feet while the other sister kept on doing traditional household tasks? But Jesus had taught her and the other women. In that regard, they were equals. And like the men, they, too, had been blessed by the Holy Spirit who empowered them and brought upon them divine gifts of leadership, eloquence in speaking, and holy insights.

Mary Magdalene, Authority Figure

Through the centuries, women symbolically and literally have brought spiritual "light" into the home. When they lit candles in religious ritual observance (symbolic) or modeled spiritual behavior through praying, obeying the commandments, living a moral life, and teaching their children through words and deeds (literal), they infused their families with spiritual light.

Mary Magdalene and the women of the movement comprehended the wife and mother as the religious center of family life. This female understanding probably made them more effective evangelizers than men, at least to potential women converts. Empowered by Jesus' wisdom teachings and the gifts of the Holy Spirit, Mary Magdalene and her spiritual sisters likely found their sacred voices could be a powerful force for change.

fallacy

It's a fallacy that the Gospel of Matthew was the first Gospel account written, although it appears first in the New Testament. Scholars say that Mark dates to 69 to 75. Matthew was written around 80 to 90. Luke and Acts date to between 90 to 100, and John was written in the ninth decade of the first century.

Mary Magdalene's modern followers complain that her contributions to Christianity have been minimized by patristic tweaking of the Gospels to clarify thorny theological questions and to correct certain difficult points as well as by a church that did not want a woman as a central authority figure. According to those who venerate her today, Mary Magdalene served as the leading female authority figure within the movement, and she might have been written out of the Christian origin story altogether were it not for her proximity to Jesus, her stature in the movement, and her contributions. She was too well known in the oral traditions during and after Jesus' lifetime. Her very importance may have contributed to her being depicted wrongly as a prostitute by the early church—a belief not supported in any historical document or the Gospels.

The Importance of Apostolic Succession

The Eastern Orthodox Church calls Mary Magdalene Holy Myrrhbearer and Equal-unto-the-Apostles. The Roman Catholic Church calls her Apostle to the Apostles. Both churches consider her a saint. Her honorific titles signify the important role she played in early Christianity. Who could be an apostle? Were there women apostles as well as men? What were the criteria? These questions have fundamental relevance to addressing the issue of apostolic succession.

What Is an Apostle?

Mention the word *apostle,* and many people think immediately of the twelve disciples of Jesus, chosen and commissioned by him to be missionaries. Yet, Paul, who never physically met Jesus but saw him in a vision during his conversion and received a call to serve, called himself an apostle. Biblical scholars have noted that a reference exists to "female apostles" from a bishop of Rome writing in the third century. This suggests that women as well as men could have served as apostles.

A simple definition of apostle that is both basic and broad is someone with authority and power who dispatches a messenger to act on his or her behalf. The Gospels of Matthew, Mark, and Luke use the term *apostle* in relationship to the twelve disciples of Jesus. John frequently uses the term *apostle* in relationship to Jesus' functions as the Apostle of God. The letters of Paul outline two criteria that must be met to make a legitimate claim of apostleship: (1) witnessing the risen Christ, and (2) receiving a call to serve him and proclaim his message. Apostles had a direct authoritative link to Jesus that rendered their message legitimate.

A tenuous, even contentious relationship between Peter and Mary Magdalene seems to emerge in the Gospel of Mary when Mary Magdalene receives a vision of Jesus and a secret teaching, which Peter asks her to share. However, when she tells him, he does not believe her. She was close to Jesus. The Savior loved her and Peter. After Jesus' ascension, both fulfilled the criteria for apostleship. Yet, according to some theologians, as the historical accounts of Christianity were written and selected for the Bible, Peter's role was magnified and Mary Magdalene's diminished.

The Great Schism

Christianity in its infancy was one church. By the eleventh century, however, theological differences over the pope and liturgical innovation caused the church to experience the Great Schism that culminated in two branches: the Eastern Orthodox Church and the Roman Catholic Church. Both trace their apostolic succession back to the original Twelve. The Roman Catholic Church claims Peter as its first pope. But some fathers of the church through the centuries (Gregory of Antioch, among them) defended women's rights to apostleship. It makes sense in the patriarchal structure to have a single doctrine of theology, illumined or attested to by Scripture, and rigorously reviewed by someone with the apostolic authority to ensure that it was valid and legitimate. A major struggle of the early church was the ascendancy splinter groups whose interpretations were deemed heretical and divisive. Today's pope traces his own apostolic authority to Peter through an uninterrupted male line. Feminist theologians assert that apostolic authority, power, and control was something patriarchal fathers did not want to share with women.

discussion question

What does it mean if a church is Christocentric?
The word suggests a church centered on Christ as its head. In Eastern Orthodoxy, the term describes a belief in Christ Jesus as the church's head and the church as his body. Eastern Orthodox practitioners trace their beliefs to oral traditions that predate the New Testament. In contrast, many modern Christian churches are bibliocentric—centered on the Bible.

Misogyny and Patriarchal Restriction

Were the first-century Jews misogynists (woman haters)? Were the Gnostics? What about Jesus' male disciples? Or, did they just view Mary Magdalene and the women in their world through the lens of an Old Testament patriarchal tradition? Though popular fiction romanticizes an ancient world in which women had a high status, scholarship of the first century tells a different tale. In the ancient pagan world, women had a low status.

A Sexualized Mary Magdalene

There were pagan cults in which temple priestesses had sex with men (some say these were magical rites to produce fertility rather than romanticized sacred masculine/feminine initiations). However, these acts did not elevate the woman's status in society. Conservative biblical scholars say that a sexualized Mary Magdalene (a conjecture found in current popular fiction), as an initiatrix into sacred mystery traditions, demeans and devalues the legitimate contributions of this remarkable woman. On the other side of the debate, some feminist theologians suggest that Mary Magdalene is the missing goddess of the Gospels, the embodiment of the Sacred

Feminine who has been virtually suppressed for the last two millennia through patriarchal restriction.

Equality Was Unknown

It is possible that at some junctures in Mary Magdalene's life, she might have encountered genuine misogynists. But it is more likely that she encountered resistance to being an independent woman who had no need of a husband and who was afire with a passionate belief in the risen Jesus—a belief that was so strong she dedicated her life to it. As for the men she met, how could they know how to be with this woman? She was the fiercely loyal confidante of Jesus while he was among them, and a bold and eloquent speaker for his message after his death. She may have seemed formidable and intimidating.

factum

The Gnostics were a sect of early Christians whose writings about the events of Jesus' life and ministry diverged from the orthodox accounts found in the New Testament. The sect's name derives from the Greek word gnosis, which means "mystical knowledge." Gnosticism may have evolved out of a Syrian/Palestinian environment in the late first or second century. Gnostic texts exalt Mary Magdalene.

In the first century, Jewish men could look back into their history and their holy texts for models of God-fearing husbands, fathers, providers, and teachers—the great patriarchs. But there were no examples of men treating women as equals—that is, until Jesus came along. The more orthodox probably were resistant to changing their long-held beliefs about women and their status in society. They may have viewed Mary Magdalene and the other women in the movement as having abandoned their womanly submissiveness for a more masculine aggressiveness that the men viewed as unbecoming.

chapter 7

Mary Magdalene in Legend

Mary Magdalene embodies the heroic figure. She risked bodily harm and even death for her love for Jesus. In Eastern Orthodox and Western traditions, she stars in the story of Christianity as an icon of love. Her legends depict her as different archetypes at various junctures in her history, however, these stories may have been so embellished that they challenge the actual historic events. For example, her legends state alternately that she died in France, Ephesus, and Rome.

Danger of Persecution

The followers of Jesus lived under the threat of persecution through-out their lives. The religious and political situation in the first century worsened around the time of the Jewish revolt from 66 to 74 and thereafter until Emperor Constantine converted to Christianity and made it the official religion in 313. If Mary Magdalene were exactly Jesus' age when he died (circa 30–33), then she would have been roughly about sixty-three to sixty-six when the revolt occurred. She may have left as the radical politics in the region started heating up or even long before, possibly right after Jesus' ascension. Her legends don't explicitly detail that part of her story.

Roman Justice

The Romans kept a close watch on the followers of Jesus. They knew about the Zealots and other groups advocating sedition. They became suspicious of any activities held at night and of groups that assembled in large numbers. Imagine the fear the early Christians must have had as they gathered in private homes for their prayer meetings. The Romans could easily imprison anyone suspected of violating their rules and civil laws. They crucified, beheaded, and stoned to death dissidents and seditionists.

factum

Stephen became the first Christian martyr when he angered some synagogue elders. He told them that Jesus would change the customs of Moses and that he would destroy the Temple.

According to accounts of the Jewish historian, Josephus, one self-proclaimed prophet stirring up the masses was beheaded, another was crucified as an insurrectionist, and others thought to be *Sicarii*, or knife-wielders, were captured and killed. It is not surprising that Jews feared the swift and brutal justice of the Romans.

Perhaps Mary Magdalene wondered where she could go within the vast Roman Empire and feel safe enough to preach the Christian message. The canonical Gospels state that King Herod, intent on suppressing the movement, "stretched forth his hands to vex certain of the church. And he killed James the brother of John with the sword. And because he saw it pleased the Jews, he proceeded further to take Peter also." (Acts 12:1–3).

Martyrdom of Christians

Many martyrs—Christian witnesses for Jesus—suffered torture and horrific deaths in the early centuries after Jesus' ascension. Polycarp, bishop of Smyrna, was martyred in 155 when he was burned alive and pierced with a spear. Some accounts say that from the hole in his flesh, a dove emerged along with a sufficient quantity of blood to put out the fire.

The torture of women through the centuries seemed particularly innovative. Perpetua, a young woman imprisoned for being a Christian, was martyred at Carthage in the third century. She gave birth to a child in her cell. Her father pleaded with her to renounce her beliefs for his sake and the sake of her newborn. Perpetua did not. She was allowed to spend time with her newborn in her cell before walking into the Roman amphitheater to meet the beasts that would tear her to pieces. Her diary reveals the love she felt for Christ.

discussion question

How were first-century apostles persecuted and martyred?
Boiled in oil (Saint John the Divine), crucified upside down (Saint Peter), beheaded (Saint John the Baptist), beaten to death with a club (Saint James), crucified on a tall cross (Saint Philip) and on an X-shaped cross (Saint Andrew), and stabbed with a sword (Saint James, son of Zebedee).

Agatha, a Sicilian girl who dared to spurn the amorous advances of Quintianus, the Roman consul of Sicily, was turned over to a brothel and made to live as a harlot for a month. Then, when she still would not renounce her love for Jesus and submit to Quintianus, she was put on a rack, bound, and tortured. Her breasts were crushed and cut off. When she still did not renounce her beliefs, her clothing was removed and she was rolled in pottery shards and smoldering coals. Such stories illustrate the brutality of Roman punishment.

Mary Magdalene may have already fled Judea before the bloody insurgency that brought the Temple of Jerusalem under the power of the Jews, who subsequently lost it. Christian persecution did not diminish until Emperor Constantine converted to Christianity. In 313 at Milan, Constantine issued his edict of religious tolerance. Only then could Christians begin to worship freely without the nagging, persistent fear of persecution.

Fleeing the Holy Land

Both Eastern and Western traditions suggest that Mary Magdalene left Jerusalem after Jesus' death, possibly to escape persecution. But where did she go? The Eastern Orthodox (including the Russian Orthodox) legends suggest that she went to Ephesus, a city in ancient western Asia Minor, to do missionary work with John the Evangelist and Mary, mother of Jesus. Other sources say she went to Egypt, where a gospel bearing her name was found in an antiquities market in Cairo in 1896. Still others assert that she went to southern Gaul (modern Provence). England, too, has strong Mary Magdalene legends and there are many churches built and dedicated to her, including at Oxford and Cambridge. In England alone, more than 200 churches were constructed in veneration of Mary Magdalene, many featuring beautiful friezes and artistic renderings of her.

She may have been in Europe because of the wealth of legends that still circulate, numerous churches dedicated to her, dozens of pilgrimage sites, and various historical Magdalene houses that were established to redeem fallen women. Although Mary Magdalene had been misrepresented as a repentant prostitute by the early church, the label led to her being deemed the patron saint of prostitutes and fallen women and thus such European houses claimed her name.

symbolism

In Byzantine iconographic images, Mary Magdalene holds an egg as a symbol of Jesus' resurrection. The egg, in Jewish custom, symbolizes promise and is one of several foods placed upon the Seder plate at Passover and mentioned in the reading of the Haggadah during the Seder service.

Still another legend asserts that Mary Magdalene went to Rome after the Resurrection where she met with Emperor Tiberias (14 to 37) and complained about Pontius Pilate. During dinner, she evangelized and defended Jesus' innocence. The icon of the red egg comes from this legend. The emperor said something like "no more could a man have died and risen after three days than a white egg could turn red." Mary Magdalene, as the legend goes, picked up the egg, and it turned red before the emperor's astonished gaze.

Mary Magdalene and John on Ephesus

According to certain legends, Mary Magdalene stayed in Ephesus, perhaps helping the apostle John (who became the first bishop of Ephesus) until her death. The Eastern Church notes that Emperor Leo VI moved her relics (from the Latin, reliquere, meaning "to leave behind") to Constantinople in 899. Some sources state that it was not until the tenth century that her veneration as the composite saint (with Mary of Bethany and the penitent sinner) took hold in Western tradition.

The New Testament Gospels do not mention the journey and death of Mary Magdalene at Ephesus. Early church fathers Irenaeus, Polycarp, Eusebius, and Clement, however, all acknowledged John's presence there. The Byzantine legends have always maintained that his tomb is there. He was buried on the southern end of Ayosolug Hill. Roughly 300 years later, a chapel was built over the apostle John's grave and named Church of St. John. A couple of hundred years after that, Emperor Justinian turned the tiny church into a beautiful basilica.

symbolism

Caves symbolize the protective womb, the unconscious, birth, and regeneration. From ancient times through today, spiritual seekers make pilgrimages to sacred caves and grottoes on hillsides or mountains. Infused with the prayers of the faithful, spiritual force was thought to permeate such caves. Mary Magdalene, as a contemplative, lived thirty years in a limestone cave in France.

As for Mother Mary, there is neither testimony, oral or written, nor any proof of her death or entombment on Ephesus. Her tomb is venerated near Jerusalem in an area known as the Valley of Cedron. However, historians also make note of a church at Ephesus in 431 that was dedicated to the Virgin. Today in Ephesus, there is evidence of an ancient cathedral called the "Double Church," in which one aisle is dedicated to Saint John and the other aisle is dedicated to the Blessed Virgin Mary. A search for churches named after or dedicated to Mary Magdalene turned up no listings.

While it is not known exactly when Mary Magdalene arrived at Ephesus, Irenaeus places John the Divine in Ephesus when he was already in exile (for his preaching of the gospel) on Patmos as the reign of Domitian was nearing its end. In Revelation, the apostle John writes "I, John, who also am your brother, and companion in tribulation, and in the kingdom and patience of Jesus Christ, was in the isle that is called Patmos, for the word of God, and for the testimony of Jesus Christ" (Revelation 1:9).

The apostle John is widely credited for his work in Asia Minor, work that seemed to be centered or based in Ephesus, a place that now claims many Christian legends. One tells the story of seven young Christian men who, when they refused to sacrifice animals at a Roman temple, faced certain persecution for their conviction. They went into a cave and fell asleep. Upon awakening, the young men went to purchase some food in the city. They were astonished when they discovered that their night in the cave had actually stretched out for 200 years. While they were sleeping, Christianity had spread across the entire Roman Empire.

When told of the incident, Emperor Theodosius II believed it to be evidence of resurrection. The lives of these men finally ended, and they were buried in that cave where they'd fallen asleep so long before. A church was built on top of the cave in honor of the seven holy men. Centuries later, excavations of the area exposed a church and hundreds of graves (supposedly because so many believers wanted to be buried near these holy beings). The church and grave walls carried inscriptions dedicated to the Seven Sleepers. One legend says that Mary Magdalene's grave is located there as well.

Arriving on the Shore of Gaul

France has many legends about Mary Magdalene. According to a popular French legend, a persecuted Mary Magdalene was placed on a boat without oars that was then set adrift at sea away from Palestine. Traveling with her was Mary of Bethany, Mary's sister, Martha, and brother, Lazarus, and perhaps others. Their boat landed where the modern coastal village of Saintes-Maries-de-la-Mer (Saints Marys of the Sea) now stands. A Romany (Gypsy) legend tells the story of their patron saint Sara-la-Kâli (also known as Sara the Black and also Sara the Gitane) rescuing the boat's survivors. They built an oratory on the site that later was replaced by Notre Dame de la

Mer. Every year during the last weekend in May, the Romany make their way to the village of Saintes-Maries-de-la-Mer to present their children to the saint and to ask for blessings on contracts and business deals. After prayers and invocations, they parade the saint in a procession to the sea.

A variant of this legend features Mary Magdalene in the company of Martha, Lazarus, Salome, Joseph of Arimathea, and Maximin as they drift in a rudderless boat toward the coast of Marseille. They were welcomed into the Jewish community. The group began proselytizing and performing miracles. Mary Magdalene made a decision to become a contemplative and found a cave in which to retire. There she fasted, meditated, and prayed while living on one holy Eucharist wafer a day fed to her by angels.

Proselytizing to the Populace

Mary Magdalene wasn't alive during the Middle Ages, but her presence was deeply felt among the common folk and they certainly talked about her. Legends from the Middle Ages make some wild claims for Mary Magdalene. Some say she was the ancestress of the Merovingian line of French kings and that she was the saintly icon worshiped by the Knights Templar (this is discussed in more detail in Part II). Medieval occultists believed she was a holy repository of secret teachings (presumably because of her proximity to Jesus). An old legend about her bearing the Holy Grail and bringing it to France has been dredged up in recent books and given a new spin.

The Golden Legend, a book of hagiographies (studies of the lives of saints) compiled in 1275 by Jacobus de Voragine, the Dominican archbishop of Genoa, tells of Mary Magdalene's evangelizing the populace of southern France. According to Voragine's story, Mary Magdalene and her siblings, Martha and Lazarus, were the offspring of wealthy and noble parents descended from kings. The three gave their wealth to support the work of Jesus. He loved Mary Magdalene completely. After his Passion, he appeared to her and, according to

Voragine's story, made her "apostolesse of the apostles." After Jesus' ascension, the friar's narrative states that Peter committed Mary Magdalene into the care of Saint Maximin but Christian persecutors rounded up Maximin, Mary Magdalene, Lazarus, Martha, and many other Christians and put them out to sea on a boat without oars or rudders. The intent was that the party would drown, but through the grace of God, Voragine explains, they landed in Marseilles.

discussion question

What exactly is the Holy Grail?
Commonly thought of as the chalice from which Jesus drank at the Last Supper, the Holy Grail has also been described as the cup that captured his blood during the Crucifixion. Some writers of popular fiction have theorized that the Holy Grail was Mary Magdalene, pregnant with his child.

When Mary Magdalene saw the local people in Marseilles preparing to sacrifice to idols, she began to preach the Word of God and commandments of Jesus. People believed, among them the provincial prince and his childless wife. The couple conceived, but the wife died in childbirth. The prince left her body on the seashore with the child suckling at its dead mother's breast. With a heavy heart, the prince continued on his journey to seek the counsel of Saint Peter in Jerusalem. Upon his return to France, he found his child alive. He gave thanks to Mary Magdalene. After prayerfully pleading for the restoration of his wife, she, too, miraculously returned to life. They sought Mary Magdalene and found her preaching with her disciples. The prince had all the idols of Marseilles destroyed, and he made Lazarus bishop of the city.

Mary Magdalene churches adorn the landscape of southern France. The French say this is a testament to the power of her presence; their region at the time was populated by pagans. In fact, even the cave at St. Baume was once thought to be the site of pilgrimage for the goddess Diana, the Light Bringer. Voragine, in *The Golden Legend*, refers to Mary Magdalene as one "who is a lighter" and "she is called the light."

Retreat from the World

After spending time in Marseille, Mary Magdalene and her disciples left to evangelize the city of Aix. They did so with great success. Thereafter, according to Voragine, Mary Magdalene became a contemplative, retiring to a limestone cave for thirty years. Each day angels would lift her up and she would hear the strains and choruses of celestial harmonies. When she died, a sweet odor permeated the space for seven days. Maximin, then bishop of Marseille, undertook the anointing of her body and oversaw the burial. He also expressed his desire to be buried next to her when he died.

News of her death brought pilgrims in such great numbers that, in the thirteenth century, a massive basilica was constructed in her honor. Some call it southern France's finest Gothic church. While her head remained enshrined at La Sainte-Baume near Marseille, her bones were scattered (according to one source) during the French Revolution. Another asserts that the duke of Burgundy had her relics moved to Vézelay. Still others say her relics remain in Constantinople, and at least one source says she was buried in Rome.

From among the rich tradition of French legends about Mary Magdalene, here is yet another. In 769, the duke of Burgundy, desiring a child, undertook the construction of a new monastery in Vézelay. He felt inspired to obtain and install the relics of Mary Magdalene in his new church. Believing the relics to be in a grave in Aix (in the south), he sent a monk to secure them and bring them back to Vézelay.

The monk arrived at the burial site and searched until he located the headstone. Then he went away to wait for darkness so no one would see what he was about to do. At night, the monk again found the grave, and removed the reliquary housing the remains of Mary Magdalene. He carried the container to his place of lodging. In a flash, Mary Magdalene appeared. The monk was frightened, but she comforted him and counseled him to complete his mission.

factum

The Catholic Church has always venerated religious relics (parts of saints' bodies). Relics can also be items that have touched the saints or with which saints have had contact. Among other places, Mary Magdalene's relics are venerated at Saint Maximin, La Sainte Baume, in Provence and at Vézelay.

On the next morning, the monk started for home. But the trip had sapped his strength. His arms felt weak and unable to carry the remains the last mile to the monastery. Perhaps through the intercession of the saint, a group of monks led by their abbot appeared from out of nowhere and in a processional carried the remains of Mary Magdalene to her new home. The legend states that the duke and his wife subsequently had a child. Vézelay monastery became a holy site for the veneration of Mary Magdalene and many miracles have been attributed to her.

Relics and Reliquaries

In Europe, the medieval holy relic trade flourished at the expense of the piety of common folk. Imagine being in the presence of a vial holding a tear of Jesus or a piece of the Holy Mother's veil. The faithful believed that the mere touch of such a holy item could have curative powers and unleash upon them untold blessings. If a church housed the relics (a finger, lock of hair, toenail, head, foot, etc.) of an important saint like Mary Magdalene, pilgrims would flock to the site and fill the church's coffers. Therefore, individual churches valued relics as highly as did the spiritual pilgrims whose devotion to a particular saint would justify the cost associated with their relic veneration. Churches engaged in stiff competition for the best relics of the holiest beings. Today, Mary Magdalene's knucklebone is said to be in Vézelay.

discussion question

What archetypes might Mary Magdalene represent?
Information gleaned from the canonical Gospels, the Gnostic texts, and her legends suggest that she represented one or more of the following archetypes at different times in her life: Hierophant, Visionary, Healer, Hermit, Victim, Prophetess, Leader, Illuminatrix, Peace Bearer, Sinner, Teacher, Lover, Goddess, and Wife (if you believe one account).

Mary Magdalene's Relics

One account asserts that she died in about 75 and was buried in the crypt of the chapel at Villalata (now Maximin) and there remained undisturbed until 710. Cassion monks guarded her relics after they founded their monastery at Maximin. When the Saracens invaded France, they destroyed all symbols related to Christianity, so the monks moved Mary Magdalene's relics to ensure their safety. The Saracens were gone by 973 and apparently so were the relics (the monks had buried them and the chapel). Then, in 1279 the nephew of King Louis IX of France uncovered Mary Magdalene's relics and transferred them to the crypt. That's the way the story is often told. However, according to Lynn Picknett's book *Mary Magdalene*, the bones of Mary Magdalene found in that fifth-century alabaster sarcophagus in the crypt of the church at St. Maximin in 1279, although highly prized, did not belong to her. In her book, Picknett wrote that further investigation proved that the documentation found with the bones and supporting their authenticity proved to be false.

In the Middle Ages, the whole business of relic possession reached near-cult status. Superstitious beliefs about magical and miraculous powers of saints' remains or holy items associated with a particular saint drew throngs of petitioners to churches claiming better collections than others. Whether the relics were authentic was another question altogether. Abuses arose in the form of fake relics or of forged authentication documents such as those at Maximin.

Collecting and Preserving Relics

The Crusaders during the eleventh and twelfth centuries contributed to the relic trade by bringing an abundance of such holy items home to Europe from their far-flung travels. It seemed fitting to have containers for these body parts and holy objects so artisans began to create a container called a reliquary (from the Latin *reliquere*, meaning "to leave behind"). By the middle of the fourteenth century, craftsmen created reliquaries of fine metal and ornate decoration to house saints' relics or objects. Sometimes reliquaries were even used in processionals through the streets of a community or along the seashore. In Maximin today, locals hoist up Mary Magdalene's skull, encased in a golden reliquary, and parade it around as part of the community's annual commemorative celebration of her life in their region.

Patroness of the Dominicans, Mary Magdalene's feast day of July 22 is commemorated during the week of July 21 through 28 in Provence. The Dominicans, originally called Dominic's Order of Preachers, established a presence at Mary Magdalene's tomb at St. Maximin. There they protected her relics and decreed in 1297 that the entire order should celebrate her feast day.

Icon Veneration

Icons (from the Greek eikon, meaning image) represent aspects of theological events and people in an art form. They are a kind of spiritual window through which believers have access to the Divine, the saints, and heaven. Icons were mentioned by early church fathers in their writings. During the eighth and ninth centuries, icons were banned. Then the acceptable representation for Christ was the Alpha and Omega symbols. Icons of Mary Magdalene, Mother Mary (referred to in the Greek tradition as Theotokos or God-bearer), the apostle John, and other saints were not intended to reflect them accurately as modern portraiture might but rather as spiritual images expressing more than just a human being.

discussion question

What are the Christian catacombs?
Early Christians buried their dead in underground burial chambers outside their city or town. Rich and poor alike were buried in these chambers with little to distinguish between them. Historians have learned much about early Christian life from the sepulcher inscriptions and the catacomb art. Some tombs are sites for pilgrimage.

Religious interest in relics was more popular in the Roman Catholic tradition than in the Eastern Orthodox where the veneration of icons was favored. In centuries-old Russian churches today, *iconostasis* (screens with icons) hide altars and sanctuaries. Other churches have entire walls of icons. Christian catacombs are also full of icons. Beginning in the eighth century and continuing through the ninth, iconoclasts (clergy and others opposing icon veneration) favored banning the veneration of icons. Certain emperors agreed. The Second Council of Nicaea in 787 declared that icons could be honored but not worshiped.

The veneration of icons remains popular in the Eastern Orthodox Church where icons of particular saints are perfumed and made available for the faithful to kiss on certain holy days. The practice is not widespread in the Western tradition although it is acceptable to pray in the presence of icons.

chapter 8

Ancestral and Apostolic Seeds Are Sown

Fractiousness in the early church arose over apostolic authority, among other things. Some held Mary Magdalene in high esteem and considered her Jesus' heir apparent, while others believed that Jesus had chosen Peter. History would show Peter prevailing as the head of the fledgling Christian church. Mary Magdalene's story would unfold as a fallen but redeemed woman, making her susceptible to diverse representations by the church over the subsequent centuries.

A Myth Is Conceived

The most persistent, yet patently incorrect, myth about Mary Magdalene revolves around her being a prostitute. Pope Gregory the Great, in 591, delivered his now famous homily in Rome at the basilica of Saint Clement. Seeking an example to illustrate the forgiving nature of Christianity, he wove together the stories of Mary Magdalene, Mary of Bethany, and the sinful woman who anointed Jesus' feet in the home of Simon the Pharisee. This composite image perfectly suited his purpose, but Mary Magdalene's reputation would bear the shame of the fallen woman redeemed for a very long time.

Historian Karen King, professor of Ecclesiastical History at Harvard Divinity School, asserted in a PBS interview that some early Christian Gnostic texts show that there was another story of Mary Magdalene. Different than the one offered in the canonical Gospels, the story revealed Mary Magdalene to be an apostle and church leader after Jesus' resurrection.

factum

When he was little more than thirty, Gregory served as prefect of Rome. Trained as a Roman lawyer, he had a brilliant mind and was skillful in grammar, rhetoric, and dialectic. Circa 574, he became a monk—the first to become pope. He relinquished his family's Sicilian estates to found six monasteries. Gregory I (or the Great) made long-lasting reforms in the Roman liturgy and was considered the father of the medieval papacy, among other things.

Other experts in biblical studies refute any argument that Mary Magdalene could ever have been a leader of the church according to the Gnostic Gospels because the Council of Nicaea deemed all the Gnostic texts heretical.

Oral traditions painted an image of a devout and loyal follower of Jesus, who loved him, who stayed with him during his death and entombment, and hurried to anoint his body on the first day of the week. Her story shifted from follower to leader when Jesus chose her to be the first to see his transcendent form and commissioned her to tell the other disciples. The theory that Jesus may have had Mary Magdalene in mind as his successor, as asserted by some biblical experts, is radical departure from conventional thought. Conservative Christians vigorously argue that no proof exists to substantiate such conjecture.

A Homily Hurts Mary Magdalene's Reputation

Pope Gregory wrote, "She whom Luke calls the sinful woman, whom John calls Mary, we believe to be the Mary from whom seven devils were ejected according to Mark. And what did these seven devils signify, if not all the vices? . . . It is clear, brothers, that the woman previously used the unguent to perfume her flesh acts" (Gregory 1: Homily XXXIII). These two sentences destroyed Mary Magdalene's reputation. A harlot, even a repentant one, would not be the first choice of men (in those patriarchal times) to build a church upon. And yet, not to have women in equal partnership with men to do the Lord's work seemed to go against Jesus' message of inclusion. He gave women equal access to the inner circle of leadership, power, and authority.

The male apostles, however, had been brought up in a culture where men and women knew their places in society. The center of the woman's world was the home. Even though Jesus had shown another approach to the gender issue, elevating women to hold the highest levels of leadership in his movement would require a major re-orientation of the male disciples' ingrained cultural beliefs. The prevailing view of women in the cultural hierarchy was still below beasts of burden. The apostles were raised in that tradition. Women, adopting an attitude of ceremonial holiness during religious ritual observances, received God's blessings just as the men did.

119

discussion question

What is the meaning of ceremonial holiness?
Ceremonial holiness is a term that suggests a covenant relationship with God brought about by worshipful activities that draw believers closer to their deity. God is characterized as the holiest of holy. When the faithful separate themselves from the material world to approach the Divine, God diminishes the sense of separation and draws them close.

Did Women Lead the Early Church?

The conservative view of what women did in the early Christian church after Jesus' death was to continue what they had been doing before his death and resurrection. They were myrrhbearers, messengers, and ministers (that is, giving to the group out of their resources and assisting in the work of the movement). Some preached and prophesied. Many made their houses available for home-churches since there were no actual buildings or houses of worship. And some women, mentioned in the New Testament—Lydia in Philippi (Acts 16:14–15) and Priscilla and Aquila in Corinth (Acts 18:2–4)—proved especially helpful to Paul by providing him with accommodations during his travels. Scholars say that Paul, *in persona Christi Capitis,* established his *ekklēsia* (home-churches) in many different communities. Women aided him in his work. In his New Testament letters, he acknowledged certain women for their service.

Hippolytus, the bishop of Rome in the third century, clearly believed that women could be apostles and expressed as much in his writings. He is credited for giving Mary Magdalene the title of Apostle to the Apostles. So, some church fathers believed Jesus intended both men and women to serve as his apostles.

Elaine Pagels, author of *Gnostic Gospels*, writes that the women in the Gnostic Gospel accounts occupy different positions than those allocated to them in the canonical Gospels and they garner different kinds of respect as teachers, disciples, and apostles. Pagels says that in early Christianity, women played strong leadership roles.

factum

To act *in persona Christi Capitis* means that clergy members and priests are authorized and empowered by Christ to serve God's people in the diaconia (work associated with their office as priest or deacon) of liturgy, charity, and words, in accordance with the bishop and presbyterate.

The Lingering Effect of the Homily

Mary Magdalene died in the first century. She was not affected by Gregory the Great's homily, but subsequent generations of women seeking ordination in the church as deacons, priests, bishops, and even pope have been severely disadvantaged by the effects of that homily. New scholarship about Mary Magdalene is giving women—especially Catholic women—renewed hope that precedent exists for women to enter the priesthood and that someday the church will change its position banning women from holding that office. One modern group representing those seeking change is Call to Action. The group stages major celebrations on Mary Magdalene's traditional feast day, July 22. The goal is to make the saint more prominent in the Roman Catholic Church.

The Church Perpetuates the Myth

In prayer sessions in private homes, Mary Magdalene, by virtue of her proximity to Jesus, her visionary abilities and keen understanding of the Lord's teachings (Gospel of Philip, Gospel of Mary), and her apostolic status, likely presided over the prayer service, perhaps even the Eucharist. Yet, her story in the New Testament Gospels seems minimalist at best. Some biblical scholars assert that her relationship to Jesus and subsequent roles in the movement were diminished. Writers and redactors, they say, pushed her story out to the margins of the infancy narrative of Christianity in order to enhance and solidify Peter's position of authority. Of course, others argue the point, saying that Jesus called Peter and gave him the name Cephas (rock) foreshadowing his role as leader of the Jerusalem church.

discussion question

Who were the apostolic fathers?
Respected leaders of the early church of the generation after the apostles were known as the apostolic fathers. They adhered strictly to the apostles' teachings. The most famous were Clement, bishop of Rome and one of the first successors of Peter; Polycarp, bishop of Smyrna; Papias (author of *Expositions of the Sayings of the Lord*); and Ignatius, bishop of Antioch.

Pope Gregory's myth was passed down through Western church fathers in their homilies and writings for nearly two millennia before the Roman Catholic Church acknowledged the inaccuracy about Mary Magdalene being a fallen woman and in 1969 corrected its Missal (a book used by the priests containing the prayers and rites of the Mass). The Eastern Church (which has always separated the women's stories) also has traditions about Mary Magdalene being a prostitute. Its legends, however, hold that she became a prostitute out of unrequited love for Saint John the Theologian (also known as John the Evangelist and John the Divine). The Eastern legends assert that she changed (presumably giving up her old ways to become more pious) once her love for Jesus was as great as the love Saint John bore for him. We are all sinners and Mary Magdalene was, too. But her sins were not sins of the flesh, and she was not the harlot the male clergy made her out to be.

factum

Early church father Irenaeus wrote a five-volume tome, *Refutation and Overthrow of Falsely So-Called Knowledge,* to counteract what he saw as growing heresy within the church. He made an important point about innovation veering away from the gospel. He advocated holding on the canon of truth given to believers in baptism.

During the first few centuries after Jesus' death, the movement underwent some growing pains. Questions arose around interpretation of theology and practice. Did Gentiles have to become Jews and the men undergo circumcision to be Christians? What about the threat women could make to male leadership? To what extent, if any, should they be equal to men to preach, prophesy, perform baptisms, and possibly dispense the bread and wine of the Eucharist? Who had the right to serve as an apostle? Anyone could claim a vision of the risen Jesus and even that he gave them secret teachings, but whose visions and teachings were true? The early apostles wrangled with issues like these. As the church continued to grow and evolve, splinter groups of early Christians (such as those embracing Gnostic ideas) began interpreting the movement's theology and practices in ways that diverged from the more orthodox. To avert a crisis or challenge to the authority of the church, one orthodox leader, Bishop Ignatius of Antioch (circa 107) drew the proverbial line in the sand. He asserted that the church, in its hierarchy, resembled that of heaven. He said that the bishop was to be respected and revered as if he were God.

Celibate Male Apostolic Succession

In the first century, most of the apostles were married, including Peter. Paul, in his first letter to the Corinthians, singles out Peter as one apostle who has a wife, "Have we not the power to lead about

123

a sister, a wife, as well as other apostles, and as the brethren of the Lord, and Cephas?" (1 Corinthians 9:5). As for the male clergy in the first few centuries, most of the priests were still marrying and having children. Yet, in 325, the Council of Nicaea decreed that priests could not marry. Peter, the "rock" upon whom Jesus said he would build his church and one of the pillars of the Jerusalem church, was married. Apostolic succession began with Peter.

fallacy

It's a fallacy that the transition from the Jesus movement to the Christian religion was a smooth and harmonious one. On the contrary, biblical experts say that the birthing of Christianity was fraught with internecine fractiousness, dissention, squabbling, gender issues, power struggles, and heresies.

Clement, bishop of Rome (possibly the third or fourth successor to Peter as Rome's bishop), wrote a letter to the Corinthians (circa 90–100) demanding that those who had deposed the church leaders in Corinth step aside and permit the former leaders to return to the leadership positions. Further, everyone had to respect and obey those former leaders who would be resuming power. Clement argued that God rules Earth through leaders and those leaders (in ascending hierarchal order) are deacons, priests, and bishops. The bishop of Rome (the office that would later be known as the pope) was at the top of that order and his word was final.

There were other married popes in that prestigious lineage, both before and after Pope Urban II decreed that anyone desiring to be ordained into the priesthood had to be unmarried. Felix III (483–492), Hormidas (514–523), Silverus (536–537), Clement IV (1265–1268), and Felix V (1439–1449) had wives and children. Hadrian II (867–872) had a wife but no child. Six other popes had illegitimate children. Precedent exists for priests to be married with families although Pope Urban II in 1095 declared that those seeking ordination into the priesthood could not be married.

discussion question

What were some of the duties of the apostles?
They were to perfect the saints, do the work of the ministry, edify the body of Christ, bear witness to the work of Jesus, start churches, and appoint elders according to Paul's letter to the Ephesians 4:11–13, 2 Timothy 2:2, Titus 1:5, and Acts 14:23.

Today Catholic priests make a promise to a bishop to remain celibate but are not forced to take a vow. Some scholars say that Mary Magdalene and her spiritual sisters may have been able to participate as leaders in the church. Other biblical thinkers assert that the women followers of Jesus had diminished roles beneath the male apostles who took the leadership positions. That would have been customary for that era. Today, women are not allowed to enter the Catholic priesthood. And in a few cases, under rare circumstances, married men are being ordained as Catholic priests today.

The Apostolic Church

Apostolic is a term that is often used to express something descended from the apostles. For example, the Apostolic Age encompasses a specific time extending from the day of Pentecost, estimated to be about 30, to the apostle John's death in 100. Also, apostolic succession (discussed in more detail in Chapter 6) refers to the unbroken papal line of succession from Peter to the present pope, who is the spiritual descendant of Peter. The Roman Catholic Church regards itself as apostolic, according to its catechism, in three ways:

1. The church was erected on the foundation of Christ's apostles and witnesses—his emissaries whom he sent forth.
2. The church teaches the apostle's salutary words and passes them on as guided by the Spirit indwelling in the church.
3. The church continues to be guided by the apostles by way of their successors (the clergy such as the priests, the bishops, and the pope) in learning and sanctity until Christ returns.

Since the church is apostolic, it is sent forth into the entire world, just as Jesus sent forth the first apostles with the Great Commission or mandate to evangelize. Through two millennia, scholars and theologians have debated the interpretation of the passages in the New Testament relating to the commandment or Great Commission of Jesus. Some of the questions raised have to do with the wording in passages of the four New Testament Gospels and Acts, about whether the words were spoken to the disciples as they were apostles of Jesus.

For example, there is a passage in Matthew that says, "Go ye therefore, and teach all nations, baptizing them in the name of the Father, and of the Son, and of the Holy Ghost: teaching them to observe all things whatsoever I have commanded you: and lo, I am with you always, even unto the end of the world. Amen" (28:19–20).

factum

All four of the New Testament Gospels present the Great Commission in some form. In the Gospel of Matthew, Jesus gives the disciples the authority, the goal, and the time frame (28:20). The Gospel of Mark reveals the method and geographical scope (16:15). The Gospel of Luke addresses the message Jesus desired them to share in their evangelical endeavors (24:45–49). In the Gospel of John, the focus is on the receiving of the Holy Spirit for the spiritual nature of the work (20:22).

These verses end the chapter of Matthew that began with Mary Magdalene arriving at the empty tomb and seeing the angel of the Lord sitting on the stone. The remainder of that section relates how the angel told Mary Magdalene and the women that Jesus had risen and that they must tell the disciples the news, and that they would see Jesus in Galilee. Of course, shortly after that the women suddenly saw Jesus, held him by the feet, and worshiped him. The eleven disciples went to a mountain in Galilee where Jesus met them and spoke the words found in the earlier quote.

Symbols of the Apostles

The Greek word for apostle is *apostolos* (messenger). The verb is *apostellein,* which means "to send forth." The apostle sent by God to save the world was Jesus. Before the Resurrection, the twelve disciples (as well as others) served as Jesus' representatives. After Jesus rose from the dead, he made apostles of the disciples and witnesses of his ministry and resurrection. In that capacity, they would proclaim the gospel, do missionary work, teach, baptize, and serve as leaders of the movement (later the church).

Judas Iscariot's symbol is a rope tied into a hangman's noose to represent how he took his own life after betraying Jesus. The betrayal of Judas reduced the number of the original male disciples to eleven. These then became the apostles:

- Simon Peter, son of Jona (Jesus called him Cephas, meaning "rock"). His symbol is an upside-down cross (he felt unworthy to die upright on a cross as Jesus died) with the keys to the gates of heaven crossed.
- James, son of Zebedee. His symbol is a group of three shells and also a bishop's hat and a sword.
- John, son of Zebedee. His symbol is a chalice containing a snake (to symbolize a cup of poison from which God spared him) and also the eagle and a book.
- Andrew. His symbol is the St. Andrew's cross in the shape of an X.

- Philip. His symbol is a basket used to feed the multitude, a tall cross, and loaves of bread.
- Bartholomew (also called Nathanael). His symbol is a knife blade or three identical knives to signify that he was skinned alive.
- Matthew (also called Levi; he was a tax collector). His symbol is three coin bags.
- Thomas (also called Didymus or Judas Thomas). His symbols are arrows, a stone, and a spear to signify his martyrdom by a spear.
- James, son of Alphaeus. His symbol is a handsaw (to signify his body being sawed apart; however, some sources say he was clubbed to death).
- Thaddaeus (also called Jude). His symbol is a ship; some sources say a gold ship against a red horizon.
- Simon the Cananaean. His symbol is a Bible with a fish on top (as he was a fisherman before becoming a disciple of Jesus). Some sources say his symbol is a book resting upon a fish.

On Pentecost, the Holy Spirit descended upon the apostles, completing them for their work in the world. Mary Magdalene was *apostola apostolorum* or Apostle to the Apostles. The symbol most often associated with her is an alabaster jar and skull. The jar holds spices or spikenard, and the skull represents the folly of hanging on to things of the material world.

Long-Term Consequences for Other Women

Spiritual women have come a long way since Mary Magdalene's time, but they still face the challenge of being negatively labeled in one way or another. In today's world, many cultures remain patriarchal. Women do not have the right to be educated, pursue work, to show their faces and bodies in public without wearing the proper covering, or to claim equality with men. In some cultures, although no longer placed out on a hillside to die from exposure to the elements when they are not wanted, infant girls are still considered inferior. Women may not have the barest necessities for survival or access to basic medical care.

discussion question

What are the seven deadly sins?
Anger, envy, lust, pride, gluttony, avarice, and sloth are popularly thought of as the seven deadly sins plaguing human life. Many are associated with female images, although they are by no means only found in women.

In more developed and open societies, the possibilities for women are brighter. Yet even women in the United States, the most developed nation in the world, struggle with ongoing gender discrimination issues. Organizations such as Human Rights for Women work to elevate the issues of female rights worldwide. Women have been trying for two millennia to shed the labels put on them. And not just in their places of work or institutes of education, but in their places of worship.

For 2,000 years, Mary Magdalene has been erroneously regarded as a symbol of repentance for pleasures of the flesh. Today, two famous colleges bear her name: Magdalen College at Oxford, and Magdalene College in Cambridge. Yet, the names of these colleges are pronounced "maudlin" for weepy sinners seeking forgiveness. The Magdalen Asylums in Ireland, where fallen women were kept as virtual slaves, were also named for her. It seems incongruous that these images are associated with an imaginary fallen woman, not the real Mary Magdalene who was Jesus' closest companion and confidante, the first witness to his resurrection, and the "glue" for the movement that enabled Christianity to take hold and thrive.

Viewed under the microscopic lens of scholars, historians, and theologians, Mary Magdalene is emerging today as a different woman than she has been portrayed for the last two millennia. As a prominent disciple, she may have been the leader of one sect of

Christians that promoted the leadership of women. The Gnostics, who believed in the equality of men and women, were followers of Jesus. They had great respect and admiration for Mary Magdalene and venerated her as their master, choosing her perceptive insights into Jesus' teachings and visionary experience over others.

Jesus showed that women and men could equally receive his teachings. He believed women were capable spokespersons for carrying his message—and maybe they did as ministers, preachers, evangelists, perhaps even as bishops. Ute Eisen's book *Women Officeholders in Early Christianity* presents evidence for women serving in leadership positions from the earliest days of the church to the Middle Ages in communities in which women led and served, including Palestine, Egypt, Asia Minor, Greece, Spain, and Yugoslavia.

Other biblical historians say that a careful reading of the New Testament suggests that the eucharistic meals were presided over by women during the earliest stages of the church and that those women were ordained. If women were leaders in the early centuries of the church, as some scholars suggest, they are not, for the most part, serving in the highest ecclesiastical levels today.

Modern Stained-Glass Ceilings

Women desiring to share spiritual gifts with their communities during Mary Magdalene's time found themselves pushing up against ages-old (Old Testament) gender biases and barriers, and in some ways, little has changed. Modern women, too, are challenged to find ways to break through the stained-glass ceilings of the ecclesiastical world. Recent scholarship of the early centuries of Christianity has unearthed evidence that supports women serving in many different roles in the early church, as ministers, apostles, priests, deacons, and bishops.

The irony is that in the first century, women in the Jesus movement may have had the opportunity to do work that they are forbidden to do today. Even in the twenty-first century, Jesus' egalitarian model for men and women does not exist in many churches. Although women cannot be priests in the Catholic tradition, they are encouraged to participate at the lay level. In the Reformed branch of Judaism, women can now be rabbis, something unheard of in the first century. Many Protestant churches welcome the leadership of women, although in some, inequality appears when it comes to sharing the pulpit. Given a choice between a man and a woman minister, women of the cloth will say that men still have the edge. Many churches struggle with a crisis of shortage: money, congregants, and clergy.

symbolism

The color red has long been a symbol for passion and sensuality. It has also been associated with holiness, love, vitality, lust, and fallen women. Red often appears in images of Mary Magdalene as the repentant prostitute. (Other paintings of her use blue, which symbolizes the spiritual life, faith, chastity, devotion, truth, and eternity.)

Working Toward Reform

A great many Christian churches have expanded leadership roles for women, allowing women who have a spiritual calling to be permitted to serve rather than being silenced as Mary Magdalene was for so long. Many denominations are calling for reform within their churches to reflect gender/cultural/societal issues facing Christians in the modern world. And Christian believers themselves, as well as groups of Christian churches, are spearheading programs to facilitate change. Organizations such as FutureChurch seek an open dialogue for reform within the Roman Catholic Church.

The church, while sticking to its apostolic and pastoral missions, has had to adapt and change to be relevant to the times. From the earliest days of the Jesus movement, a slow evolution has taken place. For example, during the Middle Ages, women belonging to holy orders were unable to travel about in order to minister to the poor, nurse the sick, and share what they had with the needy. The founding of new orders, such as the Dominicans, brought change and long-lasting benefits. The Dominicans are recognized for their invaluable contributions to education.

Modern Crises

Christian churches have always faced crises. Today, however, dissension, chaos, pathos, financial shortfalls, clergy shortages, scandals, abuses, and lawsuits are challenging the ecclesiastical status quo. Fewer men than ever are entering the priesthood, some Protestant Christian churches bemoan the lack of funds to keep their clergy, while others say they are being forced to cut church work forces because of apathy and dwindling numbers of churchgoers. The Church of England, which has more financial resources than many Christian churches in other parts of the world, has acknowledged that in many places it can't afford its clergy and may begin a tradition practiced in Mary Magdalene's time of holding services in home-churches.

factum

Mary Magdalene's feast day is July 22 on the Roman calendar. Foods made in remembrance of her include navettes, cylindrical boat-shaped French pastries commemorating her arrival at Saintes-Maries-de-la-Mer. It is traditional to make and offer these pastries on February 2 to mark the anniversary of her arrival.

Christian churches are thinking about how to move forward in the twenty-first century. Some suggest reform comes from a re-evaluation of values and priorities. Organizations lobbying for reform say it's time that exclusionary policies of the past are abandoned in favor of a spirit of inclusion as seen in the example set by Jesus when he brought Mary Magdalene and others into his inner circle.

chapter 9

Magdalene and the Early Church Crisis

N ews of Mary Magdalene's vision of the resurrected transcendent Jesus must have spread rapidly throughout Jerusalem and then quickly through the Jewish Diaspora in the region around the Mediterranean. The vision would have inspired belief in the hearts of Jesus' grieving followers that his death and resurrection were part of God's greater plan. Jesus would come again a second time and would make all things right.

The Struggling Jesus Movement

Mary Magdalene was the glue that held the Jesus movement together after the Crucifixion and the Resurrection. The canonical Gospels say Jesus appeared to Mary Magdalene and gave her the task of telling the other disciples. She honored him by faithfully carrying out her commission. The Gospel of Mary says that Mary Magdalene kissed the grieving disciples and comforted them. She turned their thoughts away from darkness and depression and lightened their hearts by reminding them of Jesus' words of comfort. At a time when some of the disciples were talking about resuming their previous lives, Mary Magdalene kept the group focused on moving forward with her words of comfort, optimism, hope, and inspiration.

factum

The Diaspora is the scattering and resettling of Jews outside of Palestine after the period of Babylonian captivity. The Jewish people often struggled with trying to acclimate to the society and culture in which they lived while still remaining true to their ethnic, cultural, and religious identity.

Certainly, the vision of Mary Magdalene must have fanned the flames of hope in the hearts of Jesus' followers. Like any other group that had lost its leader, his coterie likely went through several psychological/emotional stages—grieving, accepting, trying to make sense of his death and resurrection, and allowing the Holy Spirit to lead them as apostles and teachers. They must have reasoned that Jesus had known he must die and then rise again in fulfillment of prophecy. His followers may have believed that the Second Coming of Christ would take place within their lifetimes. Why should they write anything down? There was no need. The time was at hand.

As they spoke about these ideas with others, a clearer picture began to emerge of what had happened, of what was going to transpire, and of Jesus not as a mortal who went afoul of the Romans and was crucified but rather as the Spirit of God Incarnate as the Son. Their teacher was different from the other self-styled prophets and religious/political activists around ancient Palestine. His message of love (shown even from the cross when he said, "Father, forgive them for they know not what they do" [Luke 23:34]) contrasted with the ideology of the Zealots, the Daggermen, and others fighting for an end of Roman occupation, in preparation for the coming of the kingdom of God on Earth. Many such activists had been put to death.

discussion question

What does it mean to "keep kosher"?
Strict observance of Kashrut, Jewish dietary law, is known as keeping kosher. For example, certain animals cannot be consumed, animals must be slaughtered according to Jewish law, blood must be drained off, dairy and meat cannot be eaten together, dairy utensils cannot be used with meat, consumption of grape products made by non-Jews is forbidden, and non-kosher utensils cannot touch kosher foods.

Most Jews trusted that God could and would intervene in their history. Jesus' followers believed that he was God's instrument in that intervention. As two pilgrims on the road to Emmaus spoke about the recent events, Jesus appeared to them and said, "O fools, and slow of heart to believe all that the prophets have spoken: ought not Christ to have suffered these things, and to enter into his glory? And beginning at Moses and all the prophets, he expounded unto them in all the Scriptures the things concerning himself" (Luke 24:25–27).

A Gospel for Pagans and Non-Jews

The work of the Jesus group began. They were Jews preaching to Jews. Like their brethren belonging to the various Jewish sects, the followers of Jesus shared a belief in the establishment of the kingdom of God on Earth and the prophecies of Mica that the true prophet (Messiah) would be despised, but that the restoration of Israel to its rightful place would fill the hearts of God's chosen people with joy. Jesus' small group of spiritual brothers and sisters believed that Jesus was that Messiah. They preached to Jews of various sects but not to pagans, whom they saw neither as God's chosen nor as Jesus' elect. But that would change when Paul underwent a conversion shortly after Jesus' death to become Apostle to the Gentiles. He spoke Greek. Greek-speaking Jews, in turn, shared the Good News with the Diaspora Jews and pagans living in communities throughout the Mediterranean. The ideas and concepts of the newly converted Paul shaped the gospel that he preached. Paul's amplified ideology about Jesus' divinity appealed to Gentiles throughout the region. No longer was the kingdom of God a purely Jewish kingdom for Jews but for Gentiles and pagans as well, according to Paul. That became a source of dissension in the community of Jesus' followers, in the Temple, and among sectarian Jews.

Other conflicts arose as new Christian converts developed doctrines in conflict with the teachings of Jesus and the apostles. The apostles and the community of followers confronted issues with the leadership of some communities outside Jerusalem and had to, on occasion, rebuke false teachers, deal with divisions within their own ranks, define what it meant to be orthodox, and ensure that the new Christian churches and communities would adhere to the apostolic tradition.

Paul's views must have concerned the Jerusalem leadership of the movement after the stoning of Stephen and expulsion of his sympathizers, and they worried that the eccentric views of Paul and other evangelizers to the Gentiles might be seen as diminishing the importance of strict adherence to the Torah. God-fearers (non-Jewish converts) believed in the one God of the Jews and they tithed their half-shekels annually to the Temple in Jerusalem, but they were not Jews, did not keep the Jewish dietary laws, strictly adhere to the Torah, nor were they circumcised. Embroiled in one of the earliest and most serious conflicts of early Christianity, Paul had to defend his view and activities to the apostles in Jerusalem. According to one source, bringing into the Temple of Jerusalem an uncircumcised pagan was a capital offense.

factum

The language of the New Testament was primarily Greek. A simplified version of Greek known as Koine made communication easier between peoples of lands conquered by the Greeks. Also, this common language made it possible for the Christian missionaries to spread the gospel to disparate ethnic groups and people in different socioeconomic classes.

The Definition of an Apostle Narrows

The widest view of an apostle endows both genders with the mission of carrying Christ's message to others. In the Eastern Orthodox Church, the word apostle refers to one of seventy Disciples of Christ. Initially, there were many apostles, including Mary Magdalene and other women in Jesus' coterie. Mary Magdalene, a spiritually adept visionary with an insightful mind, fit all the criteria of an apostle, including the narrow definition given by Paul: witnessing the risen Jesus and receiving a call to evangelize others.

Most people know that the twelve disciples (with Matthias replacing Judas) became apostles. Paul, after his conversion, proclaimed himself an apostle. He declared that his apostleship was by divine authority, and he frequently defended his apostleship in his letters, the earliest writings of Christianity, emphasizing that it was by the will of God that he was called to be an apostle of Christ. This is different from the other type of apostleship in which representatives of a congregation are sent out as apostles.

discussion question

Was a presbytera a woman priest?
The feminine form of presbyter (male priest) has been found inscribed on ancient tombs. Some believe the tombs belong to female priests. Others say that the term in early Christianity meant an office bearer serving as a teacher, or priest, or someone who performed administrative duties. Through time, the term has come to mean an abbess or a priest's wife.

The original apostles appointed the first bishops. The bishops appointed elders or presbyters and deacons and deaconesses. The Montanists, a sect of early Christians, are believed to have ordained women as both presbyters and bishops.

The Hysterical Female Charge

Early Christianity was born within an ancient patriarchal society, and some anti-Christians thought the vision of the resurrected Jesus was nothing more than the ravings of a hysterical female. All four Gospel accounts agree that the first witnesses of Jesus' resurrection were women. Matthew states that it was Mary Magdalene and the "other Mary" who visited the tomb. The Gospel of John says Mary Magdalene alone went to the tomb. Mark reveals that there were three women, and the Gospel lists Mary Magdalene first. Finally, Luke says the women in the group went to the tomb, but that Gospel also lists Mary Magdalene first among them. It seems strange, given the prominence of these women's accounts in the canonical

Gospels, that they are not mentioned in the Acts of the Apostles or in Paul's Epistles (1 Corinthians 15:3–15).

factum

A Platonist and opponent of Christianity, the Roman Celsus wrote a work titled, *Alethès Lógos* (The True Word). The discourse, attacking the theology of Christian belief, was sent to Origen, a church father, with a request for him to write a refutation of the work, which he did. The refutation was titled, *Against Celsus*.

In previous chapters, the point has been made that women in first-century Palestinian and Roman cultures were considered neither reliable nor legal witnesses in Jewish courts. Celsus, who ridiculed Christians, sniped that the resurrection story was based on an account by a "hysterical female" (namely, Mary Magdalene). Celsus contemptuously dismissed the testimony of Mary Magdalene and other women in a chauvinistic style typical of the men of his time. He claimed Mary Magdalene had been deluded by sorcery. Origen, an early father of the church, refuted each point of Celsus' discourse.

Differing Views about Women's Church Roles

Women aided Paul enormously in his missionary work. He acknowledged their contributions in his letters. Yet in his instructions to Timothy, one of his associates, Paul wrote, "Thou therefore, my son, be strong in the grace that is in Christ Jesus. And the things that thou has heard of me among many witnesses, the same commit thou to faithful men, who shall be able to teach others also" (2 Timothy 2:1–2).

In this counsel, Paul is ensuring that Timothy's generation and the next two generations will have teachers (faithful men) of the apostolic tradition to carry forward the teachings Jesus gave to the apostles. What about the contributions of women? Hadn't they been faithful to Jesus during his last years on Earth? Hadn't they financed the movement, followed his instruction, carried his message to others, celebrated the Eucharist, and kept his teachings alive in oral tradition? Hadn't they helped Paul in his zealous missionary work? Some scholars have written that in women's theology of the first century, women could exercise leadership based on spiritual achievement and insights without having to conform to the gender roles placed on them by society and culture.

symbolism

Symbols of the sacraments include baptism (font, sometimes with a dove, or running water), confirmation (lamp), Eucharist (chalice and wafer or host, bread and wine), reconciliation (keys or a closed door), anointing of the sick (oil), marriage (rings connected), and holy orders (book, chalice, or keys).

Written Out of History

Spiritual maturity mattered. Yet the written Gospels and letters selected for the canon contain relatively few mentions of women in relationship to the amount of work they must have done not only to support the missionary work (in spirit and financially) but as leaders, visionaries, prophets, and missionaries themselves.

The writings of early church fathers such as Eusebius suggest that women as well as men transmitted the apostolic tradition to others. Prominent women held prayer meetings and eucharistic celebrations. There is some evidence that women interpreted the texts of their traditions and some held the title of prophet. Cyprian, an African bishop of the third century, described a particular woman prophet as performing baptisms and celebrating the Eucharist.

Women, say some scholars, initially took a variety of leadership roles in the infant Christian house-churches. By the close of the first century and the death of the original apostles, however, women began to experience resistance to their efforts. Some feminist theologians believe Mary Magdalene had a following of disciples, as did each of the apostles.

Women may have been acknowledged for their leadership in early Christianity, but the men began writing the New Testament Gospel and those accounts reflect each author's view of female importance or lack thereof in the formative stages of the infant Christian church. After the Easter story, Mary Magdalene disappears from the Gospels.

discussion question

What's the difference between a disciple and an apostle?
Many followed Jesus and all, including Mary Magdalene, were his disciples. Paul asserted two criteria for being an apostle: witness the risen Christ and receive a command to preach. The writer of Acts defines apostles as the twelve disciples who had been with Jesus from his baptism and witnessed his resurrection and ascension.

Female Priests Excommunicated

Today, Christian women continue to struggle for ecclesiastic equality in their places of worship. Without success, they have mounted challenges to the long-standing doctrine of exclusion of women from the priesthood and other high leadership positions within the Roman Catholic Church. In 2003, Father Romulo Antonio Braschi, an Argentine bishop, whom the Vatican considered the founder of a renegade community, ordained seven women as priests. The female priests were from Germany, Austria, and the United States. The ordination took place on a boat floating down the

River Danube. The Vatican excommunicated them. They appealed and the Vatican's Congregation for the Doctrine of the Faith rejected their appeal and upheld the excommunications based on the gravity of the offenses.

Oral Tradition Before Written Texts

A vibrant and established oral tradition existed during Jesus' lifetime and before any texts were written about his ministry. Of course, ancient Jews had the Old Testament books and Jesus referred to Mosaic Law and God's commandments (contained in them) in his teachings. But the early Christians, familiar with the Old Testament Scripture, received their teachings from Jesus in oral form. He did not write lessons, commandments, or commentary for them. The apostles drew on oral tradition to make theological points because they believed oral tradition to be trustworthy.

The New Testament writers drew on oral tradition for credibility, legitimacy, documentation, and examples for their Gospel accounts and letters. Oral tradition must have helped as they wrestled with interpretation and the meaning of Jesus' teachings as well as conflicting views of the roles of women and slaves in the Christian community.

factum

The expression *sola scriptura* (Latin for "Scripture alone") refers to the Protestant doctrine that the Bible alone is the source for Christian beliefs of morality and faith. The Catholic catechism teaches that oral tradition must go hand-in-hand with Scripture for support of doctrine. That oral tradition is what is declared by the church to have been transmitted by Jesus to his apostles and through the subsequent centuries by the bishops, who stand in an unbroken line of succession from the apostles.

The picture that emerges of the early Jesus movement is one in which the followers and apostles drew heavily on his oral teachings, memorizing the stories, extracting meaning, and weaving in relevant material from the Old Testament to expound doctrine. A forty-year period elapsed between Jesus' death and the completion of the first gospel. Jesus' followers, during that time, shared their oral stories, perhaps refined key points, smoothed out thorny theological questions, and framed their beliefs.

Just as oral tradition asserts that Mary, the mother of Jesus, bore him and had no other children, likewise, oral traditions of Mary Magdalene's role in the Easter story and her contributions to the foundation of Christianity must have been strong and widely known. Otherwise, she might not have been named in the four Gospel accounts or might have been eliminated altogether.

Today, early Christianity is being studied as never before. Many different academic disciplines (archaeology, textual analysis, biblical history, feminist theology) form a new lens to view, study, interpret, and reinterpret the beginnings of this worldwide religion that had its humble beginnings in ancient Palestine.

Was Mary Magdalene's Scriptural Presence Diminished?

The Gospel of Mary, considered a heretical text, reveals a Mary Magdalene highly esteemed by Jesus. The Gospel of Philip reveals that Jesus kissed her often and that the other male disciples found this distressing. These recently discovered texts, like many others excluded from the Bible, offer a widely differing view of Christianity than shown in the Gospels and letters of the New Testament.

Feminist theologians point to the old adage about history being written by the winners to explain why Gospel accounts elevating Mary Magdalene were suppressed and excluded from the canon. They also assert that Mary Magdalene's pre-eminent role in the Easter story was so important and widespread in the oral tradition that it could not be completely erased or denied in the written tradition. However, scholarly work to examine early Christian women's theology has resulted in some experts theorizing that Mary Magdalene's story was indeed diminished in the Gospel accounts, especially in the Gospel of Luke, where Peter's story and authority appears to be enhanced and elevated in importance. The more traditional Catholic view disagrees with that conjecture, asserting that Jesus nicknamed Peter "Cephas" or rock upon which Jesus would build his church, evidence that Peter was always the one chosen by Jesus to be successor and leader of the group. Apostolic tradition traces its lineage to Peter, the first pillar of the church.

fallacy

That Christianity harmoniously evolved from the teachings of Jesus is a fallacy. Biblical scholars say that the Nag Hammadi discoveries suggest Christianity was far more complicated and diverse than previously thought. Many sects and divergent theological ideas were involved in its evolution in the early centuries. Gnostic Christians, who rivaled orthodox Christianity, wrote many of the manuscripts found at Nag Hammadi.

The apostolic fathers, those who faithfully carried on the teachings of the first apostles after the latter had passed away, shared an interest in making sure that Christian practices and beliefs were consistent with the traditions found within Pauline Christianity. From the fourth century, any views divergent were considered heretical. Orthodoxy was thereby declared in contrast to all other views, which were regarded as heretical. Such works were vigorously suppressed in the early centuries of Christianity. Today, such works are believed to be either fragmentary or lost.

The writers of the New Testament Gospels and letters seem to have had little interest in detailing the contributions of women, especially Mary Magdalene. However, a spectacular discovery at

Nag Hammadi in Egypt of other ancient gospels and tracts excluded from the Bible elevates Mary Magdalene and paints a powerful portrait of her as an exceptional student of Jesus as well as his closest friend and confidante.

Presbyters, Bishops, and Women in the Early Church

Mary Magdalene, the icon and saint, inspires modern women to holy service by her example of perfect discipleship. Some modern theologians and feminists regard the service of Mary Magdalene as representing the ecclesiastical roles (presbyters and bishops) of women in the first century of the infant Christian church. The service of those women is often cited as the precedent for women in the modern Catholic Church to receive holy orders.

The Majority of Early Christians May Have Been Women

Dr. Karen King, former professor of New Testament Studies and the History of Ancient Christianity at Harvard University's Divinity School, has written widely about women in early Christianity. In an article about women, in general, and Mary Magdalene, specifically, Dr. King asserted that women served the early Christian movement in prominent roles after the death of Jesus. She noted that scholars have theorized that in the first century, the majority of Christians may have been women.

factum

One woman mentioned by Paul was Thecla. She was one of Paul's converts, who remained chaste and pure in her faith despite threats of rape and persecution. Thecla has been called an apostle and, indeed, she performed her duties as one.

In the Pauline Epistles and in the book of Acts, Paul offers glimpses into how women prayed, prophesied, and proselytized in the ancient house-churches of the Christian faithful. In his letters, Paul offers greetings, thanks, or praises to Prisca (Priscilla), Junia, Julia, Lydia, Phoebe, Mary, Persis, Eudodia, and Syntyche, women who served as leaders (deacons or presbytera), taught, and ministered. Lydia, Priscilla, and Phoebe were, according to Paul, outstanding fellow workers. Scholars also believe that Mary Magdalene served as an important and powerful leader of one branch of early Christianity, perhaps even providing a role model for women who followed Jesus' closest women disciples.

The Church Reverts to Restricting Women

Many liberal theologians say that women were repressed in ancient Jewish society, then achieved status on a par with men in Jesus' ministry, performed important roles in the early infant Christian church during the first century, but then experienced an erosion of their status as the church and government reverted back to policies restricting women after the first century. In subsequent centuries of the church, women were so restricted that their roles in churches were reduced to handling minor tasks only. This type of suppression continues today.

Women in Montanism

The Montanists, under the leadership of Montanus and two women (Maximilla and Prisca), ordained women into the movement's presbyterate. The movement espoused charismatic prophecy as a way to revitalize and renew the Christian church through the enthusiasm that existed during the first century. The movement emerged in the second century and disappeared sometime in the sixth century.

The Orthodox Viewpoint on Women Priests

Orthodox opinion refutes such liberal theological thinking on the subject of the ordination of women by noting that the idea of ancient women presbyters meaning "women priests" is erroneous at best. Those adhering to the orthodox line of thinking cite such references as Paul's Epistles in the New Testament—in particular, Titus—to suggest that a woman presbyter was simply an older woman or possibly a widow serving the church.

> *But speak thou the things which become sound doctrine: that the aged men be sober, grave, temperate, sound in faith, in charity, in patience. The aged women likewise, that they be in behavior as becometh holiness, not false accusers, not given to much wine, teachers of good things; that they may teach the young women to be sober, to love their husbands, to love their children, to be discreet, chaste, keepers at home, good, obedient to their own husbands, that the word of God not be blasphemed (Titus 2:1–5).*

The Orthodoxy maintains that priestly function from ancient Hebrew times through the early Christian period to present day has been given only to men. If women were ordained in the first century (which most orthodox Christians do not believe is the case), they were gradually prevented from continuing such practices by a patriarchal leadership within the church.

Two Views of Mary Magdalene

While liberal theologians paint a portrait of Mary Magdalene as a favored disciple and Apostle to the Apostles, the orthodox see her simply as one of Jesus' faithful followers. Many orthodox Christians believe in the absolute infallibility of the Bible as God's Word. They do not give much credence to the spectacular extra-canonical texts that include Gospel of Mary Magdalene, Dialogue of the Savior, Gospel of Philip, and the Pistis Sophia, in which Mary Magdalene's dialogues with Jesus and his disciples reveal a powerful, astute, and adept disciple whom the Lord loves more than all the others. Dr. King has noted that in the Gospel of Mary, Mary Magdalene stepped into the Savior's role after his departure. In this way, she is a powerful exemplar for both ancient and modern women.

Some Prefer the Virgin Mary

Orthodox Christians believe that the function of women in their Christian communities must necessarily conform to traditional biblical roles as wives and mothers, primary spiritual educators of their children, helpers to their husbands and families, and fellowship workers and missionaries in their communities and in the world. The mother of Jesus rather than Mary Magdalene is the model of virtue and piety that most often speaks to these conservative Christians.

chapter 10

Pivotal Events in Early Christianity

I n the political-religious milieu of the first century, spiritual traditions were complex, diverse, and evolving. While paganism flourished and Hellenistic thinking influenced other belief systems, several Hebrew sects existed within Judaism. For example, one sect of the Pharisees, extreme conservatives, believed that it was important to separate the races and that only Jews could receive salvation. Other groups espoused radical theology as well. Into this melting pot of diverse ideas, Christianity was born.

Tumultuous Timeline of Early Christianity

6–4 B.C.	John the Baptist and Jesus are born in the days of Herod the Great (Luke 1 and 2). Herod dies and is succeeded by Archelaus.
A.D. 1	The apostle Paul is born.
5	John the Evangelist, son of Zebedee and brother of James, is born.
7	Jesus, age twelve, astounds the temple priests with his knowledge and understanding (Luke 2:46–47).
8	The Shammai Pharisee sect forces a separation between Jews and Gentiles by proclaiming eighteen edicts.
26	Pontius Pilate becomes procurator of Judea.
27	John the Baptist begins his ministry (Luke 3:1–4).
28	Jesus begins his ministry (Luke 4:14; also Matthew 4:17).

29	Herod beheads John the Baptist.
30	The founder of the Shammai Pharisee sect dies. Jesus is arrested and put to death. Mary Magdalene witnesses his resurrection on the third day (John 20:15–16).
33	Stephen is stoned to death and becomes known as the first Christian martyr. The Shummai Pharisee sect expels all non-Hebrew Jews from Jerusalem. Jesus' apostles remain in Jerusalem.
34	Saul, on a mission to persecute the Christians, converts (Acts 9:1–19).
37	Caligula becomes emperor. Paul angers religious leaders in Jerusalem when he zealously proselytizes. Peter establishes the Antioch church.
44	James, brother of the apostle John is martyred by beheading (Acts 12:1–2). Paul and Barnabas work in Antioch; the word Christian comes into usage there as a term for those who follow Jesus' teachings (Acts 11:25–26).
45	The Virgin Mary dies in Ephesus. (Catholics believe that she died between three and fifteen years after the Resurrection, and that she ascended directly to heaven.)
49	Violence erupts between Christian Jews and Orthodox Jews in Rome forcing Claudius to expel all Jews from that city. James decrees that Gentiles do not have to be circumcised or follow Jewish dietary laws to be Christians (Acts 15:1–19).
62	James is clubbed and stoned to death. Simeon, the son of Cleophas, becomes leader of the Jerusalem church.

64	Matthias, who replaced Judas Iscariot as the twelfth apostle, is stoned to death (Acts 1:15–26). Rome burns. Nero blames and persecutes the Christians.
67	Nero martyrs the apostles Peter and Paul. Mark, a follower of Paul, is also put to death. The Christian Jews leave Jerusalem for the Decapolis, a region in which Jesus traveled that included Galilee (Mark 7:31).
68–69	Nero commits suicide.
73	Romans mount the final siege against Masada, and all but 7 of the 960 men, women, and children die by suicide. The Christian Jews return to Jerusalem.
81	Domitian begins to persecute Christians.
96	Domitian is murdered. Clement of Rome rebukes the Corinthian branch of the Christian church, thereby establishing the power and authority of the church in Rome.
100	John the Evangelist dies in Ephesus.

Creating the Vulgate Bible

In 382, Pope Damasus recognized a need for a standardize version of the Bible. At that time, a number of Old Latin translations existed, but they varied widely in quality. The pope wisely understood that if he could find someone to translate the Bible from the original Greek into Latin, the new translation could become a standard reference for all future copies. He picked Jerome, a widely respected scholar who later became known as the most famous biblical scholar in church history, to create the Vulgate Bible.

Who Was Jerome?

Jerome, whose birth name was Eusebius Sophronius Hieronymous, was born in 345 in the town of Stridonius, located at the head of the Adriatic. He was baptized by Pope Liberius circa 366 and became well educated, studying grammar, rhetoric, and the classics. In an effort to build a collection of literary and religious books, the young Jerome began to copy St. Hilary's books and commentaries.

factum

Tradition holds that Jerome had a dream while he was in Antioch in which he stood before a sacred tribunal of Christ and the judge condemned him for not being a Christian but rather being a Ciceronian. It was then that Jerome decided to become a hermit at Chalcis.

After traveling with some friends around Gaul, Italy, and Dalmatia, Jerome met a priest from Antioch and decided to go there in 374. He fell ill, as did the two friends accompanying him. They died but Jerome recovered, became a hermit, and remained in the Syrian desert for four or five years, giving up the study of classics for Hebrew so that he could better understand the Scriptures. Also, in Antioch, he became a presbyter (priest) but had little desire to serve as a priest within a church and, in fact, never celebrated mass.

A Commission by Pope Damasus

While Jerome was in Antioch, he translated texts, written by early church fathers Eusebius and Origen, from Greek into Latin (the lingua franca of the Western Roman Empire). Upon returning to Rome at about age fifty, he first worked as an interpreter for Paulinus at a council that was called by Pope Damasus to discuss the schism in the church at Antioch. Later, Jerome became theological adviser and secretary to the pope.

The Work of the Vulgate Version

Pope Damasus, fed up with Latin versions of the Bible that were rife with wrong copying, correction errors, and inexact interpolations, exacted a promise from Jerome that when he was translating he would remain as close to the existing versions as possible. Jerome worked diligently on the New Testament (at least as far as Acts and the Epistles, for those seem to differ very little from the Old Latin). Infatuated with the Hebrew language, he began translating the Old Testament from Hebrew into Latin—work that continued until his death in 406. Jerome was buried under the Church of the Nativity in Bethlehem but today lies in the Sistine Chapel of the basilica of Rome's Santa Maria Maggiore.

The Vulgate Endures

The only Old Testament texts that Jerome did *not* translate were the Books of Wisdom, Ecclesiasticus, Baruch, and Maccabees 1 and 2. Jerome's revised version of the Psalms, the Roman Psalter, is still in use during Matins and the Divine Office at the cathedrals of Saint Peter in Rome and Saint Mark in Venice.

In the sixteenth century, Jerome's Vulgate Bible officially became the authoritative Latin text used by the Roman Catholic Church. Today the version of the Bible most widely used in English-speaking countries is a translation of Jerome's Vulgate Bible.

The Council at Nicaea

Christians believe that the Trinity of the Godhead is defined as the Father, Son, and Holy Spirit. In 325, the Council at Nicaea was convened to resolve a dispute within the Church of Alexandria over the question of whether the nature of the Son was like the Father. While Arius, a popular presbyter of the time, did not believe in the divinity of Jesus, Bishop Alexander of Alexandria did. The council agreed with the bishop. The meeting of the council was momentous; it was the first time the church had sought consensus through an assembly representing all the Christian faithful. Other decisions and declarations were made and enacted during that historical meeting, convened by the Roman emperor Constantine and modeled on the Roman council meetings.

Formulating the Nicene Creed

The 300 assembled bishops attempted to hammer out a profession of faith written in clear scriptural language that would precisely express the church's orthodox doctrine and teachings in a way that excluded the Arian heresies. They utilized the baptismal creed favored by Eusebius of Caesarea (and used in his diocese) as a template and added further clarifications. In the end, all but two bishops signed the Nicene Creed, and the two who didn't were banished by Constantine.

Establishing the Date of Easter

Most of the bishops agreed with Constantine that Easter should be universally observed on the same day. The Eastern churches (those of Syria, Mesopotamia, and Cilicia) decided to celebrate Easter on a day relating to the fourteenth day of Nisan in the Jewish calendar. But the bishop of Alexandria, who did not want anything to do with the Jewish calendar, was given the right to choose and announce the date of Easter to the Roman curia (a sort of secretary of state). Until then, most of the bishops celebrated Easter on a Sunday (this was accepted as the day of the Resurrection of Jesus), but some celebrated on Good Friday or on other weekdays. Of paramount importance to those early Christians was that Jewish customs and celebrations were not the criteria that the Christians would follow.

Promulgating New Church Laws

The Council of Nicaea enacted twenty canons, or new laws, that were to be obeyed by the faithful. At that momentous meeting, the bishops:

1. Passed a rule that no cleric is allowed to have a young woman present in his house (she might bring him under suspicion).
2. Established a minimum amount of time to be spent on catechism.
3. Made a rule that no self-castration is allowed.
4. Declared that bishops must be ordained in the presence of three provincial bishops and confirmed by a metropolitan bishop.
5. Made it a rule that two provincial synods must be held annually.
6. Noted the supreme power and authority for the bishops of Rome and Alexandria.
7. Assured that the Holy See of Jerusalem was to receive honorary rights.
8. Established a provision for agreement with the Novatians.
9. Prohibited usury among clergy members.
10. Decided that bishops and presbyters are to be given Holy Communion before deacons.
11. Prohibited the removal of priests.
12. Agreed upon a mild rebuke of the lapsed believers that occurred during the persecution of Christians conducted by Licinius.
13. Decided against kneeling during the liturgy on Sundays (in those times, it was customary to stand for prayers).
14. Declared that any baptism done by heretics was considered invalid.

Other Actions of the Council

The bishops at the Council of Nicaea, while examining the issue that the Alexandrian See was experiencing with the schism between followers of the orthodox Meletius and the group known as the Eustathians, established a list (in order of importance) of the Christian communities. In short, the bishops decided that Alexandria would be second only to Rome in its authority and power. The Alexandrian See, it was decided, would have jurisdiction over Libya, Pentopolis, all of Egypt, and the Jerusalem church with the church at Antioch in third position. With the three main centers of power, order, and jurisdiction established, the church unified and strengthened its bases for future battles—from within and outside its ecclesiastic walls.

Apostle John Writes Revelation

A popular legend notes that Mary Magdalene joined John the Apostle in the Christian community at Ephesus. John is popularly believed to have been the "disciple whom Jesus loved," although some modern scholars have speculated that the moniker could also be applied to Mary Magdalene. The Gospel of John bears his name, as do three Epistles and the Revelation of Saint John the Divine. A key figure in the early Christian church, he helped shaped its direction through his work and in his writing.

Genealogy

John's name is often linked closely with his brother, James. Together they were called Boanerges, the Sons of Thunder. Their parents were Zebedee the fisherman and his wife, Salome. One scholarly text suggests that Salome may have been the sister of Mary, mother of Jesus; however, this hypothesis goes against the belief that Joachim and Elizabeth had only one child through God's grace after many barren years and that child was the Blessed Virgin Mary.

The name of John's mother, Salome, is linked with Mary Magdalene in the New Testament Gospels. Salome may have been one of the women with Mary Magdalene who provided for Jesus out of their substance. John is thought to have been the younger brother of James. The boys and their father plied their trade in partnership with two other brothers, Simon Peter and Andrew. Both sets of brothers may have followed John the Baptist before deciding to follow Jesus.

John's Character

John must have been ambitious and prized his relationship with Jesus because he and his brother sought places of honor at the Messiah's side when his kingdom of glory was to be established.

> *They said unto him, Grant unto us that we may sit, one on thy right hand, and the other on thy left hand, in thy glory. But Jesus said unto them, Ye know not what ye ask: can ye drink of the cup that I drink of? and be baptized with the baptism that I am baptized with? And they said unto him, We can. And Jesus said unto them, Ye shall indeed drink of the cup that I drink of; and with the baptism that I am baptized withal shall ye be baptized: but to sit on my right hand and on my left hand is not mine to give; but it shall be given to them for whom it is prepared (Mark 10:37–40).*

At least one source notes that John was the first of the apostles to believe in the Resurrection based on what he saw in the empty tomb. Also, John, the "disciple whom Jesus loved," recognized Jesus when he appeared to the apostles who were fishing. On that occasion, Jesus orchestrated the second miraculous catch of fish.

Persecution and Exile

After Pentecost, John moved into a lesser role behind Peter, the acknowledged main leader of the Jesus movement (and infant Christian church). John accompanied Peter to Samaria to witness the labors of Philip (see Acts 8:14). John also worked with the churches in Asia Minor. During the rule of the Roman emperor Domitian, John was persecuted and banished to the island of Patmos in the Aegean Sea between Crete and the shores of Asia Minor. On Patmos, circa 81–96, in the Monastery of the Apocalypse, John wrote the book of

Revelation. In the text, he mentions the persecuted churches of Asia Minor. He also mentions his own name four times.

John was alive when his brother James was beheaded and Peter was imprisoned and facing death. The apostle Paul wrote in a letter to the Galatians (2:9) that he went to Jerusalem to meet with Peter and James and John to talk about the gospel and their roles as servants. John may have stayed in Jerusalem until the Roman war with the Jews.

Interpreting Revelation

Of all the books of the New Testament, the text of the Revelation of Saint John the Divine is the most apocalyptic in symbolism, tone, and style. The texts opens with the vision of the glorified Christ and his letters to the seven churches of Asia and closes with the Last Judgment, a new Jerusalem, and eternity. The book has been interpreted by scholars in a variety of ways: (1) as depicting basic spiritual principles, (2) as detailing contemporary events, (3) as setting forth the historical view of the church and predicting forthcoming church-related events, and (4) as a prophetic scenario.

The Death of Stephen

After Jesus' resurrection and ascension, the apostles needed help to deal with the rapidly growing number of followers in Jerusalem's Jewish community, including many priests. The Hellenists, most likely Greek-speaking Palestinian Jews, complained that their widows were being neglected in the daily food distribution by the Hebrews (who spoke Hebrew or Aramaic). The Twelve Apostles chose seven deacons to address the community's spiritual needs and distribute food and alms, leaving them free to pray and minister the Word. The first Christian martyr was one of those deacons.

Who Was Stephen?

Stephen, called Stephanos in Greek, was "full of faith and power, did great wonders and miracles among the people" (Acts 6:8). His story in the New Testament reveals that he spoke eloquently with wisdom and spirit and that he was a man "full of faith and the Holy Ghost." Members of the Synagogue of Libertines, Cyrenians, and Alexandrians along with people from Cilicia and Asia debated with Stephen and found him to be a formidable opponent. Unable to win these debates, certain members of the group incited some men to accuse Stephen of making blasphemous statements about Moses and God. Stephen was brought before the Sanhedrin.

discussion question

Who were the other deacons?
The six other holy men chosen by the apostles included Philip, Prochorus, Nicanor, Timon, Parmenas, and Nicolas, a proselyte of Antioch. The apostles prayed and laid their hands upon the men, thus ordaining the first deacons of the movement that would later become the infant Christian church. Choosing deacons established a restructuring of the group, which put in place one level of organizational hierarchy.

No Turning Back

When answering charges before the high priest in the Sanhedrin, Stephen could have recanted his previous statements and distanced himself from his belief in the teachings of Jesus. Instead, his discourse diminished the importance of the Mosaic Law and the Temple and elevated the stature and importance of Jesus. His talk was not really about the charges levied at him but a homily about the fortunes of the word of God in the history of the Hebrew people. Stephen told those assembled that their ancestors had murdered those who had prophesied the Messiah's coming and then they murdered him when he finally arrived.

> *Ye stiffnecked and uncircumcised in heart and ears, ye do always resist the Holy Ghost: as your fathers did, so do ye. Which of the prophets have not your fathers persecuted? and they have slain them which shewed before the coming of the Just One; of whom ye have been now the betrayers and murders: who have received the law by the disposition of angels, and have not kept it (Acts 7:51–53).*

His Death by Stoning

The Acts of the Apostles reveals that those who heard Stephen's discourse were enraged:

> *When they heard these things, they were cut to the heart, and they gnashed on him with their teeth. But he, being full of the Holy Ghost, looked up steadfastly into heaven, and saw the glory of God, and Jesus standing on the right hand of God, and said, Behold, I see the heavens opened, and the Son of man standing on the right hand of God. Then they cried out with a loud voice, and stopped their ears, and ran upon him with one accord, and cast him out of the city and stoned him (7:54–58).*

Even as the mob set upon Stephen and began stoning him, the young man cried out to the Lord to forgive them. "And he kneeled down, and cried with a loud voice, Lord, lay not this sin to their charge. And when he had said this, he fell asleep" (Acts 7:60).

The Great Jewish Revolt

The Jews of Judea mounted a major uprising against the Roman Empire during the second half of the first century—a period during which some of the apostles were living in Jerusalem. The Great Jewish Revolt began in 66 and lasted for seven years. It was triggered by religious violence between the Judean Jews and the Hellenists. The latter were Greek-speaking Jews who lived in accordance with the Greek way of life. The Hellenists maintained their own places of worship and did not mingle with the Jerusalem Jews, who spoke Hebrew or Aramaic.

Factors Behind the Conflict

Initially, the Jesus movement was made up of Hebrew-speaking Jews, however, many Hellenists also became Christians. Nevertheless, a cultural schism existed between the two groups. The inciting incident that began the Great Jewish Revolt was the desecration of a local synagogue by a group of Hellenists; the Greek-speaking Roman troops made no attempt to stop the vandalism.

A variant of the story suggests that the revolt was due to the thievery of the last Roman procurator Florus who stole large quantities of silver from the Temple. Upon learning of this, the Jewish masses rioted, taking down the Roman garrison first.

The Jewish Retaliation

Outraged that the Roman soldiers did nothing to stop the vandalism, the son of Eliezar ben Hanania, the high priest, refused to conduct prayers and sacrifices in the Temple for the Roman emperor. He led an attack on the Roman troops based in Jerusalem. King Agrippa II, who was pro-Roman, escaped to Galilee and then gave himself over to the Romans. The emboldened Jews defeated the Roman ruler in Syria—Cestius Gallus—after he and his reinforcements tried to restore order.

factum

In 44, Agrippa I died and the Roman emperor Claudius considered giving Agrippa II the kingdom of his late father. However, Agrippa II was still a teenager, and Claudius thought the boy incapable of handling such enormous responsibility. In about 50 Agrippa II was declared the king of Chalcis and later became king of Judea.

The Jewish Zealots' membership swelled significantly after the initial success against the Romans as increasing numbers of Jews believed freedom from Roman occupation was possible. But the Romans mounted a fierce campaign against Galilee where roughly 100,000 Jews perished or were forcibly taken into custody and sold as slaves. An account in the Internet's Jewish Virtual Library (*www. jewishvirtuallibrary.org*) notes that the radicalized Galilean Jews received no help from the Jerusalem Jewish leadership. The writer of the article asserts that the embattled Jews could not win the fight against the Romans and that the Jewish leadership in Jerusalem suspected as much and wanted to minimize Jewish deaths.

Jews Battle Jews

When the Romans attacked Galilee, some Jews escaped and made their way to Jerusalem. There they assaulted the Jewish leadership that had refused to help them. By 68, angry radical Jews had killed many members of their own Jewish government. What amounted to a civil war among Jews in Jerusalem raged on while outside the city walls the Romans prepared for a final assault.

In Jerusalem, the Jews had horded a large quantity of food to sustain them for (possibly) years. Certain Zealots knew about the food supply and decided to burn it in an effort to force all Jews to participate in the rebellion against the Romans. Starvation soon followed.

The Destruction of Jerusalem and the Bar-Kochba Revolt

In the summer of 70, the Romans launched a violent assault on Jerusalem, destroying whatever was in their path. In due time, they destroyed the Second Temple. Sixty years later, Jewish life was lost in the Bar-Kochba revolt. Together, these two failed rebellions resulted in the loss of about 1 million Jews and Jewish political authority in the Holy Land until after the Holocaust in modern time.

The Bar-Kochba revolt occurred from 132 to 135. Before the revolt, the Roman emperor Hadrian, who was sympathetic to the Jews, granted them permission to return to Jerusalem and promised them that they could rebuild their temple. But when the Jewish people began the planning and preparations, Hadrian reneged, telling them that the temple site had to be changed. Further, under his watch, Jews were deported from the Holy Land to North Africa. Hadrian's treatment of the Jews led to the Bar-Kochba revolt against the Romans.

The Siege at Masada

The Bible does not say where Mary Magdalene was during the events at Masada. If alive, she would have likely been quite elderly. But Masada represented an epic moment in Jewish history, and Mary Magdalene certainly would have known about the struggle of the Zealots against the Romans.

Masada is a rocky mesa that sits opposite the Lisan peninsula, which extends into the Dead Sea. Masada has nearly vertical faces with drops of 600 to 820 feet. Herod had established himself and members of his family at Masada as a refuge after the Parthians overtook Jerusalem in about 40 B.C. A Roman garrison patrolled the fortress between Herod's death and A.D. 66.

discussion question

What was the fortress at Masada originally used for?
Fearful of the Jewish people and of Egypt's queen Cleopatra, Herod furnished the fortress as a retreat and erected storehouses to contain grains and oil and other foodstuffs. He also used it to stockpile weapons along with iron, lead, and brass materials.

The deaths of so many Jews at Masada fulfilled the prophecy of Jesus: "O Jerusalem, Jerusalem, thou that killest the prophets, and stonest them which are sent unto thee, how often would I have gathered thy children together, even as a hen gathereth her chickens under her wings, and ye would not. Behold your house is left unto you desolate" (Matthew 23:37–38).

The Defenders

In the Roman war, the Zealots gained control of Masada and held out for about three years. Numbering around 960, the Masada defenders were led by Eleazar ben Yair who became known as the Tyrant of Masada. The Romans were well aware that the Zealots holed up at Masada were the members of the group that had been revolting against the Romans since around the year 6. Historically, Masada would be remembered as the last Jewish holdout against the Romans in the ongoing conflict between the two.

The Attackers

The Roman governor, Flavius Silva, launched the siege in 72 that ended Eleazar's control of Masada. After encircling the rock on which the fortress stood, Silva's troops erected a siege tower and shot stones and flaming torches over the wooden wall. The Roman Tenth Legion, under Silva's direction, constructed the items they needed to launch a massive assault including battering rams, catapults, and ramps.

Mass Suicide

Eleazar convinced the defenders that they must not surrender to the Romans who would likely kill the men or sell them as slaves. The women could expect to become slaves or prostitutes. He inspired the Jews to take their own lives rather than allow themselves and their children to live as Roman slaves. The men then killed their wives and children before killing themselves (despite the fact that suicide is strictly forbidden by Jewish law).

factum

Archaeologists found the bodies of five children and two women in a cistern. They also found twenty-five skeletons in a cave on the south side of the mesa. These may have been Jews who were trying to hide from the Roman soldiers.

165

Discrepancies in the Account of Josephus

Josephus, the historian, left an account of Masada that in some ways is contradicted by modern archeological evidence. Josephus wrote that Eleazar ordered everything destroyed except the food-stuffs, but evidence suggests that many storerooms in the fortress at Masada containing foodstuffs were burned. Josephus noted that the Romans tossed twenty-five skeletons into the nearby cave. Scholars say that is highly unlikely. Why would the Romans launch a siege, kill more than 900 people, and then carry twenty-five to a nearby cave and toss them in? Josephus may have embellished his narrative to make certain points or to add drama; if so, that would account for some of the discrepancies noted by modern scholars.

II

Mary Magdalene
in the Gnostic Gospels

chapter 11

Gnostic Veneration of Mary Magdalene

he Gnostic Gospels portray Mary Magdalene as an evangelist, teacher, prophetess, spiritual adept, and mystic. In the Pistis Sophia, she questions the Lord with complete spiritual comprehension. The Gospel of Philip reveals that Jesus kissed her often. The Gospel of Thomas identifies her as a disciple along with Salome, Matthew, James, Thomas, and Peter. The Gnostics revered Mary Magdalene and accorded her an exalted status. However, because their texts contained ideas not supported by church fathers, their writings were excluded from the canon and purged.

An Untidy Beginning to Christianity

Mary Magdalene and the other followers of Jesus practiced what they believed to be a variant form of Judaism. Their religion had not yet evolved into the distinctive religion of Christianity. It took a long time for the practitioners of the new religion to be called Christians; some referred to their religion as "the Way" and described themselves as a "sect of the Nazarenes."

Initially, the church developed from a Jewish-Christian community of believers who met in house-churches, such as the homes of Prisca and Aquila (Acts 18:1–3) and Chloe (1 Corinthians 1:11). The host and hostess were probably first baptized by an apostle, such as Paul, and then they baptized extended family members, friends, acquaintances, and business associates who joined them for regular fellowship and prayer sessions.

Winning Converts

It seems likely that men and women followers of Jesus would have wanted to draw near to Mary Magdalene since she was one of Jesus' closest disciples. She may have officiated at house-church gatherings. Perhaps she shared her unique insights into his teachings. She may have had her own followers—spiritual seekers eager to interact with the one who had been so close to Jesus. Perhaps she gathered new converts around her.

factum

Gnostics saw Mary Magdalene as the embodiment of Sophia, archetype goddess of wisdom. Pagan philosophers revered Sophia, whose name means wisdom. Scholars say the Gospels of Matthew and Mark are thought to have drawn upon the Gospel of Q, which reveals that Jesus and John the Baptist were both messengers sent by Sophia, the Wisdom Goddess.

She would have had to deal head-on with the issues of concern to Jews. They were not so easily converted because they saw the gospel as threatening to their cultural traditions. The fledgling church, however, continued to expand and evolve into a diverse community that included Samaritans, Gentiles, and pagan converts. Increasingly, the gospel preachers took their message to Gentiles rather than focusing on the Jews. By the end of Paul's lifetime, most of the members of the Christian communities outside of Palestine were Gentiles. In the early part of the second century, some disparate groups splintered off the movement. Their interpretations of the meaning of the gospel put them at odds with the more orthodox Christians.

Before the books of the New Testament were selected, there surely was a highly contentious debate about which texts revealed the true teachings and which didn't. When the bishops at the Council of Nicaea in 325 were selecting the texts for the canon, they had many Scriptures from which to choose. Some conformed to the acceptable orthodox beliefs and others veered into alternative areas that the bishops considered false and heretical. The process of reaching consensus within Christianity continued into the early fifth century.

Variant Forms of Christianity

The Gnostics, the Ebionites, and the Marcionites were the three main groups at odds with conservative Catholic/orthodox Christians. The Ebionites believed people had to convert to Judaism, and men had to be circumcised in order to be true Christians. They traced their beliefs to James the Just, brother of Jesus. The Marcionites followed Paul's teaching, but believed that there were two Gods: one of Old Testament and the other, the God of Jesus. Marcion was excommunicated, but not before his following grew large enough to threaten traditional orthodox Christianity. Sacred texts written by the Gnostics expressed views at variance with the orthodox Christian bishops but gave rise to yet other variant forms of Christianity.

symbolism

The Sabbath in Judaism was a symbol of God's covenant with the Hebrews to create for six days but to rest on the seventh (Saturday). The Christians enjoy the Sabbath on Sunday, the day of Jesus' resurrection. Muslims regard Friday as their holy day of rest.

Although some say Gnosticism may have existed before the New Testament texts, others suggest that the New Testament had an influence on Gnosticism and point to direct quotations and allusions to sources that can be found in the many Nag Hammadi texts. The Gnostic influence gave rise to other religions such as Manichaeism, an offshoot of Gnosticism that for a time became a world religion and reached as far as China. Saint Augustine (354 to 430) flirted with ideas of Manichaeism for about ten years before rejecting the religion as false and refuting it in *Confessions*. Read more about Augustine's reasoning and conclusions in his autobiography *Confessions of St. Augustine* (Catholic Book Publishing Co., 1997).

Gnostic Beliefs

The Gnostics believed in salvation, but thought that it was the result of divine knowledge from inner work (meditation, contemplation, prayer). *Gnosis* brings soul liberation, and Jesus is the messenger who brings *gnosis* to humans. Signs of spiritual awakening, according to the Gnostics, included visions, inspired speaking and writing, and dreams. One important belief that the Gnostics held was that men and women are equal. This meant that in the Gnostic Christian congregations, women held leadership and liturgical positions.

The Gnostics gave credence to spiritually inspired visions. For Mary Magdalene, Jesus was a teacher who, after his death and resurrection, came to her in visions. In the Gospel of Mary, Jesus appears to her and tells her she's blessed because she did not waver when she beheld him. This Gospel says Mary Magdalene received a vision and secret teaching that she shared with Peter and the other disciples following Jesus' death. She modeled perfect discipleship and typified female leadership and prophethood. However, one of the issues that the early Christians struggled with was whose visions were valid and whose visions were false, and whether teachings received in visions were accurately represented. Moreover, did they truly come from Jesus?

Flourishing of Gnosticism

Gnosticism may have existed before the beginning of Christianity. Some scholars assert that signs of Gnostic systems existed independently centuries before the Christian era. Others say that Gnosticism was an offshoot of Christianity, albeit a corruption. Much scholarship during the last quarter century has been focused on Gnosticism's pre-Christian origins. Gnosticism has been called syncretistic and dualistic because it attempts to unify opposing principles of Christianity (for example, one God with both male and female aspects; and a basic dualism between spirit and matter).

discussion question

What did the first-century Gnostics believe?
Gnostic theology included radical ideas such as a belief in a transcendent deity who is pure spirit, salvation is a result of one's own inner work (not through a Savior), the soul ensnared in matter or darkness must work to extricate itself, the soul is divine but the body is polluted, men and women are equal, gnosis leads to liberation, Jesus brings gnosis to humans, and salvation is gained through living a righteous life.

Gnosticism, as a religious movement, took root and flourished from the second to the fourth centuries. The Gnostics wrote many gospels of their own about Jesus' life and ministry. Though deemed heretical by orthodox Christianity and suppressed for centuries, their diverse religious writings were discovered in 1945 when peasants found a clay jar in one of the caves in the Jabal al-Tārif mountain near Nag Hammadi, Egypt. Inside the jar were fifty-two diverse religious texts that shed light on primitive Christianity, as it existed in first-century Palestine. Among the codices and papyrus manuscripts found were the Pistis Sophia, the Apocryphon of John, the Dialogue of the Savior, the Gospel of the Egyptians, the Book of Thomas the Contender, The Thunder: Perfect Mind, the Gospel of Philip, and the Gospel of Thomas.

factum

The meaning of gnosis is mystical knowledge. The Gnostics believed God has a feminine aspect and that the spirit part of God was Divine Wisdom. The Gnostics considered Mary Magdalene as the Embodiment of Wisdom (Sophia) and the Sacred Feminine. The Gnostics particular brand of Christianity seemed to borrow elements from Platonic philosophy, Judaism, and the teachings of Jesus.

Gnosticism thrived and spread despite attempts by the Orthodox/Catholics to suppress and eradicate it. A version of Paulist Gnosticism was present up to the tenth century. Manichaeism continued into the thirteenth. The Bogomiles (a variation of Paulist Gnosticism) lasted until the twelfth century, where it evolved into the religion of the peaceful, vegetarian Cathars (Purified Ones) of France, Spain, and Italy. They maintained a devotion to Mary Magdalene but were deemed heretics and were massacred by the Crusaders.

At Variance with Literalist Christianity

Think of Literalist Christianity as the opposite pole of Gnosticism. Between these two poles is a wide range of religious beliefs and traditions. Literalist Christians believed that their spiritual tradition was unique—their "Way" was the way of truth. They embraced outward manifestations of their religious beliefs in the form of symbols, rituals, traditions, scriptural texts, and even religious leaders. They believed that their spiritual work in life was to spread Jesus' teachings and to evangelize all nations.

The Gnostics, conversely, sought an inward path to enlightenment and truth. They did not seek to convert others to their belief system. They wished to rise above cultural labels and identities in order to become one with all things. The Gnostics abhorred traditional Literalist Christianity. Even among the Gnostics were varying ideas and philosophies. Timothy Freke and Peter Gandy in *Jesus and the Lost Goddess* address the evolution of earliest Christianity from the Jewish Gnostics. Moses was considered by the Jewish Gnostics to be their spiritual ancestor and master. The Pagan Gnostics and their great philosopher Pythagoras influenced Jewish Gnosticism. In the first century, Gnostics reworked already existing myths and created new ones by reinterpreting their ancestral scriptural traditions. Gnostics used allegorical myths to encode their teachings.

symbolism

Ancient symbols of death include a skull, tomb, drummer, poppy, cypress tree, vulture, skeletal rider with a scythe, or a veiled woman. The Gnostics didn't emphasize reincarnation, but they believed that if a person had not attained liberation (union with his/her higher self and enlightenment) through gnosis while alive, he might return for another cycle of earthly life.

Mary Magdalene in the Gnostic Texts

Mary Magdalene's powerful inquisitive mind grasped the subtle nuances of Jesus' teachings (as suggested in the Gnostic text Pistis Sophia). Her subsequent retreat from the world to take up the life of a contemplative pointed to inner journey and was consistent with the Gnostic quest for inner gnosis. The Gnostics "claimed" Mary Magdalene in a way that the Literalist Christians did not. Modern scholars say the orthodox or Literalist New Testament writers marginalized her story in the Gospels. But why would they? Some say to further a patriarchal agenda and to prevent challenges to male power from females within the fledgling church.

discussion question

What sacraments did the Gnostics celebrate?
The Gnostics celebrated the sacraments of a baptism, Eucharist, sealing, chrism (anointing with olive oil), and bridal chamber. The latter might have been a sacred ritual between a man and a woman or possibly an allegory for a mystical experience such as the merging of the individual soul or bride (thought to be a spark of the divine), back into its source (bridegroom). The Gnostic texts reveal that those once joined in the bridal chamber will not be again separate.

Left Out of the Bible

When the first ecumenical Council at Nicaea convened in 325, one issue was to choose some letters and Gospels to include in the canon. The four Gospels by Matthew, Mark, Luke, and John were selected. They, coincidentally, contained the fewest references to Mary Magdalene while the Gnostic Gospels accorded her high esteem and numerous mentions. Some might say this suggests a patristic antifeminist agenda (what pope would want to trace his spiritual lineage to a woman?), while others claim the exclusion was based purely on the theology of the Gnostics, which was at odds with Literalist Christian ideology.

Mary Magdalene—as mother of the church, priestess, prophetess, and first pope—would have been unthinkable to the Literalists, although the Gnostics (who believed God had a feminine side) could have more easily embraced such thinking. Perhaps the male disciples, their followers, and subsequent generations of educated Christian men would have been embarrassed to have to trace their spiritual lineage to a woman.

Spiritual Successor to Jesus?

Some modern thinkers have postulated that Mary Magdalene may have been a spiritual successor to Jesus. Others dispute this idea, reasoning that Jesus hand-picked his twelve male disciples and made them apostles. Further, the apostles could draw many more male converts to Christianity with male authority figures such as Peter and Paul as opposed to a female wielding the power. In fact, women as the main pillars of the movement might even have brought condemnation upon the fledgling Christian church.

A woman as Jesus' spiritual successor and head of his church quite possibly would have been seen by conservative men in the patriarchal societies of the first few centuries as an embarrassment. What could be the value to men of a church with a woman at the helm? The early church fathers instead moved toward power based on male hierarchy in both organization and lineage.

The Gnostics, however, saw Mary Magdalene as someone whose visions surpassed even Peter's. She was the apostle who exceeded all the others. Her interpretations, arrived at through her spiritual maturity and insights, may have been considered deviant from the orthodox view that emerged from conservative male apostolic traditions. The Gnostics allowed women to share power with men.

The Pagan Goddess Cults

Pagan goddess veneration dates as far back as prehistoric times according to archaeologist Marija Gimbutas, author of *The Language of the Goddess*. Although some scholars believe the first pagan godesses were the fertility goddesses, others dispute the idea, suggesting that artifacts thought to depict such fertility goddesses in actuality could have been territorial markers or toys. Still, by the first century, pagan goddess cults around the Mediterranean were flourishing alongside Gnosticism and other religious theologies. During the rise of the Jesus movement and early Christianity, Isis, the Egyptian goddess of fertility, was widely venerated by pagans. A goddess (redeemed) and a Godman who dies and is resurrected were two mythical archetypes that appeared in recurring themes in some of the cultural and religious traditions in countries and communities in the first century.

A Jewish Goddess Tradition

Authors Timothy Freke and Peter Gandy suggest that a Jewish goddess tradition had always existed even though the idea was rejected at some point by Jewish Literalists. The Jewish goddess Sophia taught those who would be initiated into the mysteries of the divine. As previously mentioned, the Gnostics believed Mary Magdalene to be Jesus' consort—the Sophia to Jesus' Godman.

symbolism

Snakes were potent symbols in the Mediterranean fertility cults. Ancient Indians believed that Kundalini, a latent divine energy coiled at the base of the spine, bestowed enlightenment when raised. Some say this force is what Mary Magdalene was referring to in the Gospel of Mary when she spoke of dark powers the soul must pass through to reach its eternal resting place.

Egyptian Parallels

Mary Magdalene's role in Christianity's Easter story in some ways resonates with the Isis cult stories. Isis was the Egyptian pagan goddess and her Godman/consort/husband was Osiris. Isis searched everywhere for Osiris after he had been murdered and dismembered. Her love and magic restored him, and after three days, Osiris arose from the dead. Isis made a trip to Hades (sometimes depicted as a cave) to recover her risen Lord whilst Mary Magdalene searched for hers in the garden of Joseph of Arimathea. Mary Magdalene found the risen Jesus at a cave. Some would say that these two stories are so similar that it seems as though Mary Magdalene and Jesus were simply re-enacting the Egyptian Isis/Osiris resurrection story.

A more controversial story depicts Mary Magdalene in the Temple of Isis working to heal or help others transcend the material world so that they might enter higher spiritual realms. Temple workers used their bodies to enable others to reach these higher planes of consciousness. Not considered prostitutes, they were priestesses representing the goddess Isis in their sacred transformational acts. The Greek *heterae* also similarly served as concubines and lovers endowed with a spiritual purpose.

The Sacred Feminine in India

In India, the women who venerated Shakti, the feminine aspect of God, were known as *Shaktas* and were versed in the use of Tantric sex as a path to transcendental consciousness. In the Hindu tradition, when the sacred energy Kundalini Shakti was awakened in the human body, her goal was to merge at the top of the head with her consort/god Shiva in a mystical sacred union, an integrated wholeness. This concept of God with both male/female aspects is also occasionally echoed in Hebrew Scripture where God is like a mother protecting her child.

Early Christian Fathers Root Out Heresy

The apostles Peter, John, and Paul were intent on rooting out opinions or doctrines at odds with their versions of orthodox Christianity.

179

Later, the early church fathers Irenaeaus, Tertullian, and Hippolytus also refuted the many heresies, mainly those of Gnosticism.

Gnostic Heresies

The idea that the physical world is essentially evil as a result of the fall from God's grace and therefore should be rejected was considered a Gnostic heresy. Another heresy of the Gnostics was the belief in a good God and an "evil" God. In fact, the Gnostics were one of the earliest groups whose views were radically variant with the orthodox teachings of the Jesus movement and the earliest forms of the church.

The Gnostics weren't the only group to put forth heretical ideas. A Deism heresy held that the world was created by God who then left it to itself. A heresy found in both Manichaeism and Dualism was the concept of duality in which good and evil and dark and light are in permanent conflict. Many heretical viewpoints emerged even as Christianity was establishing itself in the first few centuries.

factum

Through the centuries, the church has had to deal with heresies and schisms. The difference between heresy and schism is that heresy occurs in the mind as a faulty thinking or reasoning that opposes religious belief or doctrine, while schism occurs as a voluntary act of will that leads to separation from some form of institutionalized Christianity in favor of a different institutional form.

The Gnostics were particularly problematic for the Orthodox/ Catholic party because they used the teachings of Christianity to further their own philosophical ideas. For example, the Gnostics embraced Paul's thinking about predestination. "For whom he did foreknow, he also did predestinate to be conformed to the image of his Son that he might be the firstborn among many brethren.

Moreover whom he did predestinate, them he also called: and whom he called, them he also justified: and whom he justified, them he also glorified" (Romans 8:29–30). The Gnostics also liked the Gospel of John statement, "You shall know the truth and the truth shall set you free" (8:32), seeing it as a justification for the idea that salvation is through *gnosis* or knowledge of the self.

Other Sources of Heresy

The orthodox Christians had to be ever vigilant to find heresies and uproot them. Irenaeus (180) wrote a text titled *Against Heresies* in which he points out Gnostic misuse of passages, ideas, and statements from what would later become the New Testament Gospels. Tertullian also challenged those who distorted Christian Scriptures to further their own brand of Christianity, be it Gnosticism or something different. Tertullian wrote *The Prescription Against Heretics* in which he mentions specifically Marcion and Valentinus, whose ideas ran counter to orthodox Christianity. The seven sources of heresies were the following:

Simon Magus

He was the leader of the Syrian cult of Gnosticism and a contemporary of the apostles. He has been described as a pagan, Gnostic Christian, magician, sorcerer, Jew, and the "father of all heresies." He was a disciple of John the Baptist and eventually succeeded him. Simon's disciples saw him as an incarnation of God's power, someone who brought salvation (through *gnosis*) from angelic tyranny and the cycles of death and birth. Simon believed that Helena, his consort, was the incarnation of the Mother of All, the Holy Spirit. He taught his followers knowledge of the Divine as male/female, mother/father, whose divided essence is found throughout all humanity. He founded a lot of churches only to lose them to the apostle Peter.

Valentinus

He was born near Carthage in Africa circa 100. He was a Christian priest (possibly even a bishop) and not considered a heretic in his lifetime, although he was thought to be a great Gnostic leader. Followers of Valentinian Gnosis celebrated a sacrament known as "bridal chamber" (union of pneuma or spirit, possibly a male/female sexual act).

Marcion

He was not a Gnostic, per se, but rather a Christian with ideas that ran afoul of the orthodox. He believed that the God of the Old Testament and New Testament were not the same being. Further, he established his own canon and rejected outright the Old Testament. He also rejected writings of all the apostles except for Paul (his favorite) and Luke.

Montanism

The church had problems with the ideas of the minister Montanus, who preached on the book of Revelation and claimed that God gave him new revelations as well. He led many Christians astray.

Mani

A true Gnostic, Mani was born circa 215 to 216 and grew up to establish the religion of Manichaeism. His followers despised Christianity because it was so full of mysteries. Salvation, Mani believed, was by the knowledge that he brought to his followers.

Donatus

Bishop of Carthage in 315, Donatus would not accept any baptisms that were performed by non-Donatists. The Donatists were condemned by the Council of Arles in 314. The Catholic Church and the Donatists were locked in constant bickering. The Donatists church was ruled illegal in 411.

Arianism

Followers of Arianism opposed what Christians believed, namely, that God could have a Son, because God was without beginning and unoriginated. They believed that God could not beget.

A Case of Medieval Heresy

The early church fathers weren't the only Christian leaders who vigilantly sought to identify and abolish heresies—with force, if necessary. One such instance occurred during 1209 in the assault against the Cathars at Beziers in the south of France.

Like the Gnostics, the Cathars believed in gender equality. They embraced ideas of the Divine Feminine. Interestingly, Mary Magdalene's cult flourished where the Cathars had settled in the Languedoc-Roussillon region of France, the area where Beziers was located. Historical accounts say this area was a magnet for heretical Christian sects in Western Europe. In fact, the Gnostic heresies grew very popular in the south of France, and increasingly, became a concern for the church. The simplicity of the Cathars' lifestyle and faith attracted many followers.

Ten beliefs of the Cathars or *Perfecti* were:

1. They practiced pacifism and consumed a vegetarian diet.
2. They believed that humans have a soul that dwells within the body but that the spirit is found in the soul.
3. The most important aspect of their lives was keeping the spirit pure so that their spirit could one day return to the Light (a term for God).
4. They despised excesses of the church.
5. Their advanced masters included women. Such masters were called Perfects or Parfaits.
6. They worshiped in nature, primarily in forested areas or on the tops of mountains.
7. They were averse to icon and relic veneration.
8. They believed in the doctrine of reincarnation.
9. They believed Jesus, as a cosmic being, could not have perished on a cross.
10. They thought the church had tampered with Christian teachings for its own benefit.

Some say that the church, smarting from criticism, felt impelled to deal with the Cathar "problem." Besides embracing heretical ideas, the Cathars refused to acknowledge the supreme authority of the pope. Pope Innocent III ordered Christians Crusaders to attack the Cathars. The assault took place on Mary Magdalene's feast day, July 22. Among the dead were thousands of Cathars as well as the local townspeople who supported them.

The Crusade continued for several years. With such darkness in that part of the world, people who sought an exemplar for beauty, light, and grace may have sought the intercession of Mary Magdalene for peace. But even though Beziers had its very own Mary Magdalene church, sadly the Cathars were exterminated.

Mary Magdalene/Holy Grail Heresy

During the twelfth century, one of the darkest periods in Christian history, the story of the Holy Grail spread across Europe. The Grail was thought to be the mythological sacred chalice that either held the blood of Christ that dripped from his body while he hung on the cross or was the cup from which he drank during the Last Supper.

An important symbol of Christianity, the Grail's popularity surged during the Crusades (1095 to 1148). A legend popular in oral tradition offered a deviation of the Holy Grail theory; namely, a pregnant Mary Magdalene was the Grail because she carried the child of Jesus in her womb. Clearly, this idea ran counter to the orthodox Christian view (thus was considered heretical), but the legend was strong in the south of France where oral traditions may have kept it circulating.

The popularity of the Cathars, the Celtic Church (associated with the Cathars), and the Grail stories deeply concerned the church. The Grail stories mesmerized many people, but the heretical thinking associated with the stories (that there might be another path to salvation through an experiential faith and *gnosis* that had little to nothing to do with the Orthodox Church) was clearly problematic for the church and necessarily had to be refuted. The Grail stories and Gnostic Christian mysteries then, according to some who have studied them, went underground and resurfaced in esoteric teachings and occultism.

184

chapter 12

Rituals and Beliefs of Early Christians

Jesus' ideas and spiritual teachings formed the beliefs and practices of early Christians. Mary Magdalene and the other disciples guarded his teachings and tried to stay close to them. The early church fathers also struggled to keep the teachings pure, rooting out heresies whenever and wherever they threatened to pollute the theology and practices of early Christianity.

Almsgiving

The early Christians shared their wealth (alms, bread, wine) for the collective good. The word alms is derived from the Greek word meaning "mercy or kindness." Most consider the term alms archaic and favor the words offering and gifts. Modern Jews and Christians, as their spiritual brothers and sisters in ancient times, make offerings or tithe money to their churches, temples, and synagogues for good works and charitable gifts to help the poor. An old tradition of the Catholic Church known as Peter's Pence was an annual tax of a penny by the Holy See upon the laity of England.

factum

Kneeling did not become a common practice until the ninth century when congregants began to drop to their knees during the part of the eucharistic celebration when the priest would raise the holy wafer and recite the words: "This is my body." Until then, Christians remained standing for prayers.

Almsgiving in the New Testament

The Old Testament book of Deuteronomy contains many references to providing for the needs of the poor, and there are many mentions in the New Testament as well. Jesus often spoke on behalf of the poor and disenfranchised. Mary Magdalene and other women funded Jesus' ministry, the New Testament Gospels reveal, out of their own resources. So, a practice that existed before the birth of Jesus and that he and his followers practiced still exists today.

References in the Gospels

The Gospels of Matthew and Luke both mention almsgiving. While Matthew 6:1–4 notes it as representative of the religious spirit and counsels givers to do it in secret, the Gospel of Luke 3:11 repeats

Jesus' guidance to give generously of what you have: "He that hath two cloaks let him impart to him that hath none, and he that hath meat, let him do likewise."

Burial

The burials of the earliest Christian-Jews usually were done on the same day (for sanitation reasons in a hot climate). Wealthy families buried their dead in rock-hewn caves with circular rolling stones to seal them. The poor were buried in the ground and covered with stones. In ancient times, the Romans did not permit the burial of Christians within Rome, so the followers of Christ placed their dead in subterranean catacombs connected by multilevel passageways and steep steps. Hundreds of thousands of early Christians were buried beneath Rome's Appian Way and other roads.

discussion question

What is the *Didache*?
Early Christians kept an instructional manual—the Didache—of their practices and beliefs to aid the instruction of converts. Composed late in the first and early second century, it presented rules about baptism, prayer, fasting, and penance and provided information about the roles of deacons, bishops, and presbyters. There are no references to women serving the church in any capacity.

Ancient Burial Rites

The bodies of Christians were washed, clothed, bound in linen, and scented with perfumed oils or ointments. For those buried in catacombs, the name and date of death were inscribed upon a slab that sealed the body inside a niche carved out of the earthen wall. Early Christian catacombs were adorned with art that included the

Chi-Rho (a monogram for the Greek word *Christos*) as well as doves and fishes. In the second century, an ossuary, or box to hold the bones, was used after the body decayed. Scientists are now studying the recently found Ossuary of James with its Aramaic inscription—James son of Joseph, brother of Jesus.

The Catacomb of Saint Priscilla

The apostle Paul called Aquila and Prisca (also known as Priscilla) "co-workers in Christ Jesus" (Romans 16:3–4). Paul acknowledged the husband and wife for opening their home as a church-house. According to one tradition, Prisca was martyred in Rome. A church bearing her name was erected on the Aventine Hill on the site of a very early Christian church, the Titulus Priscoe (built circa the fourth century).

Baptism

Many modern people believe that the ancient Christian rite of baptism began with John the Baptist, who administered the sacrament of baptism to Jesus. However, a much older tradition of immersion in water—the mikvah—to clean, purify, and sanctify existed in the Jewish faith. People became polluted by touching unclean things, and women at the end of their monthly menstrual cycle washed in the waters of the mikvah for ritual purification.

factum

During the Middle Ages, piety and purity were of utmost importance. Anyone who went against church teachings was considered a heretic and was punished or put to death. Women were especially vulnerable to charges of sorcery or witchcraft. Mary Magdalene, the fallen woman who repented her sins and became a contemplative, appealed to the medieval mind.

The word *baptism* comes from the Greek and means "to wash, bathe, or dip." The rite of purification by immersion in water existed in ancient Judaism, Christianity, Sikhism, and Mandaenism. Christians believe that baptism represents the symbolic cleansing of the person as he or she enters a covenant with Christ as one of his faithful. The baptized receive salvation and enter the kingdom of Christ forever.

Christians today baptize either through total immersion, in which the entire body is lowered into a pool or tank of water, or sprinkling, or pouring water over the head of the convert or believer. All believe that although humans perform the baptism, invisible in the act is God working through them.

Healing

Early Christians taught that God heals humans of afflictions or diseases through his infinite mercy and compassion. Throughout his ministry, Jesus performed many miraculous healings and forgave sin. His exorcism of the devils (biblical language for germs or the cause of sickness) from Mary Magdalene was perhaps one of his most famous healings.

discussion question

Of Jesus' many healings, why did only Mary Magdalene have seven devils?
Jesus may have been actually cleansing or working with the seven energy centers in Mary Magdalene's body to enable her to enter higher realms of consciousness. See a discussion of this idea in Jean-Yves Leloup's *The Gospel of Mary Magdalene.*

Jesus' followers practiced the laying on of hands and believed divine healing was the work of God. Some modern evangelists assert that Jesus the Christ bore (and bears) our sicknesses and iniquities as an oppressive weight of sadness. The Bible contains many references to sickness and the root causes. Here are four:

1. Curses—these would be visited upon people because they offended God.
2. Chastisement—illness could come upon a person in order to help him or her develop spiritual character.
3. Carelessness—sickness might come through a person's ignorance and carelessness.
4. Sin—ancient and medieval people understood that acts considered sinful (such as fornication) might cause an affliction (such as venereal disease).

Tradition says that Mary Magdalene was a conduit for healing. In particular, her French legends offer instances when she healed the sick. Following Jesus' example, she likely healed the mind as well as the body of those who petitioned her or needed her.

Conversion

The early Christians probably at first shared their message of Jesus as Lord and Messiah only with their family members, closest friends, business associates, and trusted allies. They were Jews sharing their truth with other Jews. Only later did they proselytize to non-Jews in Judea and around the Mediterranean, hoping to win over their hearts and minds. These new converts became members of the growing family of followers who ultimately converted to Christianity.

What Is Conversion?

Mary Magdalene, according to her French legends, was particularly adept at sharing the Good News of Jesus' ministry, death, burial, and resurrection. Conversion is the act of turning away from one thing and toward another. In the religious sense, it is nothing less than a spiritual rebirth—turning away from past thinking and embracing a new belief in and relationship with God. Conversion is that change in the heart that causes a person to repent from sin and to surrender faithfully to the will of Jesus Christ as Lord.

symbolism

In art, the color red is associated with life, carnal passion, and intensity. Mary Magdalene was frequently painted with red or blond hair in the image of the repentant fallen woman. Her long tresses symbolized power and vitality. Often, she was draped in red fabric, as in the works of Botticelli and the prolific Spanish painter El Greco.

Role of the Holy Spirit in Conversion

Many Christians believe that the Holy Spirit accomplishes the softening of a hardened heart, enabling the conversion of a non-believer into a faithful follower of Christ. Mary Magdalene and the apostles were empowered with gifts of the Holy Spirit. While many believe that these same gifts are available to Christians today, some question the possibility of the permanence of these gifts. Yet, indisputably, there are missionaries who have possessed exceptional gifts and extraordinary blessings from God.

Pilgrimage

A pilgrim is a faithful person who makes a journey to a sacred place (often the tomb of a holy person) as an act of devotion. Most religions have a tradition of such individuals making pilgrimages. For example, after the first century, Christians traveled to holy sites in Christian Rome to see the tombs of Saints Peter and Paul and the martyrs whose final resting places were in the catacombs.

Far-Flung Pilgrimage Sites

The Holy Land is perhaps the most popular destination for the Christian faithful, but there are sites of interest all over the world, especially wherever Jesus and the apostles lived, preached, and died. Legends purport that Mary Magdalene went to Gaul; John the Divine went to Ephesus; and others, like James, John's brother, traveled to Spain. James returned to Jerusalem where Herod had him beheaded and then refused to allow his burial. One legend says that James' Christian brethren put his body in a marble sepulcher and angels bore it to the ancient kingdom of Asturias (Spain), which remains a popular Christian pilgrimage destination even today.

Pilgrimage During Dangerous Times

The Greek Orthodox Christians traveling to Jerusalem on pilgrimage during dangerous times prefaced their names with "Hatzi," indicative of their status as a pilgrim of Jerusalem. During the Middle Ages, the Knights Templar, a militaristic religious order, protected pilgrims passing through dangerous areas of Europe on their way to Jerusalem.

The Three Pillars

From the earliest days of the movement, Christians embraced a set of beliefs that are based on Jesus' life and teachings. He taught his followers in several ways: through parables and anecdotes, through example, and through existing practices and texts of Judaism, the religion in which he was raised and from which many Christian ideas and practices come. Christians understood early on that their religion had a set of core beliefs, a particular way of living, and a community of faithful who support their religion, its churches, its followers, and its missions.

Beliefs

The most fundamental Christian beliefs can be found in the Apostles' Creed, which begins with the words "I believe in God, the Father Almighty, creator of Heaven and Earth." The creed sets forth the fundamental beliefs of the faith in twelve statements. The creed may have begun as an affirmation before the baptism of a new convert.

factum

> The catechism of the Catholic Church teaches that the Word of God has the power to save anyone who has faith and that Jesus is the Word Incarnate and the only begotten Son of God. The New Testament Gospels, according to that manual, are the heart and soul of Scripture, because they reveal the life and teachings of the Savior Jesus.

The apostles might have recited some portion or version of the Apostles' Creed as they taught new converts about the "Christian" beliefs. One major point of the Apostles' Creed affirmed the divinity of Jesus in a statement that was likely directed at the Arians who did not believe in the deity of the Christ. The second sentence of the Creed (in modern English) states: "And in Jesus Christ, his only Son, our Lord, who was conceived by the power of the Holy Spirit, and born of the Virgin Mary."

Although Christianity evolved in part out of Judaism, it quickly diverged from the older religion in two ways: (1) Christians regarded Jesus as divine (something the Jews could not do), and (2) Christians believed in the superiority of Jesus' teachings over the older Mosaic Law. The Hebrews believed they were God's chosen and that the Mosaic Law represented God's covenant with them.

Way of Life

Mary Magdalene and the other disciples left their old lives to take up new ones. Their new lives, based on love, forgiveness, and the equality of men and women to receive the blessings of the Holy Spirit, were a radical departure from their old ways. Further, others persecuted them for their beliefs; their faith had to be strong to survive any such assault. Many Christians from the first century on were martyred for their beliefs.

Dutiful Christians, as the apostle Paul pointed out, ought to practice patience and self-denial, pray for others, and be charitable to the poor and suffering. Paul emphasized that they should refrain from all kinds of immorality, adhere to the laws, and at all times follow the teachings of Christ Jesus. He warned of overconfidence and the tendency to argue. Paul emphasized the importance of giving generously of what one possessed and adhering to the call to holiness with other Christians (see 2 Corinthians 6:14–18). These practices were aligned with the teachings of Jesus.

symbolism

Mary Magdalene is often pictured with an alabaster jar or a vessel, which held the spikenard or anointing oil used on Jesus, in her girdle or belt. Aside from being associated with female chastity, the girdle also symbolized the seductiveness of the goddess Aphrodite. A rope girdle has long symbolized the binding of Christ and the scourging of his body.

Community of the Faithful

From the earliest days of Christianity, new converts were encouraged to stick together for mutual support and to strengthen their faith. The apostle Paul in many of his Epistles (in the New Testament) emphasized the beliefs and responsibilities of the faithful in their fledgling Christian communities. He told them to offer their bodies as a living sacrifice to God; they were not simply individuals but parts of the larger body in Christ, and they should make their love sincere. By obeying the higher authorities that had been established, following the commandments, and living and dying for Christ, they were part of the community of the Lord's faithful and their reward would be entering the kingdom of heaven.

Christian Holy Seasons and Prayers

Two important holidays mark the birth and death of Jesus. The earliest Christians were Jews (like Mary Magdalene and the other apostles closest to Jesus) who once observed Passover, but after Jesus' death, they marked that anniversary in remembrance of him. Christmas, of course, celebrates Jesus' birth, and the liturgical year of the church begins with Advent. It is a time when Christians celebrate the first coming of Christ and anticipate his final coming (in the end-time).

The Easter Season

An old pagan festival to celebrate the annual arrival of spring was named after Eostre, the Anglo-Saxon goddess of spring, and featured both eggs and rabbits. Art depicting Mary Magdalene often includes the icon of an egg, but as a symbol of new life and renewal. Today, of course, Easter is one of the most important Christian holy days. It is preceded by the season of Lent, forty days of preparation for Easter that begins on Ash Wednesday and culminates on Good Friday.

discussion question

What are the Stations of the Cross?
The stations are points along the path that led from Jesus' condemnation to his death: (1) Jesus is condemned, (2) Jesus bears his cross, (3) Jesus falls for the first time, (4) Jesus meets his mother, (5) Jesus receives help from Simon Peter, (6) Jesus meets Veronica, (7) Jesus falls for the second time, (8) Jesus speaks to the women, (9) Jesus falls for the third time, (10) Jesus' garments are removed, (11) Jesus is nailed to the cross, (12) Jesus dies, (13) Jesus is removed from the cross, and (14) Jesus is placed in the tomb.

Popular Christian Prayers and Recitations

Among old Christian prayers and recitations are the Lord's Prayer, which Jesus taught his followers, and the Prayer of Praise, which glorifies God, the Father, the Son, and the Holy Spirit. Both of these prayers became part of the rosary group of prayers recited by Catholics as a means of memorizing key events and the mysteries of salvation as well as a means of praising and thanking God.

The rosary is divided into four groups of five mysteries each. These mysteries are joyful, luminous, sorrowful, and glorious, and are to be reflected on as one recites the rosary. Each recitation begins by making the sign of the cross and then reciting the Apostles' Creed, followed by the Our Father, three Hail Marys, one Prayer of Praise (also called Glory to the Father), and so on. Some moderns who particularly revere Mary Magdalene have adapted and reworded the Hail Mary to reflect love and veneration for Mary Magdalene.

chapter 13

A Woman's Gospel

P eople interested in Christianity know that the New Testament is made up of four gospels—Matthew, Mark, Luke, and John—as well as the Acts of the Apostles (likely written by the author of the Gospel of Luke), various letters, and The Revelation of St. John the Divine. But what may surprise many readers is the existence of other gospels excluded from the canon. The Gospel of Mary is one of them. It is the only woman's gospel and honors Mary Magdalene.

The Manuscript Found in Cairo

German scholar Dr. Carl Reinhardt purchased a fifth-century papyrus codex (book) of the Gospel of Mary in Cairo in 1896 from a peddler of ancient manuscripts. Reinhardt took the copy to Berlin, where he began to study it. His translation, however, was not published until 1955 because of a series of misfortunes and two world wars.

factum

A codex (from the Latin cōdex, variant of "trunk") is a book of bound leaves of papyrus or parchment tucked inside a cover, often leather. Initially, the leaves were made from thin wooden strips that were coated with wax and written upon. Christians preferred these manuals for their Scriptures rather than scrolls because they could write on both sides of the parchment.

The manuscript was in the form of a book of papyrus leaves inside a leather cover and written in the Coptic language of the Egyptians. It is commonly referred to as Papyrus Berolinensis 8502. Or as it is commonly referenced in scholarly writings, *Berlin Gnostic Codex* and PB 8502. This codex is the most complete surviving copy of the Gospel of Mary of Magdala, but it is missing quite a few pages.

Neither Dr. Reinhardt nor the manuscript peddler was immediately aware that the papyrus book was not only the Gospel of Mary but also the Apocryphon of John, the Sophia of Jesus Christ, and the Act of Peter. In Berlin, Dr. Reinhardt placed the book in the Egyptian Museum. There its official title/catalogue number became Codex Berolinensis 8502.

Two other fragments from Greek editions of the Gospel of Mary have also survived and were unearthed in Oxyrhynchus in northern Egypt (along with fragments from the Gnostic Gospel of Thomas). But even after putting all the pieces of the Gospel of Mary together, no complete copy of this woman's gospel exists. What scholars now have is a partial manuscript with pages one to six and pages eleven to fourteen missing.

symbolism

> The Gnostic texts found near Nag Hammadi were located in a jar inside a cave. Plato used shadowy cave imagery to suggest that what humans take to be reality is actually just a shadow of higher reality. The cave and earthly fissures symbolize access to hidden forces, prophecy, and the womb.

A Gnostic wrote this gospel (like the others in the library of writings found at Nag Hammadi). The Gnostic view of God differs from the God of the Old and New Testaments. The God of the Gnostics can be known by *gnosis* or self-knowledge. In fact, knowledge of the self and knowledge of the divine were the same to the Gnostics. The Gnostics also portrayed the teachings of Jesus in terms of illusion (due to being trapped in matter) and enlightenment (through knowledge of the self or *gnosis*). The New Testament Gospels, on the other hand, address sin and repentance.

Other Pieces of the Gospel of Mary

In a spectacular recent discovery, another copy of the Gospel of Mary was found among fifty-two sacred texts inside a jar in Upper Egypt in 1945. The clay jar, discovered by a peasant searching for fertilizer in one of about 150 caves in the Jabal al-Tārif mountain near Nag Hammadi, also contained the Pistis Sophia, the Thunder: Perfect Mind, the Gospel of Philip, the Gospel of Truth, the Gospel of Thomas, the Gospel of the Egyptians, and the Acts of Peter and the Twelve Apostles, among others. All the texts were subsequently catalogued, preserved, translated, edited, and published. What

199

became apparent was that these texts found at Nag Hammadi were Gnostic Gospels, sacred to a particular sect of earliest Christianity. Gnosticism was eventually denounced by the Christian orthodoxy because its ideas were deemed heretical.

discussion question

What is the Papyrus Oxyrhynchus 3525?
A severely damaged, small fragment of the Gospel of Mary was found during an excavation in Oxyrhynchus, Egypt. This fragment came from a roll, not a codex, was written in Greek cursive, and contains roughly twenty lines of writing. Noted to be from the early third century A.D., it was translated and published in 1983.

Pages of an ancient text known as the Gospel of Mary (Magdalene) were also among the tractates inside the jar. Scholars already knew about two other versions of the Gospel of Mary and were interested in using the Nag Hammadi version to supplement the other two known copies. What they know now is that no complete version of the Gospel of Mary exists.

Six Missing Pages

The Nag Hammadi version of the Gospel of Mary is missing pages one to six and pages eleven to fourteen. These missing pages constitute portions of Chapters 4 and Chapters 5 to 8. What scholars have been able to piece together of the Gospel of Mary is that it portrays Mary Magdalene unflinchingly as a pre-eminent disciple and a woman of great spiritual maturity with a depth of comprehension of Jesus' teachings that is unsurpassed by his other followers. It has been documented in several sources that she never taught in her own name but rather gave all glory and honor to Jesus as she passed on his words of instruction.

symbolism

> Mary Magdalene's vision in the Gospel of Mary included seven forms. In the ancient world, seven was a mystical and magical number symbolizing completion of natural cycles, eternity, and immortality. In Judaism, the menorah has seven branches (plus a lighting candle), representing the days of the week and the seven levels of heaven. The tree of life has seven branches.

The Gospel of Mary opens on page seven with a question from the disciples to Jesus about what matter is and if it will last forever. Jesus answered them by explaining that all that is born is interwoven and thus united, but that everyone must at some point return to its roots. Then Peter asked a provocative question about the nature of sin.

A troubling aspect of the Gospel of Mary is the statement by Jesus to his disciples that there is no sin. He explained that human beings produce sin when they love (an attachment to matter) what deceives them. In this way, humans perpetually create sin through unhealthy and unenlightened imagination. Further, they then make laws to justify or to feel better about their sins. In the Gospel of Mary, Jesus' final counsel admonished his followers not to make or impose any new laws other than what is found in the Torah, least they become bound by them.

Jesus commanded his disciples to go forth and preach the good news. This section of the Gospel of Mary is often referred to as the "Savior's Farewell." The disciples, after he departed, did not immediately carry out his commission, but rather wept out of fear that they would suffer the same fate.

Peter Invites Mary Magdalene to Teach

The Gospel of Mary says that while the other disciples despaired, Mary Magdalene remained on her feet, calm, focused, and steadfast in her vision and faith. She kissed them and turned their hearts and minds from grief and hopelessness toward the "Good." She spoke eloquently on Jesus' behalf. Peter then tells Mary Magdalene that he and the other disciples know that the Savior loved her more than any other woman and asks her to share with them any words that the Savior may have told her that he didn't tell them.

Peter's request suggests that Mary Magdalene occupied the pre-eminent position of leading woman disciple as well as friend, companion, and confidante of Jesus. She was privy to information that Jesus shared only with her. She seems to have been able to step into the void left by Jesus and to refocus the disciples' thoughts and energy back on the light and goodness that was Jesus and his ministry. Peter shows Mary Magdalene a modicum of respect when he asks her to share some of Jesus' words that they have not heard.

Mary Magdalene Shares Her Vision

Mary Magdalene agrees to recount a teaching that Jesus gave her in a vision. This secret teaching focused on the ascent of the soul to its eternal resting place. She explains that as the soul (often in ancient literature referred to as a "she") moves to higher realms, she is questioned by seven cosmic powers. By overcoming these powers, the soul moves from the fetters of matter that bind her in passion and ignorance, and she becomes free to merge her spark of the Divine back into oneness with the source of her being. Mary Magdalene mentions specifically three powers the soul must pass through. When she gets to the fourth power, she discovers that it has seven forms: darkness, desire, ignorance, death wish, fleshly kingdom, foolish fleshly wisdom, and angry person's wisdom (wrath).

Could Mary Magdalene have been suggesting the possibility of a mystical spark of divine energy or breath moving upward (transcendence) through certain wheels or vortices or chakras located along the spine, from the tailbone to the top of the head (a concept found in Indian Kundalini Mahayoga)? In that belief system, the energy is divine and lies dormant at the base of the spine until the person unleashes it to rise through the body's energy centers toward the crown chakra. Once it reaches that place, the sense of duality and separation from God disappears. The soul finds completion and rests in what the Hindus call Samadhi, or a state of spiritual ecstasy. Many mystics of different religions have experienced this state of numinous transcendence, silence, and repose.

fallacy

It's a fallacy that the Acts of the Apostles tells the whole story of the beginnings of Christianity. In fact, while Acts yields some information about the problems faced by the earliest Christians, the events were of a later church after it had already begun to develop. Scholars admonish against trying to create beginnings that never actually happened.

Where the Truth Is to Be Found

Mary Magdalene explained to Peter that when she saw Jesus in the vision, he complimented her for not being disturbed at the sight of him. Mary Magdalene told Peter that she asked the Lord how she was able to see him and that Jesus replied that it was not through the soul or spirit but through the mind (also called nous) that exists between those two that she was able to see him.

In his book *The Gospel of Mary Magdalene*, Jean-Yves Leloup explains that the *nous* is the part of spirit closest to the psyche. The highest form of spirit is *pneuma*. When used to refer to the Holy Spirit, it appears capitalized as *Pneuma*. The faculty of perception in the *nous* may be the imagination, but not in its pejorative modern sense. It is in this intermediate realm of the *nous* where the resurrected Jesus meets Mary Magdalene, perhaps through a divine activation of her visionary imagination. Jesus told Mary Magdalene that where her mind/*nous*/psyche was, there, too, would be her treasure.

Some authors have asserted that this place could also be a spiritual mind or some type of imagination of the super-consciousness.

factum

The idea of transcendence was a central tenet of earliest Christianity. The term transcendence means to "rise above." Orthodox/Catholic defenders saw some Gnostics' suggestion that their resurrection (transcendence) had already taken place as a spiritual reality as a betrayal of true Christian beliefs.

Peter legitimizes the assertion that Jesus loved Mary Magdalene more than the other disciples and that his love for her was different from that which he bore for Peter and the others. Scholars have suggested that this implies the possibility that Jesus had given Mary Magdalene teachings that he had not given others.

Peter asks Mary Magdalene for the words of their teacher that he and the others had not heard. Yet Mary Magdalene does not give him words but answers him by sharing a vision and the teaching within the vision. Leloup says this shifting from the auditory to the visual relates to the primacy in ancient times of visioning over hearing. Vision is not possible for everyone, nor is it bestowed upon everyone equally by God. But people who have refined their inner "eye" of the heart through meditation, contemplation, prayer, and silence make themselves more fit to see with an inner vision rather than by means of their eyes. Peter wanted to hear words; Mary Magdalene chose to share a vision, perceived through the mind's eye between the soul and spirit. She is calm in relaying her vision, and she must have been calm when she actually received it from Jesus, for he praised her for not being disturbed (excited at the phenomenon).

The word *nous* does not appear in the canonical Gospels, yet many early church fathers, such as Clement of Alexandria, Marcarios, and Justin, mention the concept given to Mary Magdalene in her vision: that where one's *nous* is, there, too, lies one's treasure. Some biblical scholars have suggested that Mary Magdalene's teaching is revealing that the Presence of Jesus (Son of man) is in all of us. That Presence is here-and-now and is our treasure.

Mary Magdalene as a Mystic

It's nothing short of stunning that Mary Magdalene with a sense of calm and single-minded focus asked Jesus in her vision how it is that she can even see him. She knows it is not her eyes or anything related to matter or the material world that enables her to see him. She is free from the world of matter and the psychic world of excitation. She embodies the Sophia (wisdom) of the Son of man that is love itself—unconditional, limitless, and timeless.

Was her question one that only a woman would have asked, or would the male disciples have raised the question given the opportunity? In the Gnostic Gospels, Mary Magdalene outshines the others in her understanding and questioning of Jesus. Here, in the vision she relates to Peter, is proof of the kinds of questions arising in her mind. Was hers the mind of a mystic?

Seven Female Christian Mystics

In the history of Christianity, many have contacted God in the sacred temples of their hearts and souls. Sadly, many of those voices were silenced. Some of them, like Mary Magdalene in her time, revealed visions and teaching, experiences, and thoughts that did not (and do not) exactly align with orthodox Christianity. Still, the experiences are insightful to those who might also tread the path of contemplation, meditation, inward mental prayer, and the life of detachment and yearning for knowledge of the Divine. Although there are many others, the following seven Christian mystics were women who followed their hearts inward when they first heard the call of the Beloved.

Some of these women perceived God as Mother, a Sacred Feminine being, a Goddess, just as surely as the Orthodoxy worships a masculine God as Father, Creator, Friend, and Beloved. Each of these women mystics lived during the medieval period, but their ancient sister existed long before the first century. The voices of these mystics speak to the woman's soul, much as the Father God may speak to a man's soul. The important point is that Christians approach the Divine in their own ways. Christian women are taking a cue from Mary Magdalene to hear the voices of wisdom of their ancient sacred sisters. Luckily, the female voice in the Gospel of Mary Magdalene, which only recently emerged, has been recovered; others may be lost forever.

Beatrice of Nazareth

Beatrice of Nazareth (1200 to 1268) lived in Belgium and the Netherlands. She was a Cistercian mystic associated with the Beguines, women who without religious vows dedicated themselves to living a communal life of prayer and service. Her writings revealed a deep mystical connection with the Divine. In one piece, she explained how she had been transferred into oneness with God, albeit for a short time. The Beguines, considered a sacred women's movement of the thirteenth century, came under pressure from the Inquisition, which detested the independent mindedness of the Beguines.

Catherine of Siena

Catherine of Siena (1347 to 1380) lived in Italy and was the twenty-fourth of twenty-five children born into a prosperous family in Siena. At the age of seven, she had her first mystical experience. When her family tried to force her into marriage, she defied them by cutting off her long hair and retreating to a room to meditate and contemplate for three years. Her life was filled with periods of ecstasies, illuminations, and raptures. Though illiterate, she dictated letters and sermons to her disciples. She suffered the stigmata and because of her high level of mystical achievement, she had some power with the pope (whom she convinced to leave Avignon, France, for Rome). She died at the age of thirty-three after several years of fasting.

Hildegard of Bingen

Hildegard of Bingen (1098 to 1179) lived in Germany. She was a medieval mystic who was also called the spiritual genius who gave birth anew to the Sacred Feminine. In her ecstatic trances, she witnessed the Sacred Feminine as Love, Justice, Faith, Wisdom, Peace, and Truth allegorized as women. Often they were attired in beautiful white robes adorned with jewels representing the seven colors of the chakras (or energy wheels/vortices of the body). She featured some version of the Sacred Feminine in every book she wrote and she wrote several. She not only wrote books, but also composed music and created art. Her books include *Scivias, The Book of Divine Works*, and *Letters*.

Julian of Norwich

Living from 1342 to 1413 in England, Julian of Norwich celebrated the motherhood of God. In a near-death encounter, Julian experienced sixteen visions or revelations of the Divine presence. Some twenty years later, she described and discussed them in *Showings*, a book considered an example of profound English medieval writing.

factum

Within the Roman Catholic Church, there is a movement to make Julian of Norwich a Doctor of the Church. She would be the third female after Catherine of Siena and Teresa of Avila to receive recognition by the church as a pre-eminent theologian whose contributions are highly valued by the church and from whom the faithful can learn.

Marguerite Porete

Alive from 1277 to 1310 in France, Marguerite Porete was a Beguine who was burned at the stake by the church for her dangerous ideas. She might have been born in an area between France and Belgium in the south of Flanders. She wrote a book titled *The Empty Mirror*. It captured the attention of church authorities that judged her book contrary to the church's teachings. The book was publicly burned and Marguerite was officially silenced. When she did not comply, she was imprisoned in France for a year and a half while portions of her book were sent around to lawyers specializing in the canon of the church. She was found guilty of grievous doctrinal errors. Facing death by the Inquisition, she did not denounce her beliefs. She was thirty-three years old when she was burned at the stake.

Mechthild of Magdeburg

Between 1207 and 1282 in Germany, Mechthild of Magdeburg lived in a Beguignage with other Beguines or women who devoted their lives to prayer, communal living, and service to others. She composed exquisite mystical poems that offered a cosmic and symbolic vision of the union of God and soul as lovers. Mechthild is thought to have influenced the thinking of male mystic Meister Eckhart (who served at her Beguignage) and to have introduced him to the work of another German mystic, Hildegard of Bingen.

Teresa of Avila

Living from 1515 to 1582 in Spain, Teresa of Avila was a discalced (barefoot) Carmelite nun. She was known as an ecstatic mystic. She founded seventeen monasteries for women. She spoke of her soul in rapture with God's love. Her writings address the great mysteries of God that are sometimes discovered within the self, in the depths of one's being, the center of the soul. She was a close friend of St. John of the Cross. Her writings include *The Way of Perfection*, *The Interior Castle*, and *Life, By Herself.* In them, she describes various stages of the mystical journey.

chapter 14

Reaction to Mary Magdalene's Vision

The Gospel of Mary says that after Peter addressed Mary Magdalene as "sister" and acknowledged that the Lord loved her more than the other disciples, he asked her to share any words that the Savior had told to her only. Mary Magdalene agreed and shared in detail a vision of Jesus that she had along with a secret teaching that Jesus gave her in the vision.

Peter Does Not Believe Mary

When Mary finished recounting her vision and the teaching, Andrew (Peter's brother) disrupts the harmony that she had restored to the grieving disciples by challenging her that the Savior would never have told such things to a woman. He says to his assembled brethren that they can believe what they want, but he thinks her ideas are strange. Peter, known for his hot temper, questioned whether the Savior would have even addressed Mary Magdalene in private without their (the men's) knowledge. He does not believe her. Yet, this same Peter acknowledged to Mary Magdalene that they all knew the Savior loved her more, that she was Jesus' favorite. Peter wonders incredulously if they are actually expected to listen to her.

factum

Mary Magdalene is the only woman besides Jesus' mother who is mentioned in all four of the canonical Gospels by name. In every instance, except one, when she is mentioned with other women present at a particular event, Mary Magdalene is listed first, suggesting her prominence.

Did Peter have a different expectation when he asked Mary to tell him something that Jesus may have told her? Perhaps he thought she'd share some simple phrase or words of comfort. Peter apparently did *not* expect such a profound and detailed teaching accompanied by her vision of Jesus. Otherwise, why did he behave in such an adversarial way? The disciples must have known that Mary Magdalene could not have had such revelation without a pure heart, calm mind, and strong spirit—the very qualities that Jesus saw in her. Yet, perhaps the very things that set her apart from them made them antagonistic toward her.

At this point in the Gospel of Mary, Mary Magdalene begins to weep. She asks Peter if he thinks she is lying about seeing Jesus and if he believes she made everything up. The Gospel seems to suggest that Mary is disconcerted about the conflict. The harmony established after she kissed and comforted them has dissipated, replaced by the angry disbelief of two men—Peter and Andrew— who proceed to accuse her of lying. What did she do to provoke them except to comply with Peter's request to share some special words of the Savior?

Levi to the Rescue

Levi (also known as Matthew, the tax collector) comes to Mary Magdalene's defense and characterizes Peter as always being angry and treating their spiritual sister as an adversary. Levi deftly argues that Jesus found her worthy, therefore, who was Peter to reject her. Levi also reminds Peter that the Savior loved Mary Magdalene more than the other disciples.

fallacy

It's a fallacy that Mary Magdalene never stood up to Peter. Peter asks her (in the Gospel of Mary) to share some of the Savior's words. She complies with his request, but he does not believe her. Mary Magdalene then boldly confronts him by asking if he's accusing her of lying.

As the scene in the Gospel of Mary continues to unfold, Levi then stops blaming Peter and suggests that everyone present ("we all") ought to feel shame. He brought them back to Jesus' commission to go forward to teach and preach. But there is ambiguity in the ending. It isn't clear who leaves to do the preaching. Karen King reveals in her book *The Gospel of Mary of Magdala, Jesus and the*

First Woman Apostle that in the Greek version of the Gospel of Mary, only Levi leaves to spread the Good News. King raises an interesting question: What did the disciples do at that point? Did they all understand Mary Magdalene's secret teaching? Did they accept it or reject it?

Why Peter Denounced Mary Magdalene

Modern scholars who have studied the Gospel of Mary and Gnostic teachings have suggested that there is much more in the subtext of this Gospel than is obvious at first. They suggest that the scene in the text portrays what was reality for Mary Magdalene. She lived in patriarchal times. Peter and Andrew were fishermen, not highly educated, and given to emotional outbursts and judgmental attitudes toward women (females, as has been previously mentioned, were below beasts of burden in the social hierarchy of the times).

symbolism

The New Testament is full of phrases and words that contain hidden meanings coded in their sums. The gematria (or sacred geometry) of the name of Mary Magdalene totals to 342, which closely links her to the Sophia (Holy Wisdom). The Gnostics were accused of using this type of numbers theology. Read more about this in *Magdalene's Lost Legacy* by Margaret Starbird.

Peter and Andrew seem to display jealousy and antagonism toward Mary Magdalene. She had accomplished something very special—the way to transcend the world of flesh and matter to enter the quiet realms of transcendental consciousness where she heard and saw Jesus. Did Peter and Andrew also have such mystical visions? Neither the canonical Gospels nor the Gospel of Mary says they did. But in the Gnostic literature, Mary Magdalene shines as an example of perfect discipleship, a visionary, a leader who was not afraid to speak up out of her love for Jesus and the work of his earthly ministry.

Spiritual Adeptness Is More Important than Gender

In the Gospel of Mary when Peter and Andrew challenge Mary Magdalene, the implication is that they cannot accept a teaching that has come from prophecy or a vision (privately revealed to only one person, especially a woman). Perhaps Peter and Andrew thought Mary Magdalene's vision and teaching were not really from Jesus but rather from the active imagining of a woman who desired more than anything to once again see the Savior she so loved. However, even they had to remember that Jesus singled out this particular woman as a spiritual adept. Her abilities for spiritual understanding and grasping complicated theological concepts exceeded those of her brethren, a point that Jesus made to all who would hear.

factum

Pope Gelasius in 494 banned the ordination of women from leadership in the church. A model existed within the earliest beginnings of Christianity of gender equality and shared power and leadership between men and women. Mary Magdalene was believed to have been a powerful leader in the Jesus movement. Other women may have served as episcopa (bishops).

Jesus had some radical ideas when it came to women, mainly that he treated them as equal to men. But to some of the male disciples, it must have been difficult to embrace the idea that a woman (the inferior gender who was often lesser-educated or uneducated) could grasp the fullness of their teacher's words let alone see him in a vision and be present with him while he enabled her to receive a mysterious teaching. The disciples appear in the Gospel of Mary as easily excitable. Mary Magdalene, however, steps in when Jesus is gone and is calm and reassuring. How could these disciples hope to grasp the idea of the kingdom of the Father God within if they couldn't settle their emotions and calm their agitated minds in order to center and focus?

Make No New Law

In the Gospel of Mary, when Jesus first appeared to Mary Magdalene (in the part of the Gospel referred to as the "Savior's Farewell"), Jesus admonishes the disciples to let no one lead them astray. He tells them that within them is the "child of true Humanity." His disciples and apostles must first find that within them, then go forth and preach. Biblical scholars mostly agree that Jesus is talking about false prophets and messiahs leading his believers astray. He seems to be saying that already inside his disciples and apostles is the kingdom of the Father/God. This resonates with the Gospel of Luke.

> *And when he was demanded of the Pharisees, when the kingdom of God should come, he answered them and said, The kingdom of God cometh not with observation: neither shall they say, Lo here! or, lo there! for, behold, the kingdom of God is within you. And he said unto his disciples, The days will come, when ye shall desire to see one of the days of the Son of man, and ye shall not see it. And they shall say to you, See here; or, see there: go not after them, nor follow them (Luke 17:20–23).*

In the Gospel of Mary, Jesus goes on to remind his disciples not to make any new law lest they themselves become bound or dominated by it.

Jesus Tempers the Law Through Interpretation

Jesus, in the New Testament accounts, says that he came not to destroy the law but to fulfill it. His ideas, though radical, did not seek to break down the Law of Moses but rather temper the interpretations of those laws written by men—interpretations that had evolved to a point of dominating the lives of people subject to the law. For example, the woman who committed adultery and was sentenced to death by stoning got a reprieve from Jesus.

> Jesus went unto the mount of Olives. And early in the morning, he came again into the temple, and all the people came unto him; and he sat down and taught them. And the scribes and Pharisees brought unto him a woman taken in adultery; and when they had set her in the midst, they said unto him, Master, this woman was taken in adultery, in the very act. Now Moses in the law commanded us, that such should be stoned: but what sayest thou? *(John 8:1–5)*

Jesus, the Gospel of John says, stooped down and wrote on the ground with his finger as if he did not hear those who were tempting him so that they could accuse him of breaking their law. But he simply said, "He that is without sin among you, let him first cast a stone at her" (John 8:7).

fallacy

It is a fallacy that the Jesus' followers knew exactly how to establish their new religion and set about doing it and building churches. The truth is that they faced the prospect of persecution and death, struggled with challenges to their beliefs from within their group and without, fought off other popular religions trying to usurp them, and faced major divisions from within their own ranks.

This story is very likely one that was inserted later into the Gospel (possibly to clarify the meaning of John 8:15 ". . . I do not judge anyone."). The story of the adulteress is missing completely from all the early Greek manuscripts. Bible experts say this story fits better (in terms of language, style, and motifs) in the Gospel of Luke than it does in the Gospel of John, however the passage has been accepted as canonical Scripture by the Roman Catholic Church.

In the early centuries after Jesus' death and resurrection, his admonition to make no new law seemed to be overlooked for many new laws were made to condemn the ideas of some Christians, whose variant views went against the more orthodox Christian positions.

Conflicting Attitudes Toward Prophecy

Irenaeus was one of the early church fathers who asserted that the apostles did not have any secret or hidden mysteries or teachings from Jesus given to them in private. Yet, Irenaeus charged those whom he thought to be heretics with creating lies and fabricating and preaching their own stories.

A major issue for the apostles and later leadership of the early Christian church was the reliability and veracity of revelations and visions that came to people calling themselves Christians. How could the apostles and those in leadership positions ascertain that the messages, teachings, words received in individual private prayers or meditations were inspired truth?

factum

Jeanne d'Arc (Joan of Arc) and Marguerite Porete were two medieval mystics burned at the stake. Twenty-five years after she was put to death, charges of heresy against Jeanne were rescinded, and she was declared a saint. Her feast day is May 30, and she is France's patron saint.

One school of thought is that the Holy Spirit activates within the individual supernatural gifts. Yet the expression of the gifts (inspired seeing, hearing, speaking, intuitive or psychic knowing, prophecy) caused many (women, in particular) through the centuries to be called witches or sorceresses or magicians and to be stoned, crucified, hanged, banished, or burned at the stake.

Gifts of the Holy Spirit

The Holy Spirit distributes and bestows "gifts" to empower Christians in their tasks as workers of the Lord. Also called charisms or charismatic gifts, these are not ordinary abilities but rather supernatural powers, and they manifest in each individual according to the will of the Holy Spirit. The Holy Spirit is the third being of the Trinity (and is also called the Holy Ghost). Paul states in his first letter to the Corinthians (12:4–10) that, although they come from the same Holy Spirit, the gifts are exceedingly diverse and include knowledge, faith, and words of wisdom along with the ability to heal, work miracles, prophecy, speak in tongues (*glossolalia*), and interpret the meaning of words spoken in tongues.

discussion question

What is Pentecost?
Originally a grain harvest festival in Old Testament times and also known as Feast of Weeks (Deuteronomy 16:10), Pentecost in the New Testament refers to the day of the outpouring of the Holy Spirit upon the apostles, completing them with gifts (signs and supernatural abilities) to aid them as teachers and preachers of Jesus' message of salvation.

Who knows what transformation might have come over Mary Magdalene when the Holy Spirit descended upon her to empower or transform her to do the Lord's work. The canonical Gospels reveal nothing about how the Holy Spirit worked through Mary Magdalene. However, Gnostic texts (deemed heretical by the church and therefore excluded from the approved canon) reveal that she was a spiritual adept, a prophetess who had visions, and a powerful and effective communicator for the messages of Jesus.

Paul's Vision Yields Apostolic Authority

Paul, whose letters constitute the earliest texts of Christianity, never met the earthly human Jesus. Before his conversion, Paul, known as the Pharisee Saul, sought to threaten and slaughter Jesus' disciples. However, on the way to Damascus, a bright light from heaven shone on Saul. He fell to the earth and heard a voice.

> *Saul, Saul, why persecutest thou me? And he said, Who are thou, Lord? And the Lord said, I am Jesus whom thou persecutest: it is hard for thee to kick against the pricks. And he trembling and astonished said, Lord what wilt thou have me to do? And the Lord said unto him, Arise and go into the city, and it shall be told to thee what thou must do* **(Acts 9:4–6).**

Saul was blinded for three days until Ananias (whom Jesus told in a vision to go to Saul) called for him. When Ananias put his hands on Saul's shoulders and told him that Jesus had sent him, Saul regained his vision and was baptized in the Holy Spirit.

Saul became Paul. He, who once spoke vehemently against Jesus and his followers, spoke boldly in favor of them after his conversion. The time came, however, when Paul claimed and defended his right and authority as an apostle. In his second letter to the Corinthians, Paul claims that his visions are his apostolic credentials.

Paul had a vision of Jesus and claimed apostolic authority based on it. Peter and the other disciples accepted him as apostle to the Gentiles. Mary Magdalene had a vision of Jesus and was rebuked by Peter who doubted her truthfulness and the veracity of her vision and the secret teaching. Clearly, there had to be some subjectivity in deciding which visions were legitimate and which weren't. Feminist theologians suggest that since the early Christian orthodoxy established their authority upon apostolic succession, the Gospel of Mary would fall into the realm of heresy, since the gospel itself questions apostolic authority's validity.

Founding the Church on Peter

Another instance of Mary Magdalene's not being believed is found in the Gospel of Luke 24:10. Mary Magdalene and some of the women went to the tomb and found the stone rolled back. They did not find the body of Jesus. They saw two men standing nearby in shining garments.

> *Why seek ye the living among the dead? He is not here, but is risen: remember how he spake unto you when he was yet in Galilee, saying, The Son of man must be delivered into the hands of sinful men, and be crucified, and the third day rise again. And they remembered his words, and returned from the sepulchre, and told all these things unto the eleven, and to all the rest. It was Mary Magdalene, and Joanna, and Mary the mother of James, and other women that were with them, which told these things unto the apostles. And their words seemed to them as idle tales, and they believed them not (24:5–11).*

The Gospel goes on to say that Peter ran to the tomb, looked into it, and saw the linen clothes lying there. He left "wondering in himself at that which was come to pass" (Luke 24:12).

Both the Gospel of Mary and the Gospel of Luke reveal a tenuous relationship between Mary Magdalene and Peter. He didn't seem to put much value in anything she said. Some sources say that Peter was patriarchal in his thinking. In his world, women could not be trusted to be legal witnesses and men didn't put much value in their "tales." He neither believed Mary Magdalene when she reported the tomb empty nor when she had a secret teaching and vision of the Savior. It may have been difficult for him to respect and value her spiritual and leadership abilities, as Jesus did. She may have been

219

too bright, too spiritual, too calm, and too close to Jesus for Peter to feel comfortable. Still they both found their own ways to continue the Lord's work through the rest of their lives. Peter became a pillar of the Jerusalem church and community. As previously mentioned, Mary Magdalene left Palestine.

chapter 15

Mary Magdalene Shines in Other Gnostic Texts

ary Magdalene stars in the Gospel of Mary, but she is also mentioned in other Gnostic texts, including the Pistis Sophia, the Dialogue of the Savior, the Apocalypse of James, and the Sophia of Jesus Christ. Her name appears as Maria, Mariaham, Mariam, Mariamne, and Mariamme. Jesus calls her "blessed beyond all women upon earth," "All-blessed Pleroma, who will be blessed among all generations," and "she whose heart straineth toward the Kingdom of Heaven more than all her brothers."

Mary Magdalene in the Inner Circle

What roles might Mary Magdalene have filled as one included in Jesus' inner circle? People usually think of the twelve men as the ones closest to Jesus. But the modern discovery of some Gnostic texts supports the notion that the inner circle of Jesus also included women. Chief among them were his mother, Mary Magdalene, and Salome. The women served him in many ways. Jesus' mother along with Mary Magdalene and other women traveled with him, ministered to him and his followers, and financially supported his ministry.

Courage and Revelation

Mary Magdalene did not fear showing her support for Jesus, as did some of the male disciples, even under the watchful gaze of Roman authorities and at the risk of losing her life. Rather, she defiantly, with his mother, accompanied him to his death at Golgotha. A group of women that included Mary Magdalene went to the tomb to anoint his body. Mary Magdalene wept at the sepulcher on the first day of the week and was blessed to be the first eyewitness of the resurrected Jesus.

factum

The two fishermen from Capernaum—Simon Peter and his brother Andrew—as well as James and John, sons of Zebedee, were among the first to follow Jesus. The latter two were called the Sons of Thunder. John is thought by many modern Christians to be the Beloved Disciple or "the disciple whom Jesus loved."

The Gnostic texts also referred to her being present and participating with the other disciples when Jesus was teaching. The Gospel of Mary, a text despised by early Christian church fathers who dismissed it as heresy, mentioned her comforting Peter, Levi, and Andrew after Jesus left Earth and sharing with them a teaching she had received in a vision. Only Levi understands what Mary Magdalene has revealed, but Andrew and Peter do not.

Serving in Many Roles

Some say that Mary Magdalene may have been a powerful leader in the early Christian church because she was the first to see and proclaim Jesus' resurrection, she eloquently articulated Jesus' words, she was a spiritual conduit for his teaching, she saw him in her vision and received inner teachings, she was his benefactress or patroness, and thus she served many roles in his inner circle. Tradition refers to her as the Apostle to the Apostles, and few would begrudge her recognition as a model disciple.

Each disciple had his or her job to do after Jesus died, but the work brought people together with different temperaments and abilities. The conflict between Peter and Mary Magdalene may have represented a wider struggle between patriarchal male dominance and female struggle for power.

Conflict with Peter

Some writers suggest that Mary Magdalene's relationship with Peter may have been contentious because of his hot-headedness and volatility, traits for which he was well known. In some of the ancient texts, Peter appeared at times a little dense and unwilling to grasp what Jesus was saying. In the Gospel of Matthew when Jesus revealed to his disciples that he was Jesus the Christ, Peter refused to believe that Jesus would be killed and raised again on the third day.

> Then Peter took him, and began to rebuke him, saying, Be it far from thee, Lord: this shall not be unto thee. But he turned, and said unto Peter, Get thee behind me, Satan: thou art an offense unto me: for thou savorest not the things that be of God, but those that be of men (Matthew 16:22–23).

But Jesus also saw something in Peter that inspired him to call Peter Cephas, meaning "rock." In fact, Peter did become a pillar of the early church, representing the strict orthodoxy of the early church.

Beginnings of a Rift in the Movement

The contentiousness between Peter and Mary Magdalene was not evident (or noted in the Gospels) in her relationship with Jesus, his other women followers, and Levi. Rather, it seems that the source of conflict she encountered came from two men within the inner circle—Peter and his brother, Andrew, the two brothers Jesus called to be fishers of men (Matthew 4:19). They were not scholarly or well educated; they were fishermen. Yet, Jesus chose his disciples not for what they did, but for what they were to do as his representatives on Earth. All his disciples were devoted to him and probably tried to do their best to follow his examples and teaching. Still, on one end of the spectrum were Peter and Andrew (who likely represented what would later become Orthodoxy) and on the other end was Mary Magdalene, whom some scholars believe to have been well educated, calm, insightful, intellectually agile, loyal, and deeply devoted to Jesus (and possibly representing the nonorthodox among his followers).

Two Distinct Camps

The rift between Mary Magdalene and Peter may have possibly placed their followers in two camps: those who embraced Gnostic ideas (especially equality between men and women) and saw Mary Magdalene as having the apostolic authority for the Gnostic beliefs, and those who followed Peter's more orthodox thinking and patriarchal beliefs.

What scholars have learned from close examination of the canonical and Gnostic texts is that Mary Magdalene exemplified a perfect model of discipleship: she remained calm when Jesus departed, stepped up to fill the void when he left, comforted the frightened and distraught disciples, instructed them with the authority of one who understood Jesus' teachings with a superior comprehension, and took no credit for herself but gave all honor and glory to Jesus. At the same time, Peter was insightful, yet dense (Matthew 16:21–23), impulsive but also cowardly, denying that he was a follower of Jesus (Matthew 14:30, 26:69–74), and was rebuked by Jesus when he complained that Mary Magdalene took up too much time with her questions, depriving the others disciples time to ask their questions.

discussion question

Why did the Gnostics reject the God of the Old Testament?
The Demiurge, according to Gnostic belief, was identified with either the God of the Old Testament or Satan, and thus the Gnostics rejected the Old Testament, believers in the Old Testament, and Judaism.

The Ancient Story of Sophia

Mary Magdalene has been associated with Sophia, an ancient archetype of holy wisdom who brings knowledge. In the Gnostic tradition, especially Valentinian Gnosticism, followers believed in an unknowable God from whom lesser beings emanated. Together these beings or Aeons in pairs made up the wholeness of God and were known collectively as the Pleroma. Sophia (wisdom) and Christ were the lowest of these pairs. In the Byzantine liturgy of the Eastern Catholic Church today, the name of Sophia is intoned before reading passages from the Gospels.

Meaning of the Word

Though some may associate Sophia with pagan roots, the name is anchored in Christian spiritual tradition and Scriptures. According to some sources, Sophia inspired elements of Jewish, Gnostic, Christian, and pagan theologies. The word *Sophia* means "wisdom" in Greek. In fact, the term *philosophy*, first used by Pythagoras, means "lover of Sophia." Some sources say the earliest Christians (perhaps the Gnostics) equated the Divine Masculine with Jesus

225

while the Divine Feminine was Sophia. Many saw Mary Magdalene as the embodiment of Sophia. In Greek philosophy, some saw Sophia as the goddess of wisdom who, in her aspect as the creative force, formed the entire cosmos from chaos.

Gnostic Interpretation of Sophia

In the Gnostic's myth, Sophia is in a fallen state because, out of a compelling desire to know where she comes from, she illicitly creates another being known as the Demiurge (from the Greek word *demiurgos*, meaning "one who shapes"). At least one source notes that some Gnostics associated the Demiurge with Satan, and that contributed to orthodox Christians regarding the Gnostics with a great deal of suspicion. The act of illicit creation brings shame upon Sophia. She is exiled in matter as long as humans, too, are separated from the Divine. When humans attain knowledge (*gnosis*) and return to the divine state or realm, so, too, does the fallen Sophia (or what some might refer to as a lower aspect of Sophia).

Timothy Freke and Peter Gandy offer a different explanation in their book *Jesus and the Lost Goddess*. They assert that the Virgin Mary and Mary Magdalene in the Gospel accounts represent, respectively, the higher Sophia and the fallen Sophia—aspects of the same character in the Sophia myth.

Mary Magdalene as Sophia

Greek pagans searched for Sophia or holy wisdom and truth just as did the early Christians and as do modern people. Some Gnostics believed that Mary Magdalene embodied holy wisdom. In the Pistis Sophia (sometimes translated as Faith Wisdom), Jesus answers questions asked by his disciples—namely, Mary Magdalene, his mother, and Martha. Mary Magdalene asks most of the questions. The discussion covers the hierarchies of heaven that are consistent with the Gnostic teachings. Scholars date the Pistis Sophia at circa 250 to 300. A simpler version of a Sophia found at Nag Hammadi, the Sophia of Jesus Christ, features Jesus' explanation of the name Pistis. He points out that in coming down from the immortal world to the world that dies, the Son of man with Holy Wisdom revealed a magnificent androgynous light. The Gnostics referred to light as divine soul ensnared in matter. Jesus explained that the male name was Savior, Begetter of All Things and that the female was called All-Begettress Sophia, or "Pistis" as some would say.

discussion question

In the Gnostic systems, what is the role of Sophia?
Sophia represents the supreme female principle who was thought to be identical to the pagan goddess Astarte or Istar. Her other role is as the virginal goddess who falls from purity in the realm of light into darkness and thus causes this sinful, material world to come into being.

Mary Magdalene exhibits an insightful inquisitiveness in the Gospel of Thomas, whose authorship is attributed to Didymos Judas Thomas (also known as the twin). Peter wants Mary Magdalene to leave because she is a female, and females, he points out, "are not worthy of life." But Jesus, instead of telling her to go, says that he will enable her to become more male so that she might enter heaven. Jesus wasn't talking about gender but rather about her spirit (male being a metaphor for "divine," so Jesus will make her spirit resemble the Divine). In another Gnostic text, Jesus refers to Mary Magdalene as the Woman Who Knows the All. Perhaps because of her excellent grasp of the subtle nuance and meaning behind Jesus' words, she was equated with his Sophia (holy wisdom) and became a fitting spiritual conduit for his message.

Mary Magdalene and the Sacred Feminine

Some people believe that the woman in the New Testament Gospels who anointed Jesus with a costly perfume, though unnamed, was Mary Magdalene. The act itself may have been the re-enactment of the Sophian tradition of the priestess-queen preparing the priest-king for the religious ritual of sacred sacrifice. This would have been in keeping with the pre-Christian mystery tradition found in certain countries around the Mediterranean in the first century, including Greece. According to this theory, Mary Magdalene would have been serving in the capacity of the consort/Sacred Feminine to Jesus.

symbolism

> Light is a spiritual symbol that means an outpouring of divine force or presence of God. When the light turns into lightning, it means divine wrath. The most ancient image of light is the sun, symbol for knowledge, truth, and spiritual illumination. Mary Magdalene has been called Illuminatrix or Light Bearer.

Jesus Defends the Anointer

The canonical Gospels reveal that when the anointing was taking place, the woman was rebuked for her extravagance because the spikenard (ancient aromatic substance like scented oil) could have been sold for a substantial amount of money that could have benefited Jesus' ministry. Jesus protected her by telling those present: "Why trouble ye the woman? for she hath wrought a good work on me. For ye have the poor always with you; but me ye have not always. For in that she hath poured this anointment on my body, she did it for my burial" (Matthew 26:10–12).

The Questioner Outshines the Others

Several Gnostic texts, including the Gospel of Thomas and the Pistis Sophia, reveal the tension and conflict between Mary Magdalene and Peter. In the Pistis Sophia, Mary Magdalene shines as the brilliant and insightful questioner during a session when Jesus is teaching about how Sophia (divine wisdom) falls from the place of Light or holy presence of God. In that text, Mary Magdalene asks thirty-nine of the forty-six questions that are asked. This upsets the male disciples, especially Peter, who speaks out against her usurping the men's time with her questions and not letting any of them speak.

discussion question

Who were some of the early Christian women prophets?
Those who served as leaders of the church as well as visionary prophets included Mary Magdalene, Philip's daughters, the Corinthian women, Ammia, Philumene, and Perpetua (a young mother/martyr.

In the Gospel of Thomas, Mary Magdalene's inquisitive nature is again revealed with insightful questions. Peter complains that she should leave. His reason is that as a woman, she isn't worthy or deserving of life. Jesus addresses Peter's concern, but says that he will make Mary Magdalene more "male" (asexual, spiritual, divine) so that she can enter heaven. In fact, Jesus goes on to say that every woman can enter the kingdom of heaven if she makes herself "male." All are equal in spirit.

Examples Predate Christian Scripture

Some feminist theologians see a pre-Christian connection between the anointing of Jesus at Bethany with expensive perfumed spikenard and his death. Also, some assert that various of Jesus' sayings and his works were not new but drew upon records and documents of religions preceding Christianity. Orthodox Christian thinkers argue that the anointment at Bethany had no particular symbolism associated with it. Mary Magdalene used expensive spikenard, not sacred oil for the anointing. Also, there were no examples in the Old Testament of anointing before (or in anticipation of) another's death. As Jesus was careful to fulfill Scripture, it is doubtful that he would have allowed Mary Magdalene to perform a pagan religious rite upon him.

The Jewish people of the Old Testament made anointing part of an offering for a meal and called it a peace offering. They also anointed the sick. Jesus was not sick. Finally, the Old Testament sacrificial system allowed for sin offerings, but use of oil with a sin offering was forbidden. "But if he be not able to bring two turtledoves, or two young pigeons, then he that sinned shall bring for his offering the tenth part of an ephah of fine flour for a sin offering; he shall put no oil on it, neither shall he put any frankincense thereon: for it is a sin offering (Leviticus 5:11). Following this argument, conservative Christians might suggest that Mary Magdalene was simply aware that Jesus was about to face his destiny, and she felt such emotion that she wept and anointed him with perfumed oil for his pleasure.

A Sacred Marriage?

Some scholars have suggested the anointing preceded the *hieros gamos* (sacred marriage). One of the five sacraments of the Gnostics, the *hieros gamos* remains a mystery. Ideas abound as to what it entailed—perhaps it was a sacred sexual act or some sort of religious rite to accomplish a spiritual merging of the Sacred Feminine with a Sacred Masculine or Godman or king—but it is shrouded in mystery. It might have been a merging of energies within one's self. Still, there are those who hold the controversial view that Mary Magdalene and Jesus shared a sacred relationship, possibly engaging in an intimate ritual, and some even believe that perhaps they were married. However, the orthodox and the canonical Gospels do not support such radical and provocative ideas as a married Jesus and Mary Magdalene.

Missing Text

The Gospel of Philip says that Jesus kissed Mary Magdalene often on the [. . .]. The brackets indicate that a piece of the papyrus is missing and thus the word that would have been written on that piece. In their translations and commentary, scholars either leave a blank where that word should be or insert the word *lips*.

discussion question

What is a lacuna?
It is a gap in the text. The gap could be a hole or an illegible written word. In the Gospel of Philip, a lacuna exists at the word that identifies where Jesus kissed Mary Magdalene. At least once source asserts that ants damaged the manuscript during the time the text was buried in the desert.

That account goes on to say that the disciples asked Jesus why he loved Mary Magdalene more than them. Jesus, by way of explanation, asked them why did he not love them like her. Then he spoke about how a blind man and a sighted man who are both in darkness see darkness. With the coming of the light, the sighted man will see, but the blind man will remain in darkness. Some who have studied this passage suggest that Jesus loved Mary Magdalene more than the others because she could "see" what the others could not.

Jesus' Promise to Mary Magdalene

What kind of promise did Jesus make to Mary Magdalene and why? In several of the Gnostic texts, Mary Magdalene is held in much higher esteem than given her in the canonical Gospels. The Gnostics did not devalue her contributions because of her gender in the way that the patriarchal Orthodoxy did. But the Gnostics weren't particularly interested in a person's gender, particularly the female, because that would be associating that individual with sex and procreation.

The Gnostic spiritual ideal leaned toward becoming a spiritual being that was asexual or genderless. In the Gnostic view, men and women were equal in many ways, including having the ability to experience *gnosis*. Jesus, too, showed a belief in the equality of men and women to grasp his teachings. Choosing to make his first resurrection appearance to Mary Magdalene suggests her favored status.

231

The Gospel of Philip says that three women always walked with the Lord: Mary, his mother, her sister, and Mary Magdalene, his companion. That Gospel reveals that Jesus often kissed Mary Magdalene. That text suggests a close relationship between Mary Magdalene and Jesus. Some authors have asserted that she was his closest friend and confidante.

symbolism

> The Gnostic Cross (or Celtic Cross) is a circle quartered. Humans must symbolically bear this cross as they struggle to free themselves from entrapment by matter. The four points of the cross symbolize the four elements (fire, air, water, and earth) and four directions. Several Gnostic sects, particularly the medieval Cathars in France, used this symbol.

Jesus makes the supreme promise to Mary Magdalene in the Pistis Sophia when he tells her that because her heart is pure and strains toward heaven more than her brother disciples he will complete her in all the Divine mysteries. This suggests that Mary Magdalene held a special place in his heart and that he saw something in her that made her worthy to receive the spectacular blessing that he promised—that is, to complete her in all the Divine mysteries.

chapter 16

Mary Magdalene in the Gospel of John

Among the four Gospels included in the canonical New Testament, the Gospel of John is unique. It stands apart from the synoptic Gospels in a variety of ways. The conventional view is John son of Zebedee and disciple of Jesus wrote the account or was the source for it. However, some modern writers have asserted that perhaps Mary Magdalene was either the eyewitness source for this Gospel or possibly its author.

What's Different about the Fourth Gospel?

At least five characteristics differentiate the Gospel of John from the other three synoptic Gospels. First, this Gospel is simply different in character and tone. It uses a highly literary and symbolic style. It does not produce the same stories as the synoptic Gospels. Neither does it follow the same order as the other three. Close examination reveals a grasp of theology that seems to have evolved out of a different tradition—one with a fairly sophisticated and well-developed theology, not one undergoing the rigors of being birthed and refined.

factum

Both orthodox Christians and Christian Gnostics believed that God is Love. Christians believe that men and women are created in the image of God who is Love (see Catechism of the Catholic Church Article 7:1604). In the First Letter of John (written by the apostle and found in the New Testament), those who live in God live in Love and, therefore, Love lives in them.

Many scholars date it to the first century, perhaps during the decade of the 90s, and believe that more than one person wrote or edited this Gospel. In particular, the Greek style of writing in Chapter 21 is different from the remainder of the text. Scholars also assert that because of the inclusion of certain specific details the author or source for the Gospel had firsthand knowledge of the events written about and that the writing itself was sophisticated.

Peter seeing him saith to Jesus, Lord, and what shall this man do? Jesus saith unto him, If I will that he tarry till I come, what is that to thee? follow thou me. Then went this saying abroad among the brethren, that that disciple should not die: yet Jesus said not unto him, He shall not die, but, If I will that he tarry till I come, what is that to thee? (21:21–23).

The Gospel features one disciple who is variously called as "the one whom Jesus loved," "Beloved Disciple," and "the other disciple." This individual is never named yet makes a "center-stage" appearance. "Now there was leaning on Jesus' bosom, one of his disciples, whom Jesus loved " (13:23). Interestingly, Jesus refused to answer Peter's question about the exact nature of this disciple's role.

Questions about the Anonymous Beloved Disciple

The author of the Gospel of John noted that the one "whom Jesus loved," or the Beloved Disciple, remained at the cross with Mother Mary while the other disciples fled. Jesus spoke from the cross to his mother and to the one whom he loved. Who was this Beloved Disciple? As already noted, Mary Magdalene was certainly there with Mary. The Gnostic Gospels revealed that Jesus loved Mary Magdalene more than the other disciples. Perhaps this is what inspires some writers to believe that the Beloved Disciple was the disciple Jesus loved most—Mary Magdalene. Orthodox Christians, however, believe such thinking is erroneous and assert that John, son of Zebedee and a member of Jesus' inner circle, was the unnamed disciple in the Gospel of John.

The Gospel of John also states that on the first day of the week, Mary Magdalene went to the tomb while it was still dark. She found the stone that blocked the opening had been removed. She believed the Lord's body had been stolen. "Then she runneth, and cometh to Simon Peter, and to the other disciple, whom Jesus loved, and saith unto them, They have taken away the Lord out of the sepulchre and we know not where they have laid him" (20:2).

Peter and the "other disciple whom Jesus loved" ran to the tomb. The "other disciple" arrived first, looked inside, and saw the burial clothes and the napkin (which had been around Jesus' head). Then

Peter arrived and went inside. The other disciple followed Peter. The Gospel of John states that the other disciple went in, "saw, and believed." In other words, the Beloved Disciple believed that Jesus had risen. The Gospel of John says that Mary Magdalene visits the sepulcher again and sees the two angels who ask her why she is weeping. It is then that Mary Magdalene mistakes Jesus for the gardener until he speaks her name. Then she recognizes him and he tells her not to cling to him because he has not yet ascended to his Father. So Mary Magdalene in the Gospel of John is the sole eyewitness to the risen Christ. Do the four Gospels agree on who first saw the resurrected Jesus? The Gospels of Matthew, Mark, and John each state that Mary Magdalene first saw the risen Christ. Those accounts differ from Luke—the only Gospel that states that the group of women, including Mary Magdalene, went to the tomb and saw two men in dazzling white clothing who reminded them of the prophecy of the death and resurrection. The women rushed back and told the apostles, but Peter did not believe. He ran to the tomb, saw the burial clothes, and went home amazed.

discussion question

When do scholars say the Fourth Gospel was composed?
John was persecuted and banished to Patmos in the last year of Domitian's reign in 95. In 96, the emperor (before he died) stopped persecuting Christians and recalled those exiled. Scholars believe that the Gospel of John dates to circa 96 or immediately after.

Luke does not place the Beloved Disciple with Peter when he rushes to the tomb. Peter is alone. Some say the writer of the Gospel of Luke and the Acts of the Apostles (one author wrote both accounts) may have had an agenda of making certain Peter's status and power exceeded Mary Magdalene's, but others dispute this idea.

factum

Orthodox tradition equates the anonymous "disciple whom Jesus loved" with the apostle John, whose other appellations in the New Testament Gospels are John son of Zebedee, John the Revealer, Boanerges (Son of Thunder), John the Evangelist, John the Theologian, and John the Divine. He died in Ephesus and his feast day is December 27. He is the patron saint of Asia Minor.

Not only does the Gospel of John never reveal the identity of the Beloved Disciple, it also does not reveal the exact nature of the relationship between Jesus and this individual. So while there are plenty of questions and speculation about the identity of the unnamed disciple in the Gospel of John, there is no proof that that individual and Mary Magdalene are the same person.

Founder and Leader of the Johannine Community

The founder of the Johannine Community is referred to in the Gospel of John as the Beloved Disciple. The traditional thinking is that the Beloved Disciple is John son of Zebedee. A more radical and provocative concept asserts that the identity of the Beloved Disciple and the founder and leader of the Johannine Community is none other than Mary Magdalene. Ramon K. Jusino wrote an interesting Internet article presenting a strong case for ascribing the authorship of the Fourth Gospel to Mary Magdalene. He based his theory on the research of Roman Catholic scholar Raymond E. Brown, a highly respected Catholic biblical scholar who has studied the ancient Johannine Community.

Jusino argues that a basic disagreement must have resulted in a schism between the early Christian community (orthodox) and the

Christian Gnostics. According to his article, apparently both communities possessed the Gospel of John. As would be expected, in the Gnostic version, Mary Magdalene held a position of prominence whereas the orthodox version favored a patriarchal apostolic hierarchy with Peter as founder and leader. At some point, a redaction to diminish the portions referencing Mary Magdalene was necessary. The Gospel of John that appears in the New Testament today is believed to be a redacted work.

discussion question

What is a redaction?
When a text is edited or revised to correct information or position the information in a more suitable literary form or to frame a particular statement, argument, or meaning, that revision is called a redaction. The opinion of many scholars is that the Gospel of John had some redaction.

Who Wrote the Gospel of John?

A widely held view of the authorship of the Gospel of John is that John, the son of Zebedee and Salome, wrote this text. Before becoming Jesus' disciples, John and his brother, James, with their father, Zebedee, earned their living as fishermen. John, James, and Peter made up the core of Jesus' inner circle. John could be vengeful and fiery. Jesus rebuked John for asking God to rain fire upon a Samaritan village. "And when his disciples James and John saw this, they said, Lord wilt thou that we command fire to come down from heaven, and consume them, even as Elijah did? But he turned and rebuked them, and said, Ye know not what manner of spirit ye are of. For the Son of man is not come to destroy men's lives but to save them. And they went to another village" (Luke 9:54–56).

But John could also be compassionate, loving, and bold, especially after Pentecost. "Now when they saw the boldness of Peter and John, and perceived that they were unlearned and ignorant men, they marveled; and they took knowledge of them, that they had been with Jesus" (Acts 4:13). The author of the Gospel of Luke also wrote the Acts of the Apostles; this scribe made these observations about John. It is interesting that this author also makes a point of noting that those gathered around John and Peter observe that they are ignorant men.

That John might be considered ignorant or at least not highly educated has relevance to the Gospel bearing John's name. Why? This Gospel is the most theologically symbolic and sophisticated of all the Gospels in the New Testament and was written in a literary style that some biblical scholars and feminist theologians say is inconsistent with the abilities of a simple fisherman. Yet, the language style suggests that the author was a Palestinian Jew. Further, the author knew the Hellenic Greek spoken by the upper classes. Through his writing, he appears to have had personal contact with Jesus. He seems to have had eyewitness experience to most of the events he recorded. Finally, he avoids using the appellation, the apostle, and mentions of his own name.

Some believe the apostle John is also the author of the book of Revelation, the last book of the Bible. The language in the latter text is also highly symbolic, which was typical of apocalyptic literature of the first century. For many modern readers, it is difficult to understand the book of Revelation. The author refers to himself as John, one who had been exiled to the island of Patmos (because of his belief in Christianity), which was a Roman penal colony.

In Revelation, the author does not distinguish himself as John the Apostle of Jesus, yet many of the early church fathers (Justin, Irenaeus, Clement of Alexandria, Tertullian) asserted that he was. However, other church fathers (Denis of Alexandria, Eusebius of Caesarea, Cyril of Jerusalem) disputed that assumption. An alternative theory suggests that the author of Revelation might have been a disciple of the apostle John. Some modern thinkers believe that the New Testament Gospel of John and book of Revelation are too dissimilar to have been written by the same person despite some affinities in language and theology. The book of Revelation has been dated to circa 81 to 96, which puts the writing near the end of the lifetimes of the first apostles.

A final thought about the apostle John as the author of the Gospel bearing his name: The Bible also contains three Epistles of John. Critics generally agree that the same person wrote these three letters as the Gospel of John because of language, style, and the Johannine teaching that is put forth.

Did Mary Magdalene Write the Fourth Gospel?

Some modern scholars do not believe the apostle John (the fisherman) could have written this elegant and theologically sophisticated Gospel. Orthodox critics say that modern scholars disputing the Gospel's authorship are putting forth views that cannot be supported either in the Gospel's text or in the critical interpretations and explanations of its history.

symbolism

In the Fourth Gospel, Jesus is hailed as "the bridegroom." The church is his "bride." When wine and bread were consumed ceremoniously in pre-Christian pagan mystery tradition, they represented a mystical marriage between Consciousness and Psyche. Some sources say the Gnostics interpretation of the Last Supper was as a re-enactment of this mystical marriage. Jesus (Godman/Bridegroom) officiated while Mary Magdalene (the Beloved Disciple/Bride) leaned on him.

Since the nineteenth century, biblical researchers have theorized that the Gospel was written decades after some of the events that it details. Also, some believe that it was written in at least two or three stages with the last stage around the end of the first century since the last chapter deals with the death of the Beloved Disciple. John was based (as were the other Gospels) on other texts, once in existence and now lost.

At Variance with the Synoptic Gospels

Compared with the synoptic Gospels, the Gospel of John features numerous unique elements, including a focus on the mystical relationship of Jesus (as the only Son of God) to the Father more than on the work of Jesus and his role as the Son of man (so characteristic of the other three Gospels). Also, the Gospel of John follows a sequence that chronicles Jesus' ministry with special emphasis on the first miracles and the attention given to Jesus' claims of divinity.

Unique Elements

There are many elements unique to the Gospel of John, including Jesus referring to himself metaphorically seven times as "I am . . ." Also, two miracles or "signs" are signified numerically (see John 2:11, 4:54). The disciples do not believe the Beloved Disciple will die (21:23). The "disciple whom Jesus loved" states that these are things he witnessed and his testimony is known to be true (21:24).

Orthodox Versus Gnostic

Some view the synoptic Gospels more in line with orthodox Christianity as represented by Peter. Others viewing the Fourth Gospel through the lens of Gnosticism suggest that it seems to favor that early sect of Christianity rather than Christian Literalism.

Mary Magdalene may have had her own followers who believed she had the apostolic authority for a Gnostic form of Christian belief. The Gnostic Gospels portrayed her as highly intelligent and intuitive, and as a close friend and confidante of Jesus, indeed the Sophia to Jesus' Godman. For some moderns, that is enough to suggest that Mary Magdalene should be considered as possibly the writer or the eyewitness source for the Fourth Gospel.

Suggestions of Redaction

Some scholars who have critically studied the Gospel of John have theorized that more than one person wrote this Gospel. There are three reasons for this theory. First, there are some inconsistencies within the text that likely occurred from editing the manuscript and using materials to augment what was initially a shorter version. Second, the prologue may have been adapted to serve as a preface. Third, Chapter 21 features a Greek literary style that some view as different from the style found elsewhere in the work.

fallacy

It's a fallacy that the apostle John died a martyr. Under Domitian's persecution, John was immersed in boiling oil but remained unharmed. He was then banished to the island of Patmos where he is believed to have written the Revelation of Saint John the Divine. He returned to Ephesus and died a natural death, the only apostle not martyred.

Some feminist theologians have suggested that any redaction shows how Mary Magdalene's position as the pre-eminent disciple of Jesus and leader of the fledgling Christian church was edited out of the Gospels (by patristic scribes) to marginalize her presence, leadership, and power. Further, they suggest that history's winners are able to write historical accounts and exclude those that don't suit their agenda. These scholars are encouraged by the discovery of ancient sacred texts in Egypt (that were once suppressed as heresies). Scholarly examination, they say, allows for a more complete understanding of the complexity of Christian origins and allows them to construct a new narrative about the beliefs and views of the early Christians.

chapter 17

Her Place in Esoteric Christianity

I n the Gospel of Mary, Mary Magdalene comes across as a spiritual adept who possesses knowledge of esoteric teachings. She shares this knowledge with Peter and Andrew who do not grasp it. They do not believe that Jesus would have told her such things. Yet, her relationship and proximity to Jesus (who, the Gnostics believed, brought the means of salvation through mystical esoteric teachings) meant that she was in a unique position of authority to lead and teach others.

A Goddess Archetype

For some, Mary Magdalene, as a human repository of wisdom, embodied the goddess archetype. Numerous modern writers have called her the lost Christian goddess in the Gospels. As noted in Chapter 11, Mary Magdalene was associated with Sophia, the wisdom goddess of the pagans. At one time, the Jews had also worshiped Asherah, the goddess/consort of Jehovah, so the god/goddess union was not unheard of in Judaism, the religion in which Jesus and Mary Magdalene were raised.

factum

Some devout Catholics and Christians assert that there was a powerful woman in Jesus' life who served as a spiritual leader—the Blessed Virgin Mary. According to the Catholic Church, she was born without sin and represents the ultimate feminine model of piety and purity.

Some modern spiritual seekers have embraced the idea of a female consort to the Son of God, suggesting that the only figure appropriate for that role would have been Mary Magdalene. Further, they say, restoring the legitimacy of the goddess in Christianity means a return to a healthy sacred masculine/feminine balance in the religion. A sacred myth in which a female goddess shares power equally with her god/consort offers a different model to ordinary women who desire to serve—one that values them and celebrates their contributions of spiritual leadership and wisdom.

In the sacred Scriptures of many different religious traditions, wisdom is allegorized as a woman. In the Christian myth of Sophia, the goddess (Mary Magdalene) who became lost by misidentification with her body (matter) was rescued, redeemed, and restored by Christ Jesus. Literalist Christians eschewed the idea of a goddess in the Gospels as dangerous fanciful thinking. Gnostic ideas of the god/goddess, sacred masculine/feminine, and its mystery traditions were denounced as heretical. The patriarchs of early Christianity advocated destroying texts promoting such radical ideas.

symbolism

In the Hebrew's theology, Shekinah was the presence of God (or a symbol of the presence such as an emanation) upon Earth. Sometimes allegorized as female, Shekinah represents the light of God, his word, or Holy Spirit that comes down into his representatives (priests). They, in turn, serve as oracles of the Word.

Supporters of Mary Magdalene say that by the third and fourth centuries, male church leaders suppressed the discipleship and strong leadership of women as they moved out of private house-churches (where they had led small groups in prayer and lessons, and it was considered appropriate for them to do so) into public buildings and forums (where their presence and power butted up against prevailing norms of societal behavior for women). In public, women teaching and preaching was considered shameful; yet, scholars say they are able to discern from certain texts that women held ecclesiastical positions immediately following Jesus' death that they were to unable to hold in later centuries. As already mentioned, the Gnostics venerated Mary Magdalene, and women as well as men held leadership positions in their sects.

Heavenly Mother

From Literalist Christian beliefs, it was a radical departure to goddess mythology and Mary Magdalene representing Sophia (wisdom, God's spouse) as did the Old Testament goddesses Asherah and Shekinah. Mary Magdalene's path to the Divine was a direct personal relationship with the God/Goddess through gnosis rather than through the Savior, priests, or other intermediaries.

factum

Asherah, revered as the household goddess of the Canaanites (ancient Palestinians) and Hebrews, was also known by other names and titles, including Astoreth, Ashratum, Atharath, and Eliat, as well as "Queen of Heaven." Altars dedicated to her have been unearthed in ancient kitchens. King Solomon, according to some sources, worshiped her.

Some modern writers assert that Mary Magdalene was the "bad girl" counterpart to the Blessed Virgin Mary as the "good girl." Some of the more esoteric spiritual seekers suggest that these two archetype figures (good girl, bad girl) represent a splitting of the goddess into two aspects: the Heavenly Mother and the redeemed penitent prostitute. Of course, now it is widely known Mary Magdalene was never a prostitute.

Timothy Freke and Peter Gandy, in their book *Jesus and the Lost Goddess, The Secret Teachings of the Original Christians*, wrote that when Jesus was about to die on the cross, he united the two aspects of the goddess when he united the two Marys as mother and daughter. Of course, you have to believe first that Mary Magdalene was the Beloved Disciple at the foot of the cross with Mary and that the pronoun in the scriptural passage was originally "she" and not "he." This is the way the passage reads in the King James Version of the Gospel of John.

Now there stood by the cross of Jesus his mother, and his mother's sister, Mary the wife of Cleophas, and Mary Magdalene. When Jesus therefore saw his mother, and the disciple standing by, whom he loved, he saith unto his mother, Woman behold thy son! Then saith he to the disciple, Behold thy mother! And from that hour that disciple took her unto his own home (19:25–27).

Most Christians believe that the words "behold thy son!" make the meaning obvious and that there is no confusion about gender. For them, the scriptural passage could not be clearer. And yet, the idea that Mary Magdalene could have been the Beloved Disciple is titillating, controversial, and sparks the imagination of those who believe she was much more to Jesus than a loyal and devoted follower.

Vesica Piscis—Sacred Feminine

Imagine two circles of the same diameter with half of one overlapping the other. The elliptical shape produced in the area where the overlap occurs is the shape of an almond standing upright on end. This is the shape of a vesica piscis (literally meaning, "bladder of a fish"). If you search for this term in the dictionary, you will discover it is a figure used in fine art. It was also called a mandorla, and early Christians placed the image of Christ inside.

Gematria or sacred geometry, mentioned in Chapter 10, links Mary Magdalene not only with holy wisdom but also with the *vesica piscis*. Its ratio designation is 265/153, according to Margaret Starbird writing in *Magdalene's Lost Legacy, Symbolic Numbers and the Sacred Union in Christianity* (page 140). Starbird explains in her book that the Greeks, not possessing a square root symbol, used "whole-number ratios" to designate irrational numbers so that the ratio for *vesica piscis* is 265/153.

To Christians, the Ichthys (fish) represents Jesus. The *vesica piscis*, an important symbol in the ancient world, symbolizes the doorway of life, the yoni, the Earth Goddess, the Sacred Feminine. One could associate Jesus with the fish and Mary Magdalene with the *vesica piscis* (bladder or vessel of the fish). Mary Magdalene was Jesus' complement or vessel (to hold and pour forth his teachings). One might take this kind of thinking one step further to the ancient rite of *hieros gamos* between Jesus, the Son of God, and

Mary Magdalene, the Sacred Feminine. If there were a child of their union, as conjectured in the bestselling novel *The Da Vinci Code*, Mary Magdalene would then be the Holy Grail, the vessel that held the blood of Jesus. Such thinking is clearly at odds with orthodox Christianity and its Scriptures, yet it fires the imagination of those who believe that the whole story about Mary Magdalene has been suppressed and perhaps is yet to be revealed.

factum

In the Gospel of John (21:3–11), the risen Jesus makes an appearance to the disciples while they are fishing. They had fished all night and caught nothing. Jesus stood on the shore and instructed them to cast the net to the right side of the boat whereupon they hauled in a net full of fish. How many? Exactly 153.

Magdalene in Other Doctrines

Those who want to re-establish the Goddess/Sacred Feminine in Judaism and Christianity might appreciate learning about the link between Mary Magdalene and the goddesses in ancient Judaism. The cults of those goddesses had been obscured by Mary Magdalene's lifetime; although in many pagan polytheistic religions some goddess cults (Isis, for one) were still around.

Although first-century Palestinians may have been exposed to Greco-Roman beliefs and religious practices, Jewish men did not want a goddess within their religion nor a woman upstaging them in real life. Orthodox Jewish men during Mary Magdalene's time did not allow women to participate in their religious discussions. Perhaps they viewed women as somehow compromising the holiness of the temple as well as their devotions and discourses. Yet evidence exists in the form of tablets from the fourteenth century

B.C. that Yahweh had a wife/consort in Asherah, the fertility goddess. Lynn Picknett, in her book *Mary Magdalene*, mentions the discovery of those tablets along with the fact that the identities of Asherah and Astarte (another, perhaps more famous, goddess) were interchangeable. The worship of Yahweh was closely associated with the cult of Asherah. As zealous Yahweh worshipers destroyed the pagan shrines, heretics continued to try to revive goddess worship. Later, the goddess re-emerged in Judaism as the Shekhina, the emanation of God on Earth. Initially Shekhina was female and served as God's wisdom, somewhat akin to the Greek Sophia or Holy Wisdom that is associated with Mary Magdalene.

symbolism

Ichthys is the Greek word for fish. As early as the second century, church fathers called Jesus the "Fish." The term derives from using the first letters of the Greek words in the phrase "Jesus Christ, Son of God, [our] Savior." The resulting acronym is Ichthys. From catacomb art to modern church materials, the symbol of the fish is understood to represent Christ.

The Mystery Traditions and Magdalene's Role

Throughout history, practitioners and teachers in the mystery traditions have preserved esoteric knowledge and the means for achieving it. They have passed on inner teachings, rituals, initiation rites, and metaphysical training from one generation to the next, often in secret.

In the first century, some of the Roman mystery traditions had initiations into more than a half-dozen levels of spiritual knowledge. From ancient Sumerian fertility cults to New Age spiritual seekers, certain groups have always had mystery traditions. Examples include the Freemasons, Hermetic Orders of the Golden Dawn, the goddess traditions, shamanism, the Greek Eleusinian and Orphic schools, the Egyptian Hermeticists (Isis and Osiris cults), the Celtic Orders, the Knights Templar, Jewish mystics working with the Kabbalah, and the Essenes and Gnostic Christians.

discussion question

What is the *hieros gamos* ritual?
This was a religious rite performed by members of ancient fertility cults. Two people—a priestess and a male "king" were joined in sacred marriage to symbolize the rebirth of the land. The king would be anointed before being ceremoniously and symbolically "slain." In the Gnostic tradition, the priestess represents the soul and the king signifies God in the union of the two.

The Gnostics taught their initiates that they must pass through one level in order to ascend to the next. The Gnostics believed that there were seven heavens ruled by archons (rulers), whose forces kept humans ensnared in the world of matter. They evidently believed that Mary Magdalene had transcended the lower levels to the highest—she "understood perfectly" and was the woman "who knew the All"—and, with Jesus as her teacher, had attained the state of enlightenment.

The pre-Christian mystery traditions of Greece, ancient Egypt, and lands around the Mediterranean included a practice of a priestess-queen anointing a priest-king for a symbolic mythical sacred sacrifice. Some modern writers suggest that Mary Magdalene's role may have been to re-enact this ancient rite with Jesus in keeping with a pre-Christian pagan tradition. One theory suggests Mary Magdalene served in the cult of Isis, perhaps in the role of priestess or as an initiatrix into the obscure practice of *hieros gamos*. This obscure ritual (which may or may not have been sexual) was performed in ancient fertility cultures around the Mediterranean and throughout Mesopotamia.

factum

The Egyptian Hermeticists, followers of the mythological god Hermes, were spiritual relatives of the Gnostics. While the Hermeticists believed that salvation came through the initiation and teachings derived from Hermes, the Gnostics embraced the Savior Jesus and his teachings. Gnosis or inner truth and knowledge was crucial to both groups.

However, the idea that Mary Magdalene could ever be associated with sexual acts outside marriage, sacred or otherwise, is offensive to many Christians who revere her as a saint and the holy companion, confidante, and devoted follower of Jesus. Still, speculation swirls around this theory even though the church and scholars have declared that Mary Magdalene was never a prostitute.

Esoteric References in the Apocrypha

There are individuals with esoteric inclinations, such as New Age practitioners, who have theorized that Mary Magdalene possessed knowledge of the deeper mystery of the *hieros gamos* and the Sacred Feminine. They believe that there are hints of it in the canonized scriptures as well as in the apocryphal literature.

Of the apocryphal literature, the Gnostic texts, in particular, do not shy away from such references. The Gospel of Philip alludes to Mary Magdalene being Jesus' consort, one whom He loved (and surely taught) above all others. The term *bridal chamber* was one of the sacred rites of the Gnostics and connotes the *hieros gamos* or mystical union of the Sacred Masculine and Sacred Feminine. When there is a split between these two, there is a fall from Divine

Grace into cosmic ignorance. In the Gnostic text, the Pistis Sophia (Faith Wisdom), Mary Magdalene shines as the primary questioner of Jesus, serving as a kind of divine muse who draws out secret knowledge from the Son of God.

discussion question

What is the apocryphal literature?
The Apocrypha designates a collection of texts not included in the canon of Scripture. The term apocrypha literally means, "hidden things." Interestingly, early usage of the word meant roughly the same as esoterikos, or writings not intended for the masses but rather for a select inner circle of believers who alone were capable of understanding them.

Depending on the orientation of the school or tradition of esoteric thought, Mary Magdalene served Jesus and humankind through her deeper knowledge of divine mysteries. And as some of those organizations of mystery traditions survive even today, there are people who are learning teachings that may have been conferred by Mary Magdalene to those in her innermost circle. In this way, teachings survive from one generation to the next.

III

Mary Magdalene
in Modern Times

chapter 18

Mary Magdalene
Through Artists' Eyes

Mary Magdalene has inspired artists for centuries. Whether portrayed as the archetypal fallen woman, the weeping penitent sinner, the distraught and vulnerable devotee of Christ, the voluptuous and seductive temptress, or the contemplative, whose ankle-length tresses hide her nakedness, Mary Magdalene has unquestionably stoked the fires of artistic imagination. From ancient iconography to modern magical realism, her images seem to evoke strong feelings and resonance for the creator and viewer alike.

Early Portrayals and Icons of the Magdalene

One of the earliest surviving images of Mary Magdalene is a fresco that dates to circa 240. It was found in 1929 in a house-church in Dura-Europos, located along the west bank of the Euphrates River in Syria. The image is of three women. Each woman carries a container of myrrh and a lighted torch and walks toward a sarcophagus.

discussion question

What is an ampulla?
In ancient catacombs where Christians were buried, fragments of vessels (ampulla) have been recovered. Of particular interest to archaeologists are the vessels containing a dark red color. One theory is that the material is the blood of the martyr to whom the object belonged or from whom the vessel was obtained. The ampulla often bore the image of that person.

Susan Haskins, in *Mary Magdalen, Myth and Metaphor*, describes the work and its significance in detail. In fact, Haskins discusses the portrayals of Mary Magdalene in the world of art throughout her work. Another early image she mentions is of Mary Magdalene with the other Mary at Jesus' empty tomb meeting the angel. That image was found on an ampulla dating from sometime in the sixth century.

Nurith Kenaan-Kedar, in her writing about the images of women in early Christian art, noted that in the early church period, images of saintly women show the women in despair, love, or ecstasy. She mentions specifically three ivory panels that date to the fourth and fifth centuries. In each of them, Mary Magdalene's image is meditative and her gestures are stylized. The author suggests that the panels' creators relied upon earlier Hellenistic pictorial traditions.

Before the Middle Ages, the iconography of Mary Magdalene was as the archetypal penitent saint, preacher/teacher/evangelist, and first witness to the Resurrection—often in the *Noli Me Tangere* (touch me not) scenes that included Jesus. During the Middle Ages (and also the Renaissance period), her image transformed to reflect theological shifts and popular culture.

symbolism

Angels lifting Mary Magdalene symbolizes divine protection and guardianship. The image of angels also carries with it the connotation that they are messengers. For Mary Magdalene to be lifted suggests that she is leaving behind the world of matter for higher celestial realms where she can commune with the Divine.

Artist Renderings During the Middle Ages

The period that extends from roughly the fifth century until about 1350 and perhaps even a century later is known as the Middle Ages. During this time between classical antiquity and the Renaissance, the image of Mary Magdalene was captured and venerated in many art forms and renderings. Mary Magdalene's popularity as the archetypal fallen woman and the spiritual icon remained strong from the twelfth to the sixteenth centuries, especially in the Low Countries, France, Italy, Germany, and Spain.

Gothic Art

The Gothic style prevailed from 1201 through 1300 (part of the High Middle Ages). The eleventh and twelfth centuries, in particular, were one of the bleakest periods in history because of the Crusades, followed shortly by the Inquisition. The world needed light bringers like Mary Magdalene who was highly revered and a popular icon of piety.

Manuscript illumination was a type of Gothic art in which the pictures and decoration around the text unified the entire composition. The Paris school was center of Gothic painting for nearly two centuries. Stained glass and tapestry work evolved into high art. Fresco painting was another popular expression of Gothic art. Frescoes were not yet done on a monumental scale, except in Italy where buildings still had massive walls; towering skeletal structures of Gothic buildings and cathedrals became the style elsewhere in the world.

Evidence exists of medieval frescoes in old English churches. On the wall of a parish church in Great Tew in Oxfordshire, England, are a series of paintings depicting the Passion of Christ. Painted in about 1290, they are arranged in strips and tiers. Among them is an image of the risen Jesus holding the Resurrection Banner and standing before a kneeling, reverent Mary Magdalene.

factum

Fresco paintings are made on moist lime plaster surfaces using colors that have been mixed or ground into water or a mixture of lime and water. Since the fresco technique can be used on tombs and walls, many old European churches have fresco paintings adorning their interiors and exteriors. Fresco painting has been around for centuries.

Giotto's Work

The image of Mary Magdalene being fed a single holy Eucharist wafer each day while being lifted into the air by angels (as claimed by at least one French legend) was a favorite for medieval artists such as Giotto (1267–1337). In the 1320s, he painted an image of her kneeling and being transported upward by angels.

People suffering from the scourges of the Middle Ages such as pestilence, war, and the plague may have drawn an uplifting and inspirational message from Giotto's fresco *Nolo Me Tangere*. Since Mary Magdalene had suffered terribly and had been spiritually reborn in Christ, people saw her as an icon of hope. Another work Giotto created during that period—*Voyage to Marseille*—features Mary Magdalene and her traveling companions on the way to Gaul. This fresco and many others adorn the walls of the Magdalen Chapel in the Church of San Francesco, Assisi, Italy.

Renaissance Depictions of Mary Magdalene

The Renaissance era lasted from the fourteenth to the seventeenth centuries and represented a new flowering of spiritual and artistic ideas throughout Europe. The art world experienced a tremendous vitality and revival. Some of the Renaissance's greatest artists chose Mary Magdalene as their subject. The Flemish artist Rogier van der Weyden produced several paintings of Mary Magdalene between 1435 and 1450. In the Penitent Magdalene, he depicted Mary Magdalene reading a book. This was an uncommon occurrence for medieval women. Some sources say he may have been influenced by the Beguines, a movement of spiritually minded Christian women, who advocated the literacy of women.

discussion question

Is Mary Magdalene present in Leonardo da Vinci's painting of *The Last Supper*?
John, the Beloved Disciple, appears particularly effeminate in that painting, perhaps suggesting that this disciple isn't a man but rather a woman. One can make out the letter M from Jesus' and John's body positions. Perhaps Leonardo was suggesting the symbolic presence and importance of Mary Magdalene.

An English church painting that dates to around 1400 found in Little Witchingham, Norfork, is similar to the house-church work found in Dura-Europos in 1929. It, too, is made up of a series of scenes depicting Christ's Passion, arranged in tiers. One is of Jesus' resurrection appearance to Mary Magdalene.

Albrecht Durer, like Giotto before him, was enchanted with the contemplative Mary Magdalene. In 1504 or 1505, he immortalized her in a woodcut titled *Mary Magdalene Taken Up into the Air.*

Renaissance painters moved away from the dark colors and the stylized Gothic style into somewhat brighter palettes. Also, the Renaissance painters increasingly painted eroticized images of Mary Magdalene.

symbolism

Mary Magdalene's nakedness symbolized the sacramental aspect of the body reborn in the spirit. Artists depicted her with little or no clothing to suggest that she had transcended her own physicality to become a spiritual being who communed with the Divine. While some saw her nakedness as provocative, others understood that it was to suggest innocence, not sexuality.

Titian's painting, *Penitent Magdalene* (circa 1565), features Mary Magdalene with her hand resting on her partially exposed bosom and her eyes turn toward heaven. Rubens, in his painting *Christ at Simon the Pharisee,* portrayed Mary Magdalene as a woman kneeling, her honey-colored tresses tumbling suggestively over a bare shoulder and back. Botticelli's painting, *Magdalene at the Foot of the Cross,* depicts a repentant Magdalene draped in a cloak of red to symbolize, perhaps, carnal passion subdued as she is prostrated at the base of the cross. In *Christ in the House of Mary and Martha,* a painting by Tintoretto, Mary Magdalene's hair is concealed yet she appears stunningly covered in an opulent blue garment. In fact, Jesus and she are both thusly covered. Was the artist suggesting that the two had covered themselves with the same cloth of sacred belief since the color blue symbolizes truth, spiritual life, eternity, devotion, and faith?

The Renaissance painters seemed to focus mainly on images of Mary Magdalene as the first witness to the Resurrection or as the nude contemplative. Rembrandt, too, found Mary Magdalene an irresistible subject for in A.D. 1651 he masterfully painted her in *The Risen Christ Appearing to Mary Magdalene.*

Nineteenth-Century Symbol of Eros

During and after the Reformation, artists began to portray Mary Magdalene, not as the first witness or the deeply spiritual contemplative, but rather as the lover and sinner as portrayed in the Gospel of Luke. That text tells the story of the anointing at Bethany in which Jesus has been invited to dinner at the home of Simon, the Pharisee.

> *And, behold, a woman in the city, which was a sinner, when she knew that Jesus sat at meat in the Pharisee's house, brought an alabaster box of ointment, and stood at his feet behind him weeping, and began to wash his feet with tears, and did wipe them with the hairs of her head and kissed his feet, and anointed them with the ointment. Now when the Pharisee which had bidden him saw it, he spake within himself, saying, This man, if he were a prophet would have known who and what manner of woman this is that toucheth him: for she is a sinner (7:37–39).*

Even while Simon was judging the actions of the woman, Jesus defended her.

> *And he turned to the woman, and said unto Simon, Seest thou this woman? I entered into thine house, thou gavest me no water for my feet: but she hath washed my feet with tears, and wiped them with the hairs of her head. Thou gavest me no kiss: but this woman since the time I came hath not ceased to kiss my feet. My head with oil thou didst not anoint: but this woman hath anointed my feet*

with ointment. Wherefore I say to thee, Her sins, which are many, are forgiven: for she loved much: but to whom little is forgiven, the same loveth little (7:44-47).

Nineteenth- and twentieth-century artists' works reflected this archetype of the "woman who loved much." The pre-Raphaelite painter Dante Gabriel Rossetti, obsessed with the beauty of the female face and form, was one such artist. In 1858, he portrayed a beautiful Mary Magdalene as the woman longing to see Jesus in his *Mary Magdalene at the Door of Simon the Pharisee.* In the composition, Mary Magdalene arrives at the door of the home of Simon. She knows Jesus is inside the house. She casts flowers from her hair while her lover and a woman from her procession try to turn Mary Magdalene away from the door at Simon's house. Jesus waits for her approach. This painting was clearly about the conversion of Mary Magdalene, and the artist portrayed her as a fallen woman soon to repent and become Jesus' follower.

Antonio Canova, apparently finding inspiration also in the sinner, sculpted an image of a woman kneeling with open palms and head bowed which suggests a supplicant seeking forgiveness in his marble sculpture of the *Repentant Mary Magdalene,* now housed in the Hermitage Museum in St. Petersburg. Henryk Siemiradzki was another nineteenth-century artist who worked with the repentant sinner image of Mary Magdalene in *Christ and Sinner: First Meeting of Christ and Mary Magdalene,* painted in 1873, now housed in the Russian Museum of St. Petersburg.

Jules-Joseph Lefebvre, in his *Mary Magdalen in the Grotto,* depicted a sensuous, supine, nude Mary Magdalene. Her thick red hair is splayed wildly over the rock upon which she lies. Flowers are strewn about her feet. Mary Magdalene seems to be an exquisite example of womanhood who is unaware of the power of her own flesh, so absorbed is she in the world beyond the mind.

A Model for Twentieth-Century Artists

While organizations such as FutureChurch.org and others continue to work diligently to rectify the centuries-old false image of Mary Magdalene as the penitent prostitute, artists continue to be inspired by her dramatic personal story—her proximity, love, and devotion to Christ and her power to endure and lead. The brilliant Spaniard Pablo Picasso depicted her as a weeping woman, the maudlin archetype *Weeper*, but more recently, artists have moved away from such images, returning to the art of the icon. Such artists include Sister Mary Charles McGough in her piece *Mary Magdalene Announces the Resurrection* and Sister Marie-Paul Farran in *The Risen Christ and Mary Magdalene*.

discussion question

Which icons are often found in paintings of Mary Magdalene?
The jar in which she carried her perfumed oil or spikenard was Mary Magdalene's primary possession. In some paintings, the unguent jar is a work of art itself. In others, it is bulky and angular with sharp edges. Her other icons are a skull, a book, and a cave or grotto.

Ethnically True Image

Scholars say that Mary Magdalene as imagined by artists has yielded a very different image of her than what would be expected as accurately reflecting a woman from her area of the world in ancient times. Consider whether a Hebrew woman born of parents in first-century Palestine would have alabaster-white skin with long red or blond hair. Would she have exposed breasts? Hardly. And she certainly would not be wearing a shirt with lace and blousy sleeves as portrayed in at least one major work. Nor would she have a modern woman's face. An image that perhaps better matches her ethnic lineage to her time and her gene pool might better serve modern artists interested in a more accurate representation of Mary Magdalene, Jesus' beloved friend and loyal follower.

Noli Me Tangere Still Inspires

A popular image of Mary Magdalene painted by artists through the centuries is the *Noli Me Tangere* scene found in the Gospel of John 20:11–18. Giotto painted his version in the 1320s, Fra Angelico in the 1400s, Tiziano Vecellio in 1512, Correggio in 1525, Rembrandt in 1638, Alonso Cano in 1640, and Sir Edward Coley Burne-Jones in 1882.

fallacy

It's a fallacy that Mary Magdalene was always portrayed respect-fully in art. The truth is that artists have portrayed her in less-than-flattering ways. The art of Mary Magdalene runs the gamut from beautiful spiritual images to sensuously seductive and what some might judge as little more than pious pornography.

While some artists are still inspired by the images of the *Noli Me Tangere* scene revealed in the Gospels and by the repentant sinner, many other painters are returning to portrayals of Mary Magdalene as the saint icon, the woman from first-century Palestine who has served as an exemplar to women of all time and places, someone who was not afraid to stand up for truth, to lead others to the word of God, and to be a faithful disciple as well as a leader and voice for Jesus' ministry. Christians today want to see images that reflect the truth of her life and her roles in the founding of early Christianity.

chapter 19

Under the Scholars' Microscope

Many experts think that Mary Magdalene had a more intimate relationship with Jesus. They also concede that the church suppressed early Christian writings that offered a different version of New Testament events than the canonical Gospels. Popular interest in Mary Magdalene has escalated to a fever pitch thanks to the success of *The Da Vinci Code* novel and movie, but scholars, too, are taking a new interest in Mary Magdalene.

Historical Reinterpretations of Magdalene

When the Roman Catholic Church in 1969 reversed its position and its missal to correct the miscasting of Mary Magdalene as a penitent prostitute, it stopped short of doing anything further. It did not acknowledge her service in any role beyond eyewitness to the Resurrection and messenger to the apostles. What the church accomplished was separation of the identity of Mary Magdalene from Mary of Bethany and the sinner of Luke 7:37–38 who anointed Jesus' feet at the dinner party. This, subsequently, aligned the Western Church of Rome with the Eastern Orthodox Church that has always adhered to the belief that there were three separate Marys.

discussion question

Why does the Catholic Church still refuse the ordination of women?
The catechism (teaching and rules) of the Catholic Church (revised in accordance with the official Latin Text and promulgated by Pope John Paul II), states that Lord Jesus himself chose men for the Twelve Apostles. The church is bound by the choice of the Lord, states the catechism, until he returns.

While scholars are reinterpreting Mary Magdalene's role in the birth of Christianity, some believe that the early church in later centuries oppressed women who may have been following the tradition already established by Mary Magdalene and others who had previously served as deaconesses and priestesses. If that were the case, the suppression of Mary Magdalene as a leader may have been a deliberate attempt by church fathers to exclude women of their own time from serving in such roles. When Pope Gregory I cast Mary Magdalene as a prostitute, his action tarnished her reputation. When church fathers persisted in using the penitent prostitute image as a powerful example of the forgiving nature of the church, it fostered a tradition of suppressing women. Rather than becoming powerful exemplars, women were expected to be pious, virtuous, and submissive.

The Magdalene and Unwed Mothers

The image of Mary Magdalene as a harlot made her the most likely candidate for the symbol of repentance from temptation and vanity. Although scholars have never found evidence to support the contention that Mary Magdalene was unchaste, her name was invoked for the Irish asylums that took in wayward women who had given birth to children out of wedlock or who had left abusive husbands. Catholic nuns of various orders ran the asylums.

From the 1800s to more recent times, thousands of unfortunate women became virtual prisoners and were used as slave labor mainly in convent laundries. However, they also cooked, cleaned, and cared for aging nuns. Admonished to hide their shame, the women were locked inside convent walls and forcibly separated from their newborns who were placed in orphanages after birth. Working under the most Spartan conditions, many died behind convent walls and were buried in unmarked graves. Ironically, they were called the "Magdalenes," the name of Jesus' pre-eminent woman disciple, the one he forgave, and loved, and taught. However, the Irish "Maggies" received no such redemption.

factum

Oxford's Magdalen College has a tower where each year the college holds ceremonies for the welcoming of spring. Mary Magdalene was from Magdala, and that place name, as pointed out in previous chapters, means "tower." Fans of C. S. Lewis and the movie *Shadowlands*, which portrayed his life, will recall images of the tower ceremonies at Magdalen College.

In 1993, when the Order of the Sisters of Charity in Dublin was about to sell back its property to the Republic of Ireland, more than a hundred unmarked graves were found in the convent cemetery. The remains belonged to women who had worked in the convent throughout their lives. When the news broke, it traveled quickly throughout the world. Families identified some of the bodies, but the others are unknown to this day. The discovery marked the close of a sad chapter in the history of the church. That Mary Magdalene's name was associated with it makes it doubly distasteful to the saint's most ardent admirers.

Feminist Theologians Have Their Say

Feminist scholars assert that Mary Magdalene shared a closer relationship with the Jesus than many people believe. Furthermore, she served as an influential leader of a branch of the early church that promoted women's leadership. These scholars believe that what happened to Mary Magdalene reflected a wider pattern of what generally occurred within the early church. Jesus gave women prominent roles. But in the early centuries, their power and authority steadily eroded due to patriarchal cultural and societal beliefs of female inferiority: Women were not as learned, as capable, or as holy.

In essence, the church fathers cast Mary Magdalene much like a second Eve, who brought disgrace upon the whole of humanity through her action in the Garden of Eden. By allowing herself to be tempted by the snake into eating an apple from the tree of knowledge and then offering a bite to Adam, she and Adam both lost their original holiness and innocence. Their action is now called the original sin. That sin was then transmitted to their descendants (according to Catholic belief) through human nature by propagation, not imitation. As a result of original sin, humans are destined to have weakened powers of human nature and to suffer pain, ignorance, and death.

Mary Magdalene, like Eve, sought knowledge, and she paid a high price for it. In many ways, women still suffer as did their ancient spiritual sisters, Eve and Mary Magdalene, who hungered for knowledge. Some feminist theologians say that what happened to Mary Magdalene is indicative of the fate of women in the early Christian Church and that diminished leadership roles for women still exists in modern churches. They see her as a strong and wise woman who enjoyed a close, personal relationship with Jesus.

fallacy

It's inaccurate to think of Christian women as having an easy time in the first few centuries of early Christianity. The reality is that Christian women, just like the men, were put into arenas to be attacked and torn to pieces by beasts. Regardless of their gender, they were tortured and persecuted for their beliefs.

What Some Progressive Catholics Think

Many modern progressive Catholics believe that the ongoing shortages in the clergy and the increasing numbers of women lay leaders (particularly in U.S. churches) will reach a critical mass and put pressure on the Vatican to ordain women. Although some women hope that change will come from within the highest levels of dioceses and Catholic colleges, others suggest that change will come only from the grassroots level and will only happen when the pressure builds to a level that the Vatican can no longer ignore. Still others complain that the papacy of the last two-dozen years (one that has refused to consider the idea of women in the priesthood) will not likely change its position.

FutureChurch Envisions Change

FutureChurch, an organization that works for reform within the Catholic Church, has been working hard to repair damage done to Mary Magdalene's miscasting as a prostitute. The organization provides information to those who seek the truth about Mary Magdalene as well as historical accuracy about the practices of the early church. FutureChurch, on its Web site, has proposed three solutions to solve the problem of a worldwide priest shortage. The three solutions are to get rid of the celibacy requirement for priesthood, to permit the return of those men who left the priesthood and married, and to allow qualified women to enter the diaconate. The three possibilities seem like new ideas but were a reality in the infant church.

Male Gender, Status, and Power

Catholic teachings emphasize that Scripture not only contains the Word of God, but it was also inspired by the Word of God. Further, God is the author of the Scriptures because he inspired the human authors. The human authors of the canonical Scripture of the Old and New Testaments were all men. There is no woman author visible in the New Testament writings and texts. Does this mean that women were left out of the Scriptures by male writers who were educated (when women were not) and had the benefit of religious discourse (that women did not have) and were made holy by their participation in the temple (where women could not participate in the same way as men did)? Jesus taught women equally with men, and women were mentioned in both the Old and New Testaments. But until the discovery in 1896 that a "woman's gospel" existed—the Gospel of Mary Magdalene—in which a woman revealed her visionary experience was not part of any official biblical record.

Today, orthodox writers accuse forward-thinking feminist theologians of trying to reinterpret history and base their reinterpretation upon texts such as the Gospel of Mary and others found in Egypt. The Gospel of Mary Magdalene reveals a vision experienced by Jesus' foremost female disciple and shows the tensions that existed between leaders such as Peter and Andrew, who discounted and denounced the visions of those whose views and visions might be at variance with theirs. In the Gospel of Mary, they did not believe the Savior would have given such a teaching to a woman, especially without men present.

Strife and Conflict in the Early Church

Visions and revelations were at the very heart of the Christian movement. Without them, some scholars assert, the religion would not have begun. By the end of the first century and beginning of the second, the fledgling Christian communities continued to experience internal and external conflict over this issue. An early church father Irenaeus, in the second century, complained harshly against new converts and believers for their false prophecies, calling them frauds. But he struggled with how to differentiate between revelations and visions truly inspired by the outpouring of the Holy Spirit and those that seemed to be nonsense. It was in part because of the tales of miracles and the "gifts" of the Holy Spirit that people were attracted to Christianity. Certain early Christians believed that prophecy and vision were important gifts. Following the Resurrection, the risen Jesus had remained with his disciples for forty days, during which time the Holy Spirit blessed them with gifts of tongues, healing, preaching, understanding, and visions. Other noted that after Jesus' forty days on Earth had passed, so too did the gifts of the Holy Spirit. Some leaders in the early church encouraged visions while others did not.

fallacy

It is a fallacy that the Apocrypha provides authentic details about the missing years of Jesus' life or secret information about his teachings or the Bible. Such texts—which include infancy Gospels, apocalyptical writings, Epistles, and Gnostic texts of Nag Hammadi—may simply spread the views of their ancient writers in opposition to Scriptural canon.

The apostles possessed such gifts. Could the gifts of the Holy Spirit bestowed upon the apostles be transferred to their followers?

Some Christians struggled with that issue. Others noted that ancient prophecy was fulfilled in every way by Jesus' birth, death, and resurrection and would always be available to true believers. In the second century, Irenaeus argued that the church possessed the truth and passed it from bishop to bishop. Many Christians were inclined to believe Irenaeus because he had known Polycarp, the Asia Minor bishop who had known John and the other apostles.

Irenaeus wrote to his friend Marcianus against Gnosticism saying that their belief that one needed hidden inner knowledge to save one's soul was false. The flourishing of ideas variant to the teachings of the apostles worried Irenaeus; he saw it as divisive, disruptive, and destabilizing to the new religion.

factum

Irenaeus was sent to Rome in 177. While on his trip, his bishop was martyred with numerous other Christians, including a woman slave named Blandina and her Christian mistress. Blandina was tortured and burned to death and her ashes were thrown into the Tiber River. Catholics celebrate her feast day on June 2.

Divisiveness in the Time of the Apostles

Divisiveness was one of the earliest problems the church faced. It was one of the primary issues that Paul tackled in the Corinthian church. He wrote:

Now I beseech you, brethren, by the name of our Lord Jesus Christ, that ye all speak the same thing, and that there be no divisions among you; but that ye be perfectly joined together in the same mind and in the same judgment. For it hath been declared unto me of you, my brethren, by them which are of the house of Chloe, that there are contentions among you. Now this I say, that every one of you saith, I am Paul; and I am of Apollos, and I of

Cephas, and I of Christ. Is Christ divided? was Paul crucified for you? or were you baptized in the name of Paul? I thank God that I baptized none of you, but Crispus and Gaius. Lest any should say that I had baptized in mine own name **(1 Corinthians 1:10–15).**

Whether it caused disorder, confusion, or simply contentiousness, Paul believed that division could not be tolerated within the fledgling Christian communities. Paul continued in his first letter to the Corinthians that their dissent was not godlike. He wrote: "For God is not the author of confusion, but of peace, as in all churches of the saints" (1 Corinthians 14:33).

Paul's Position on Women in the Church

Jesus, as previously noted, treated men and women equally. Although he did not meet Jesus in the flesh, Paul knew about Jesus' ministry and certainly would have heard about his policy of inclusion of women. Still, in the same letter in which he counseled the Corinth church members against divisiveness and discord, Paul also offered this advice: "Let your women keep silence in the churches: for it is not permitted unto them to speak; but they are commanded to be under obedience, as also saith the law. And if they will learn any thing, let them ask their husbands at home: for it is a shame for women to speak in the church" (1 Corinthians 14:34–35).

While modern Christian women might find that passage offensive, remember that Paul was Jewish, raised to obey Mosaic Law, and lived in patriarchal times when the voices of women were routinely silenced. And yet Paul also wrote, "Now if Christ be preached that he rose from the dead, how say some among you that there is no resurrection of the dead? But if there be no resurrection of the dead, then is Christ not risen: And if Christ be not risen, then is our preaching vain, and your faith is also vain" (1 Corinthians 15:12–14). It is curious to read these words, especially since the eyewitness to the Resurrection was a woman—Mary Magdalene. Paul does not mention her in his letter to the Corinthians, but rather in Chapter 15 where he explains the certainty and manner of the Resurrection he states: "For I delivered unto you first of all that which I also received, how that Christ died for our sins according to the Scriptures; and that he was buried, and that he rose again the third day according to the Scriptures: and that he was seen of Cephas [Peter], then of the twelve" (1 Corinthians 15:3–5).

All four Gospels mention Mary Magdalene in association with the Resurrection story. Paul mentions, not Mary Magdalene, but Peter as the eyewitness. He told the Corinthian Christians to be of one mind. If they did not believe in the risen Jesus, then all their preaching and even their faith was in vain.

The Roman Catholic Position

The Roman Catholic Church, like the Eastern Orthodox Church and many other Christian denominations, has an internal movement called Charismatic Renewal. The movement encourages petitioning the Holy Spirit to bestow upon the church's faithful such charisms (from the Greek word charis, which means "grace or gift") as prophecy, speaking in tongues, and healing. The late Pope John Paul II noted in 1979 in a speech before an international audience that he believed the movement was an important part of the church's entire renewal. He also said that he felt that the charisms constituted a part of the richness of the Lord and his action.

discussion question

What are the fruits of the Holy Spirit?
Twelve fruits can manifest upon those who accept the pouring forth of the Holy Spirit and its action: charity, generosity, gentleness, goodness, modesty, self-control, kindness, patience, joy, peace, faithfulness, and chastity.

Modern churches experienced a burgeoning renewal of interest in supernatural gifts of the Holy Spirit, especially in the decade between 1960 and 1970. Modern Christians believe the Holy Spirit calls people to faith and empowers them to lead a holy, Christian life. But the phenomenon is by no means new. The apostles received the outpouring of the Holy Spirit. The church from its earliest inception has emphasized healings, visions, prophecy, and speaking in tongues. The Gospel of Mary reveals that Mary Magdalene had the charism of vision. She showed charity of spirit when she complied with Peter's request to share some words of the Lord with him and the others. She exhibited kindness and self-control when Peter and Andrew challenged her after she'd shared her vision and special teaching.

factum

The four Gospels of the New Testament became the standard sources and measures for revelation during the time of Irenaeus. All visions and revelations had to agree with the truths put forth in these four Gospel accounts. In effect, doing so safeguarded the canon and ensured that future generations who might render their interpretations of the Scriptures would not introduce lies or wrongful thinking.

Mary Magdalene Is the Glue

Many biblical scholars agree that Mary Magdalene served as the "glue" for the Jesus movement and the infant Christian church. If she had failed in her role as the eyewitness to the Resurrection and in Jesus' commission to spread the Good News to the others, the church might well have disintegrated. Without a visionary and a spiritual adept such as Mary Magdalene to keep the members focused on carrying forth Jesus' ministry, the disciples would have gone back to their familiar worlds. Andrew and Peter desired to return to fishing, according to at least one source. Mary Magdalene reminded the others to reflect on the "good" and the important work Jesus had already accomplished on Earth. She never wavered but was always dedicated to doing his work and giving him all the glory and credit.

discussion question

How are women serving the church today?
In the United States, women make up the majority of religion instructors and, in addition, are increasingly becoming theologians, canon lawyers, and chancellors for dioceses. Women are also serving as advisers to the U.S. bishops who are responding to the sex abuse crisis within the Catholic Church. In many other Christian denominations, women are increasingly fulfilling leadership roles.

When the disciples went into hiding after the death of Jesus, they may have been afraid to show their faces out of fear that they, too, would be put to death. Mary Magdalene assuaged their fears. One account says that she kissed them all and talked with them gently, perhaps to pull them out of the throes of grief and ameliorate their sense of defeat. With Jesus' death and without Mary Magdalene, some wonder whether Christianity could have survived to become one of the most popular religions in the world.

chapter 20

Relevance and Resonance
for Modern Women

The status of women in the early Christian church has been hotly debated. This is due to the passionate work of scholars and to the women's movements in the United States and elsewhere. In the New Testament, Paul called women coworker, deaconess, and apostle. The prevailing thought today is that women in the infant church served in various ways. They stand as exemplars to modern women who also desire to serve but are not permitted to by a rigid male hierarchy.

Speaking with Authority and Conviction

Mary Magdalene lived her life as a beacon for Christ. Though she dwelled under Roman occupation and faced the risk of persecution and death, she faced her adversaries—among them, those who tortured and crucified Jesus. She did not hide her loyalty and love for Jesus as others did. She was an exemplar for women then and remains so today.

factum

Regardless of what form it takes—lantern, flashlight, candle-holder—a lamp symbolizes the power of light to illuminate darkness. In spiritual terms, the light of a flame illuminates spiritual truth in the presence of human ignorance and despair. In churches and temples everywhere, candles are ritually kindled to represent humanity reaching for the Divine.

There are women in the modern world who live in constant fear of expressing their voices and points of view. Some have been deprived of an education and any chance of advancement in their societies. Others live in cultures where they remain trapped in subservient roles with no hope of escaping. From across the centuries, Mary Magdalene's light inspires them to speak with authority and conviction as she did in her roles as Jesus' insightful questioner during his life and his eloquent spokesperson after he departed. Her voice did not fall silent when Peter and Andrew challenged her.

Hollywood Offers Its Distorted View

Hollywood stories about Jesus often include his mother and Mary Magdalene as two of his most loyal supporters. Those two women's lives were closely linked to his, and they played prominent roles in his life and ministry, supporting him in different ways. Both women were included in the story of *The Passion of the Christ* and necessarily so for the biblical accounts say that both women accompanied Jesus to his death.

The Passion

The Passion of the Christ focused on the last twelve hours of Jesus' life. The movie made quite an impact when it was released. The story started in the Garden of Gethsemane and ended with his condemnation to death. The movie showed the sadistic treatment of Jesus during his torture and crucifixion and the graphic imagery of those scenes was the most difficult part of the movie to watch for many viewers. Some viewers felt the film distorted this aspect of the Passion story.

The Mel Gibson film was released in 2004 amid controversy and critical acclaim. In the movie business, that translates to higher ticket sales and interest in related items such as DVDs with additional film clips or the complete soundtrack, pictorial books, and in the case of *The Passion of the Christ,* a tear bottle.

The Last Temptation

Martin Scorsese's 1988 film adaptation of the *Last Temptation of Christ* (based on Nikos Kazantzaki's 1951 novel of the same name) also focused on Jesus and his crucifixion. *The Last Temptation of Christ* centers on the last temptation of Jesus in which he longed for a normal life with a wife and family. His dream included Mary Magdalene, who tempted him to want to live a pleasant life with her as an ordinary man and to forsake his divine mission and ultimate fate. He dreams an entire lifetime before finally accepting his fate of death on the cross. Critics of this film say it would have been unlikely that Jesus would suddenly be seduced by such sensual hunger, understanding as he did that his path and purpose on Earth were unique and divinely ordained and required him to make the ultimate sacrifice for humankind.

discussion question

Would it be sinful for Jesus to have been married?
The Da Vinci Code suggests Jesus and Mary Magdalene were married, but no evidence exists. Biblical scholars say that sex within marriage is not sinful. According to the Epistle to the Hebrews 4:15, Jesus was without sin. So technically, if the two were married and had conjugal relations, he would remain sinless.

Questions of Accuracy

Both *The Passion of the Christ* and *The Last Temptation of Christ* sparked controversy over claims that the films distorted the historicity of the biblical characters and events. Yet these films were not documentaries that were meant to be factually accurate. The purpose of both projects was to entertain audiences through their storytelling. Such projects always put forth the view of the writer, director, and producers, so some distortion is expected.

The Da Vinci Code Sparks Heated Debate

Writers seeking dramatic stories and interesting characters need look no further than the Bible. It is a rich resource packed with tales about people who receive and accept a call to action that forever changes them. Mary Magdalene accepted such a call when she began her journey with Jesus. Two thousand years ago, the Gospel writers gave her minimal attention in their stories, but today bestselling novelist Dan Brown has been able to capitalize on the mysteries surrounding her life.

The Da Vinci Code phenomenon started with the release of the book and the publicity/promotion surrounding it. Publishing giant Bertelsmann released a short statement in December 2004 saying that for the first time in the history of bestseller lists, Dan Brown had taken positions one, two, three, and four in the *London Sunday*

Times. The Da Vinci Code topped that list and Brown's other books filled the other three slots.

The Da Vinci Code readers must sort through myriad mysteries, puzzles, codes, and conspiracies. This triggered other books revealing how the "code" could be broken or mysteries and puzzles might be solved. In short, a whole cottage industry sprang up around this one amazing novel. That, in turn, kept churning out publicity for *The Da Vinci Code.*

The Controversy

Perhaps more than any other written material featuring Jesus and Mary Magdalene, *The Da Vinci Code* has lifted Mary Magdalene's profile to pop star status. The book reveals among other shocking assertions that Mary Magdalene and Jesus were married, and she was actually the Holy Grail containing the blood of Jesus by way of carrying his child in her womb. The novel has broken publishing records in the United States and abroad. With such a large, international audience for the product, Hollywood couldn't help but notice. In 2006, the book became a film under the direction of Ron Howard and Akiva Goldsman, Oscar-winning director and writer respectively of *A Beautiful Mind.*

While the novel has many orthodox Christians riled up over its wild assertions, lovers of the thriller genre and Dan Brown's previous novels think this is his best work. They say readers must keep an open mind and enjoy the fictional ride that the author has created for them in this novel. Also, novels are works of fiction that create a sense of verisimilitude or reality. That's what makes the reader suspend disbelief and buy into the story. In that sense, the author succeeded and perhaps somewhat explains why so many readers around the world enjoy this particular book.

Other Writers Debate and Debunk

Critics of *The Da Vinci Code* claim the author of the novel makes outrageous claims that include a woman-hating church that eliminated the Sacred Feminine from the Gospels, that the author's Christology is false, that his view of the Bible is patently negative, and that he wildly distorts the image of Jesus from that of a carpenter who becomes the Messiah to a Jesus who is trained in religious studies and is intent on regaining the throne of David. Those are only a few of the falsehoods critics say are in the pages of the novel. Perhaps the most egregious assertion for the novel's critics is that Mary Magdalene was Jesus' royal consort and the one Jesus intended to be head of his church.

Dan Burstein's book, *Secrets of the Code, the Unauthorized Guide to the Mysteries Behind the Da Vinci Code*, spent twenty-one weeks on the *New York Times* Bestseller List and differs from the other *Da Vinci Code* "tag-along" books in that it offers a collection of scholarly opinions and criticisms. The *U.S. News and World Report* largely based its special edition on Burstein's book.

factum

A plethora of articles and books, many focusing on correcting errors of fact found in *The Da Vinci Code*, has escalated interest and sales of the spectacularly successful novel. It landed in the number-one position for sales at Amazon.com and spent thirty-two weeks at the top of the *New York Times* Bestseller List. There are now more than 35 million copies in print.

In June 2005, *U.S. News and World Report* produced a collector's edition of its popular magazine, calling it the *Unauthorized Guide to the Bestselling Novel*. It featured articles written by Elaine Pagels, Margaret Starbird, and Timothy Freke and Peter Gandy, some of the many authors of source material for *The Da Vinci Code*. These authors have written books that touch on the subject of Mary Magdalene as well—her role in the Jesus movement, possible leader of the Gnostic branch of early Christianity, and prophetess and preacher. Their works portray Mary Magdalene in a highly favorable light.

Newspapers, too, have devoted column space and ink to the controversial claims of *The Da Vinci Code.* Such illustrious publications as the *New York Times,* the *Christian Science Monitor, Time Magazine, Vanity Fair,* and *Newsweek*, as well as many metropolitan newspapers around the country have done features or articles about Mary Magdalene. In the words of one woman for whom Mary Magdalene is her personal patron saint, "It's about time!"

Modern Seekers Exchange Ideas

Modern Christian and non-Christian women alike are calling for recognition of the women in the Bible, especially Mary Magdalene. They are forming reader's discussion groups and establishing Bible study sessions. Some women are establishing rituals to celebrate Mary Magdalene's contributions to women's spirituality. With FutureChurch.org, women can get help in putting references to Mary Magdalene back into religious services and orthodox liturgy or planning celebrations to honor Mary Magdalene. Women, increasingly, are searching out new ways to integrate appropriate references to Mary Magdalene into their devotional practices and scriptural readings and faith-sharing with others.

Mary Magdalene aficionados are creating Web sites and campaigning for change by repairing her tarnished reputation, sharing information about her, and lobbying for more inclusion of her in church liturgy, homilies, and rites. Increasingly, they are posting their opinions on Web blogs (Internet sites with logs that cater to readers). The Internet is fecund with blog commentary and Web articles about Mary Magdalene.

A blog that targets the Anglican Church faithful, among others, is Magdalen's Rose and Compass at Herbert House. Subscribe to it at *http://herberthouse.org*. The site's creator describes it as a place for discourse, much as one would find in a traditional English pub. The rules are simple: comments must be consistent with being a follower of Jesus. While the site is intended mainly for Anglicans, others are welcome.

fallacy

It's a fallacy that Mary Magdalene has had little presence except in modern popular culture. The truth is that she has been written about for centuries. She has been included in music as well, from Gregorian chant to modern rock operas such as *Jesus Christ, Superstar*, and her character has been written into movie scripts since the beginning of the cinema.

Since the publication of the translations and commentary of the texts found at Nag Hammadi, as well as *The Da Vinci Code* book and movie, many bloggers are turning to the Internet to express their opinions about Mary Magdalene and the controversial material and mysteries swirling about her. Without listing many sites here that may or may not be of interest, go to Google and type into the subject line the words *Mary Magdalene+Blog*. Hit the search key and from the list that comes up, select those you find most interesting.

A New Generation Looks Beyond the Myth

Some of the issues facing women of Mary Magdalene's time have continued through the centuries. In particular, the modern woman is faced with the challenge of breaking through the glass ceilings in many modern corporations and institutions of higher learning as well as in churches and temples. Those seemingly impenetrable boundaries perhaps had their earliest origins in ancient cultures in which women were considered inferior and men occupied the highest positions of the social order.

As the early Christian church established its identity, unified, and strengthened its hierarchal order, the roles of leadership and authority for women became increasingly diminished and narrowly defined. One way to keep a woman down in the early centuries of Christianity, according to some theologians, was to call into question her moral purity. This, some speculate, is precisely what happened to Mary Magdalene and also to women during the Middle Ages whose visions and spiritual gifts brought accusations of sorcery, black magic, and demonic possession.

factum

My Magdalene is the name of a play written and produced by Laura Lea Cannon and David Tressemer. The work builds upon their vision of the Sacred Feminine. Through contact with Mary Magdalene, the protagonist—a young woman named Clara—undertakes a journey and experiences a kind of self-discovery or gnosis.

Old myths aren't so easily forgotten. But today, with Mary Magdalene's star rising in popular culture, a new generation of Christians sees beyond the female stereotyping and the false myth. Increasingly, Mary Magdalene is becoming a role model for women desiring to serve and who believe there are more important roles for them in their places of worship.

Restitution Worldwide

Men and women who feel that Mary Magdalene may have been badly treated by Orthodox Literalists and who are interested in learning not only about her but about the origins of the church and the role of women in early Christianity are establishing study groups, organizing religious observances on Mary Magdalene's feast day and at Easter, and undertaking pilgrimages to sacred sites that venerate her.

Biblical and historical scholars, archaeologists, feminist theologians, and faithful Christians are all working to better understand Mary Magdalene's life in the context of the infant Christian church and the times in which she lived. She is suddenly the focus of books, articles, Web sites, blogs, movies, and plays. There is even a Magdalene encyclopedia underway on the Internet. The Catholic Church and various Christian denominations are working with their branches throughout the world to erase the non-biblical image of Mary Magdalene as the repentant fallen woman. In the last few years, travelers interested in undertaking a pilgrimage/vacation have many Mary Magdalene–focused trips from which to choose.

Mary Magdalene Pilgrimage Sites

There are numerous sites where pilgrims can honor and venerate Mary Magdalene. Many are found in southern France, the Holy Land, and Ephesus, Turkey. Some sites have been receiving pilgrims for a long time and have procedures in place to make a visit efficient and effective while others are now becoming known through Mary Magdalene's increasing popularity. Included here is a list of pilgrimage sites of special significance.

- Visit the Russian Church of Mary Magdalene on the Mount of Olives. Tsar Alexander the Third built this beautiful old church in 1886. Constructed in the style of traditional Russian architecture, the church features classic onion-shaped domes or cupolas.
- While in Jerusalem, see the site of the Lord's ascension and the Via Dolorosa where Jesus walked to the site of his crucifixion accompanied by his mother and Mary Magdalene.
- See the Church of Mary Magdalene in the remote village of Rennes le Chateau in southern France. The site was once the ancient Temple of Isis, the goddess with whom Mary Magdalene has most often been associated.
- Visit Les Saintes-Maries-de-la-Mer, a fishing village on the Mediterranean where Mary Magdalene and her companions arrived on the shores of ancient Gaul.

- Journey to the Saint Maximum-La Saint Baume grotto where legend says Mary Magdalene spent her last years as a contemplative. Her skull is still housed there.
- Go to Vézelay in the region of Burgundy in southern France where there is a shrine dedicated to Mary Magdalene.
- Make a trip to Salt Lake City, Utah, to see the Cathedral of the Madeleine (the French spelling of Mary Magdalene's name).
- Visit the Church of St. John on Ephesus where the apostle was buried on the southern end of Ayosolug Hill. The apostle John and Mary were said to have spent time together in Ephesus evangelizing.
- Make a pilgrimage to see the paintings of Mary Magdalene in the National Galley of Art in Washington, D.C.

In addition to these trips, reading a book such as Phil Cousineau's *The Art of Pilgrimage, The Seekers Guide to Making Travel Sacred* is an excellent resource for understanding sacred travel and providing insights to ensure a successful pilgrimage experience. Information on all the sites mentioned above is available on the Internet.

Diverse Ways She Is Venerated

Mary Magdalene is venerated today in a variety of ways. Protestant, Catholic, and Eastern Orthodox faithful mark the occasion of her feast day on July 22 with a service in remembrance of her. Others honor the saint with prayers, novenas (a nine-day prayer), and affirmations. Some individuals find ways to create sacred space in their homes, installing a little altar or fountain or painting. There they can do their devotions and spend time in adoration of Mary Magdalene. Often they will mark a period of devotion by lighting a candle, placing a flower in water, and perhaps even anointing themselves with perfumed oil such as frankincense and myrrh to symbolize her intent to anoint Jesus' body in the tomb.

Some people venerate Mary Magdalene through food preparation, offering, and consumption. In France on February 2, bakers make navettes, a type of cylindrical pastry resembling a boat. They are prepared and consumed in honor of Mary Magdalene and her friends' arrival on French soil in the village of Les Saintes-Maries-de-la-Mer. Others make red egg salad, using beet juice, to commemorate the legend of Mary Magdalene evangelizing the emperor Tiberias. As noted previously in this book, she told him the story of Jesus' death and resurrection and when she got to the part about how he rose on the third day, the emperor declared incredulously that no man could rise after being dead for three days anymore than a white egg could turn red. Mary picked up the egg, and it changed from white to red.

symbolism

Bread has long been a symbol of nourishment and life. In Christian symbolism, bread is a metaphor for the body of Christ. In Jewish households in ancient times as today, women kindle the candles on the Sabbath and bless the bread. Unleavened bread was used as a symbol of purity during Passover.

Some like to honor Mary Magdalene through the making of craft projects for churches, homes, and gardens. Projects might include a floor cloth, rug, or garden pathway maze or labyrinth; a mask; or even a holy tears bottle in remembrance of the tears Mary Magdalene shed for Jesus during his Passion. Garden enthusiasts might plant a rose garden and include at least one Mary Magdalene rose bush. They might also add a statue of her or a beautiful piece of mosaic art created in her image. For other ideas, see *Mary Magdalene: The Modern Guide to the Bible's Most Mysterious and Misunderstood Woman* (Adams Media, 2005). This book offers numerous ideas at the end of every chapter on ways to venerate Mary Magdalene and to bring her blessings of goodness into your life.

Recounting Her Many Roles

Looking beyond the religious icon of saintliness that Mary Magdalene represents for many modern Christians, one can see that she, in fact, served in a variety of roles important to Jesus' ministry. The Gospels reveal that she was one of the women who supported Jesus and his movement out of their resources. As such, she may have been his patroness or wealthy benefactor. She served as Jesus' faithful and loyal follower, was his closest companion and confidante, acted as his expert questioner and muse, accompanied him to his death, was eyewitness to his resurrection, and carried out his commission to tell the others. She turned the grieving disciples' thoughts back to Jesus and his words and works. She communed with the Lord in her meditation and shared with Peter and others a vision and a secret teaching that Jesus had given her. Mary Magdalene was the venerated leader of one branch of early Christianity that supported leadership roles for women. She served as a powerful role model and spiritual example for ancient women. Modern women, too, see her as a sacred sister—someone to turn to in times of trouble, confusion, and daily challenges.

Some of the same issues facing women of Mary Magdalene's time continue to be challenges for modern women. The glass ceilings in modern corporations had their origins in ancient cultures in which women were considered inferior and men occupied the highest positions of social standing. Men ran most of the business enterprises in ancient times and wielded the power and authority in the Jewish temples in first-century Palestine. So, stained-glass ceilings in modern ecclesiastical institutes such as churches and religious schools also had their origins in ancient times.

appendix A

Glossary

Anoint: To smear with oil as an act of consecration.

Apostle: One of Jesus' twelve disciples commissioned to teach the Gospel.

Apostola apostolorum: Apostle to the Apostles—title of Mary Magdalene honoring her role as messenger to the other disciples following the Resurrection of Jesus.

Aramaic: The language of first-century Palestine spoken by Jesus.

Cathar: A member of one of a number of ascetic Christian sects in medieval Europe (especially southern France) that believed in a dualistic theology. Cathar means "purity."

Contemplative: A person devoted to contemplation or thoughtful reflection.

Coptic: An ancient Egyptian language, considered extinct, but still in use liturgically in the Egyptian Coptic Church.

Crucifixion: Jesus' death upon a cross; also a form of capital punishment practiced by the Romans.

Domitian: A Roman emperor who lived A.D. 51–96. During his reign, the Apostle John was tortured and exiled to the rocky island of Patmos.

Ecclesia: Church or congregation (from the Greek *ekklēsía*).

Ephesus: Ancient city with an early Christian community associated with the ministry of John the Divine and Mary Magdalene.

Essenes: A sect of ascetic Palestinian Jews who lived during the first century. They practiced celibacy and advocated spiritual and physical purity and piety. The Dead Sea Scrolls were discovered near their base at Qumran; scholars believe these scrolls belonged to the Essenes.

Eucharist: The sacrament of Holy Communion; the celebration of the Lord's Supper.

Exorcism: To cast out an evil spirit through a ceremony (especially a religious rite).

Gematria: Literary device of the ancients utilizing numerical values assigned to Greek and Hebrew letters to compute sums that, in turn, yield symbolic meaning.

Gnosis: Self-knowledge as the path to salvation and enlightenment.

Gnosticism: Belief system that relies on individual self-revelation as a path to salvation and knowledge rather than relying on outside forces.

Hieros gamos: Literally "sacred marriage." An ancient religious belief or possibly a ceremonial rite practiced by the Gnostic Christians.

Irenaeus: A Literalist Christian who lived from A.D. 130 to 202. An opponent of Gnosticism, he wrote a book titled *Against All Heresies*. He served as bishop of Lyons in 178.

Josephus: Jewish historian who lived from A.D. 37 to 107 and who wrote about the Jews in the first century.

Kabalah: Esoteric teachings that make up a system of Jewish mysticism developed by rabbis from the seventh to the eighteenth centuries.

Liturgical: Associated with public worship and the eucharistic service.

Martyr: An individual who dies rather than give up his or her religion.

Martyrology: Collection of information about the lives of martyrs such as their histories.

Merovingian: A line of rulers in Gaul (France) during the fifth to the eighth centuries.

Messiah: Usually a reference to Jesus; literally means "anointed one."

Montanism: Movement founded by Montanus and two women who prophesied the impending apocalypse and practiced a strict asceticism. Followers of Montanism were called Montanists.

Myrrhbearers: Women, especially Mary Magdalene, who used perfumed oil, spices, spikenard, or unguents to anoint someone else (especially Jesus) in an act of consecration or religious ritual.

Mystic: A person who contemplates, meditates, prays, and engages in other practices with a goal of developing a personal relationship with the Divine.

Noli me tangere: Latin for "touch me not," the admonition Jesus gave Mary Magdalene when she reached for him before he had ascended to his Father.

Pagan: A non-Christian who believes in polytheism. For example, the ancient Romans and Greeks were pagans.

Pascha: The term in the Easter Orthodox tradition that is synonymous with Easter.

Passion, the: Jesus' suffering after the Last Supper until his death by crucifixion.

Patriarchal: Systems, cultures, or institutions under the domination and control of men.

Penitent: Someone who repents of sins and seeks forgiveness.

Pharisee: A particular Jewish sect consisting mainly of laymen and scholars who lived prior to and during the first century.

Pistis Sophia: Literally means "faithful wisdom" and is the title of a collection of four Gnostic texts most likely written sometime in the third century.

Pythagoras: A Greek philosopher who lived 581–497 B.C. and had a profound effect on Plato and the Greek philosophical traditions.

Relic: Human remains or possessions that belong to a saint and are venerated by the faithful.

Reliquary: The container holding a sacred relic.

Resurrection: Most often refers to the risen Jesus. He was put to death, entombed, and on the third day rose from the dead.

Sadducee: A particular Jewish sect during the time of Jesus whose members strictly adhered to the written Mosaic laws.

Sepulcher: The tomb in which Jesus' body was laid for burial.

Sophia: Wisdom allegorized as the sacred feminine consciousness. Sophia is also associated with the Jewish Shekhinah, or an emanation of God's glory, and the Holy Spirit.

Synoptic Gospels: The New Testament Gospels of Matthew, Mark, and Luke because of their similarities in content, suggesting they may have relied on the same source material.

Tertullian: An early Church father who lived from A.D. 155 to 220. He became a Christian circa 195 and a Montanist circa 207.

Thecla: A highborn, first-century woman who was a companion of the Apostle Paul. She traveled about preaching and baptizing and eventually was martyred.

Torah: The Pentateuch or the first five books of the Bible containing the Law of Israel.

Valentinus: Greek Gnostic poet who lived from A.D. 100 to 180 and whose brand of Christianity spread all over the Roman Empire.

Vesica piscis: An elliptical almond shape with points at the top and bottom. In early Christian art, the figure often contained an image of Christ. Also, the figure symbolizes the orifice in the female anatomy through which new life is brought forth.

appendix B

Web Site Resources

To view the painting of Mary Magdalene by nineteenth-century artist Henryk Siemiradzki:

www.abcgallery.com/S/semiradsky/semiradsky.html

For articles about the Grail legends:

www.altreligion.about.com/od/thegrailquest/

For information about the Didache:

www.antioch.com.sg/th/twp/bookbyte/hermas/didache.html

For more information about the world of the Gnostics and Mary Magdalene:

www.bcrecordings.net/store/index.
php?main_page=index&cPath=12

An excellent article by Karen King, professor of Ecclesiastical History at Harvard Divinity School:

www.beliefnet.com/story/131/story_13186_1.html

For a recipe for Navette à la Fleur d'Oranger:

www.beyond.fr/food/navette.html

For more information about the Hagia Sophia:

www.byzantines.net

To see some beautiful icons of Mary Magdalene:

www.catholic-forum.com/saints/saintm11.htm

For a list of mystics and a brief synopsis about them:

www.clas.ufl.edu/users/gthursby/mys/alpha.htm

To read the book of Revelation of St. John the Divine in both English and Greek:

www.ellopos.net/elpenor/greek-texts/
new-testament/revelation/1.asp

For information on epilepsy (which Mary Magdalene may have suffered from):

www.epilepsyfoundation.org

For dozens of interesting facts about Mary Magdalene:

www.factbites.com/topics/Mary-Magdalene

The Internet Medieval Sourcebook Web site at Fordham University:

www.fordham.edu/halsall/basis/goldenlegend/

For a recipe for the traditional Provence version of navettes, Navettes de la Chandeleur:

www.frenchfood.about.com/library/blnavettes.htm

To find Gnostic texts:

www.gnosis.org

For information on Simon Magus:

www.hermetic.com/sabazius/simon.htm

For more information about the Jewish holiday Pesach (Passover):

www.jewfaq.org/holidaya.htm

For an image of Masada and a brief historical account:

www.jewishvirtuallibrary.org/jsource/Judaism/masada.html

An account of the Jewish revolt in the Jewish Virtual Library:

www.jewishvirtuallibrary.org/jsource/Judaism/revolt.html

See images of Mary Magdalene's shrine, reliquary, crypt, and basilica frieze:

www.magdalene.org/vezelay3.htm

For more information about Celsus:

www.newadvent.org/cathen/03490a.htm

To read a discussion of the question of authorship of the Gospel of John from the Catholic point of view:

www.newadvent.org/cathen/08438a.htm

Orthodox Christian Information Center's Web site posts informative articles about icons and iconography:

www.orthodoxinfo.com/general

Read about the women in early Christianity:

www.pbs.org/wgbh/pages/frontline/ shows/religion/first/women.html

For information on the Emperor Domitian:

www.roman-emperors.org/domitian.htm

To read the Gospel of Mary:

www.southerncrossreview.org/35/gospel-mary3.htm

To read Nurith Kenaan-Kedar's writings:

www.tau.ac.il/arts/projects/PUB/assaph-art/ assaph2/articles_assaph2/06Kenaan.pdf

To see many images of Mary Magdalene:

www.textweek.com/art/mary_magdalen.htm

The Web site of The Passion of the Christ movie:

www.thepassionoftheChrist.com/splash.htm

For more information on the Vulgate of St. Jerome:

www.thesacredheart.com/sts/jerome.htm

To see some of Giotto's frescoes depicting Mary Magdalene:

www.wga.hu/index1.html

appendix C
Bibliography

Scriptural Texts
The biblical texts quoted in this book are drawn from:

The Holy Bible: Old and New Testaments
Self-pronouncing edition, conforming to the 1611 edition, commonly
known as the Authorized or King James Version. Cleveland and
New York: The World Publishing Company. (No copyright or publication date available.)

The New Testament of our Lord and Saviour Jesus Christ
Translated from the original Greek, Dutch-English edition.
New York. American Bible Society, 1869.

Other Texts

Baigent, Michael, Richard Leigh, and Henry Lincoln. *Holy Blood, Holy Grail.* New York: Bantam Doubleday Dell Publishing Group, Inc., 1983.

Brock, Ann Graham. *Mary Magdalene, The First Apostle: The Struggle for Authority.* Cambridge: Harvard University Press, 2003.

Compton-Hernandez, Maria. *The Catholic Mother's Resource Guide, A Resource Listing of Hints and Ideas for Practicing and Teaching the Faith.* Goleta, CA: Queenship Publishing Company, 2002.

Cousineau, Phil. *The Art of Pilgrimage, The Seekers Guide to Making Travel Sacred.* Berkeley: Conari Press, 1998.

Dues, Greg. *Catholic Customs and Traditions: A Popular Guide (More Resources to Enrich Your Lenten Journey).* New London, CT: Twenty-Third Publications, 2000.

Eisen, Ute. *Women Officeholders in Early Christianity.* Collegeville, MN: Liturgical Press, 2000.

Farmer, David. *Oxford Dictionary of Saints*. Fourth edition. Oxford: Oxford University Press, 1997.

Fox, Matthew. *Illuminations of Hildegard of Bingen*. Rochester: Bear & Company, 2002.

Freke, Timothy, and Peter Gandy. *Jesus and the Lost Goddess*. New York: Three Rivers Press, 2001.

Gaffney, Mark H. *Gnostic Secrets of the Naassenes, The Initiatory Teachings of the Last Supper*. Rochester: Inner Traditions, 2004.

Giles, Mary E. *The Feminist Mystic and Other Essays on Women and Spirituality*. New York: The Crossroad Publishing Company, 1982.

Gimbutas, Marija. *The Language of the Goddess*. New York: HarperCollins Publishers, 1989.

Hanegraaff, Hank, and Paul L. Maier. *The Da Vinci Code Fact or Fiction?* Carol Stream, IL: Tyndale House Publishers, Inc., 2004.

Haskins, Susan. *Mary Magdalen, Myth and Metaphor*. New York: Berkeley Publishing Group, Riverhead Books, 1993.

Higgs, Liz Curtis. *Unveiling Mary Magdalene*. Colorado Springs: Water Brook Press, Division of Random House, 2001.

King, Karen. *The Gospel of Mary of Magdala, Jesus and the First Woman Apostle*. Santa Rosa, CA: Polebridge Press, 2003.

Klein, Peter. *Catholic Source Book, a Comprehensive Collection of Information about the Catholic Church*. Dubuque, IA: Harcourt Religion Publishers, 2000.

Leloup, Jean-Yves. *The Gospel of Mary Magdalene*. Rochester: Inner Traditions International, 2002.

L'Engle, Madeleine, and Carole F. Chase. *Glimpses of Grace, Daily Thoughts and Reflections*. Harper San Francisco, 1998.

Lockyer, Herbert. *All the Women of the Bible*. Grand Rapids, MI: Zondervan, 1967.

Markale, Jean. *The Church of Mary Magdalene, The Sacred Feminine and the Treasure of Rennes-le-Château*. Rochester: Inner Traditions International, 2004.

Meeks, Wayne A. *The First Urban Christians, the Social World of the Apostle Paul*. Second Edition. New Haven and London: Yale University Press, 2003.

Meyer, Marvin. *The Gospel of Thomas, The Hidden Sayings of Jesus.* New York: HarperCollins Publishers, Inc., 1992.

Meyer, Marvin with Esther A. De Boer. *The Gospels of Mary, The Secret Tradition of Mary Magdalene, the Companion of Jesus.* New York: Harper Collins Publishers, Inc., 1994.

Pagels, Elaine. *Beyond Belief, The Secret Gospel of Thomas.* New York: Random House, 2003.

Pagels, Elaine. *The Gnostic Gospels.* New York: Random House, Vintage Books Edition, 1989.

Picknett, Lynn. *Mary Magdalene.* New York: Avalon Publishing Group, Inc., Carroll & Graff Publishers, 2003.

Picknett, Lynn, and Clive Prince. *The Templar Revelation, Secret Guardians of the True Identity of Christ.* New York: Simon and Schuster, 1998.

Robinson, James M, Ed. *The Nag Hammadi Library in English, The Definitive Translation of the Gnostic Scriptures Complete in One Volume.* New York: Harper Collins Publishers, 1990.

Starbird, Margaret. *Magdalene's Lost Legacy, Symbolic Numbers and the Sacred Union in Christianity.* Rochester: Bear & Company, 2003.

Starbird, Margaret. *The Feminine Face of Christianity.* Wheaton, IL: Godsfield Press, Quest Books, 2003.

Starbird, Margaret. *The Woman with the Alabaster Jar, Mary Magdalen and the Holy Grail.* Rochester: Bear & Company, 1993.

Videos

Mary Magdalene: An Intimate Portrait
1995. V.I.E.W. Video.
http://www.Amazon.com.

Mary Magdalene: The Hidden Apostle
2000. A&E Home Video.
http://www.Amazon.com.

Rediscovering Mary Magdalene, The Making of a Mythic Drama
2001. StarHouse.
http://www.thestarhouse.org/MMVideo.html

Index

A

Almsgiving, 186–87

Ampulla, 256

Ancestral seeds, 115–32

Anointing, 18, 140, 176, 194, 229–30

Apocalypse of James, 221

Apocrypha, 251–52, 271

Apologists, 66–70

Apostles, 20, 33–35, 44–49, 91–92, 98–99, 105, 125, 137–38, 141

Apostolic church, 125–28

Apostolic fathers, 122, 123

Apostolic seeds, 115–32

Apostolic Succession, 98–99, 123–25

Apostolic symbols, 127–28

Archetype, 114, 244–45

Arianism, 182

Arius, 60–62

Art inspiration, 255–64

Artist renderings, 257–64

B

Baptism, 11, 86, 140, 176, 188–89

Beatrice of Nazareth, 206

Beloved Disciple, 235–37

Bible, 142

Bishops, 145–46

Bread, 288

Burial rites, 116, 187–88, 256

C

Catacombs, 116, 256

Cathars, 183

Catherine of Siena, 206, 207

Catholic Church, 17, 99, 113, 125, 193, 207, 266, 274–75

Celsus, 139

Ceremonial holiness, 119–20

Challah, 81, 82

Chiliasm, 68

Christian goddess, 244–45

Christian mystics, 205–8

Christian struggles, 94–96

Christianity, 80, 99, 143–44, 149–66, 170–73, 203, 243–52, 269

Christianity timeline, 150–52

Christocentric, 100

Church laws, 156. *See also* Laws

Clement of Alexandria, 56–58

Codex, 198–99

Confirmation, 140

Constantine, 72–74

Conversion, 190–91

Conviction, 278

Council of Nicaea, 155–57

Cross significance, 29–30

Cross stations, 195

Crucifixion, 26–30, 38

D

Da Vinci Code, The, 248, 265, 280–83

da Vinci, Leonardo, 259

Deacons, 159, 160

Dead Sea Scrolls, 77–78

Demiurge, 225

Dialogue of the Savior, 221

Diaspora, 133, 134

Didache, 187

Diocletian, 64–66

Disciples, 5, 12–15, 24, 37–49, 90–93, 141, 222–23, 235–37

Diversity, 77–79

Domitian, 70–72

Donatus, 182

E

Early Christianity, 80, 149–66, 170–73, 203, 269

Early Christians, 185–96

Early Church conflict, 271–74

Early Church crisis, 133–48

Easter, 155–56, 179, 195

Eastern Orthodox Church, 17, 99, 106, 274

Ephesus, 107–9

Eros, 261–62

Essenes, 77–78

Eucharist, 82, 140, 176

Eusebius of Caesarea, 62–64

F

Feminist theologians, 268–70

Fish, 248, 249

Fourth Gospel, 233–42

Fruits of Holy Spirit, 274

G

Gamaliel, 47

Gaul, 109–10

Giotto, 258–59, 264

Glossary, 290–92

Gnosis, 174, 175, 199

Gnostic beliefs, 172–73

Gnostic Cross, 232

Gnostic Gospels, 169, 198–205

Gnostic texts, 32–33, 176–77, 198–205, 220–32

Gnostic veneration, 169–84

Gnosticism, 173–74

Gnostics, 101, 169–84

Goddess archetype, 244–45

Gospel of John, 233–42

Gospel of Mary, 198–205, 211–14

Gospels, 25–27, 94, 97, 126, 136–37, 196–208, 275

Great Commission, 34–35, 126

Great Schism, 99

Gregory, Pope, 13, 118–19

H

Hail Mary, 39

Healings, 84–86, 189–90

Heavenly Mother, 245–47

Heresy, 179–84, 219

Heretics, 188

Hermeticists, 251

Hieros gamos, 230, 250, 251

Hildegard of Bingen, 206–7

Hippolytus, 70

Hollywood, 278–80

Holy Grail, 111, 184

Holy Land, 106–7

Holy orders, 140

Holy seasons, 195–96

I

Ichthys, 249

Icons, 18, 96, 107, 115–16, 256–57, 263

Illumination, 228, 278

Influential people, 52–74

Irenaeus, 70, 123, 216, 272

J

James, the Lord's brother, 40–42

Jerome, 153–54

Jesus

background of, 10–11

baptism of, 11

Crucifixion of, 26–30, 38

death of, 12

early years of, 11

followers of, 5, 12–15, 37–49, 84–88, 90–93, 141, 222–23, 235–37

on laws, 214–16

love of, 21–35

Passion of, 12

promise to Mary Magdalene, 231–32

relationship with, 265–76

Resurrection of, 12, 24–27, 30–34, 89–92, 138–39

Jesus movement, 124, 134–35

Jewish Diaspora, 133, 134

Jewish Revolt, 161–64

Joan of Arc, 216

Joanna, Wife of Chuza, 15, 26

Johannine Community, 237–38

John the Apostle, 157–59,
    238–40, 242

John the Baptist, 42–44

John the Divine, 107–9

Josephus, Flavius, 52–53, 166

Judaism, 76–79, 88

Julian of Norwich, 207

Justin the Martyr, 66, 68–70

K

Kosher, 135

L

Lacuna, 231

Last Apostle, 49

Last Supper, 23

Last Supper, The, 259

Laws, 4–5, 79–80, 83–84,
    104–5, 156, 214–16

Lazarus, 15, 19

Legends, 103–16

Levi, 211–12

Literalist Christianity, 175, 176

Love, 21–35, 234

Loyalty, 278

M

Magdala, 4, 6–7

Male apostolic succes-
    sion, 123–25

Male power, 270

Male resistance, 93

Manuscript, 198–201, 230–31

Marcion, 54–56, 182

Martha, 15, 19, 26

Martyrs, 105–6

Mary Jacobi, 5, 14

Mary Magdalene
    background of,
        xii–xiv, 3–20
    companions of, 14–15
    facts about, xi
    feast day of, 132
    financial status of, 15–18
    as "glue," 275–76
    healing of, 7–9
    as leader, 22–24, 96–98
    lineage of, 18–20
    myths about, 13,
        118–23, 284–85
    portrayals of, 96, 107, 131,
        191, 194, 256–64
    promise to, 231–32
    reinterpretations
        of, 266–67
    roles of, 22–26, 77,
        222–23, 249–51, 289
    in society, 80–83

teachings of, 201–2

titles of, 16

veneration of, 287–89

vigil of, 27–30

visions of, 202–3, 209–20

Mary, Mother of James,
5, 14, 24–25, 28

Mary, Mother of Jesus, 5, 14,
28, 38–40, 108, 148, 210

Mary, Mother of John
Mark, 5, 14

Mary of Bethany, 5,
15, 17, 19, 26

Mary, Wife of Cleophas,
5, 14, 26, 28

Masada siege, 164–66

Mechthild of Magdeburg, 208

Medieval heresy, 183–84

Millennialism, 68

Miryam, 4. *See also*
Mary Magdalene

Misogyny, 100–101

Modern thinkers, 5–6

Modern times, 255–89

Montanism, 66–67, 146, 182

Mosaic Law, 4–5, 79–80

Myrrhbearers, 23, 25, 26, 120

Mystery traditions, 249–51

Mystics, 205–8

Myths, 13, 118–23, 284–85

N

Nicaea Council, 155–57

Nicene Creed, 155

Noli Me Tangere, 32, 257, 264

Nous, 203–5

O

Oral traditions, 142–43

Origen, 58–60, 139

P

Pagan Goddess
veneration, 178

Pagans, 136–37

Papyrus Oxyrhynchus
3525, 200

Passion, 12, 279

Passover, 24, 288

Patriarchal entrench-
ment, 92–93

Patriarchal paradigm, 86–88

Patriarchal restriction, 100–101

Patriarchy, 87–88, 92

Paul the Apostle, 46–49,
91–96, 218

Pentecost, 217

Persecution threats, 104–6

Peter the Apostle, 44–46,
210–13, 219–20, 223–25

Pharisees, 78–79

Pilgrimage, 191–92
Pilgrimage sites, 286–87
Pillars, 192–94
Pistis Sophia, 32, 221, 226–28
Pneuma, 203–5
Porete, Marguerite, 207–8, 216
Prayers, 39, 186, 196
Presbytera, 138
Presbyters, 138, 145–47
Priests, 138, 146–48
Promise, 231–32
Prophecy, 216–19, 229
Proselytizing, 110–12

R

Reconciliation, 140
Redaction, 238, 242
Relics, 113–15
Renaissance art, 259–61
Resources, 293–95
Restitution, 285–86
Resurrection, 12, 24–27,
    30–34, 89–92, 138–39
Retreating from world, 112–13
Revelation, 157–59
Roman Catholic Church,
    17, 99, 113, 125, 193,
    207, 266, 274–75
Roman Law, 79–80,
    83–84, 104–5
Rosary, 196
Rosh Hashanah, 81

S

Sacraments, 140, 176
Sacred Feminine, 227–29,
    247–48, 251–52
Sadducees, 78
Salome, 15, 24–26, 28, 33
Samaritan, 85–86
Sanhedrin, 47
Saul, 46–48
Scripture, 143–45
Seven deadly sins, 129
Shabbat, 82
Shaktas, 179
Shekinah, 245
Simon, 181
Snakes, 178
Sophia, 170, 174, 212,
    221, 225–27
Spiritual adeptness, 213–14
Stephen, 104, 159–61
Stoning, 29
Susanna, 26
Synoptic Gospels, 25–26

T

Talmud, 76
Teresa of Avila, 207, 208
Tertullian, 29, 66–68, 70
Three pillars, 192–94
Torah, 76, 81, 88
Transcendence, 204